XNA 4 3D Game Development by Example Beginner's Guide

Create action-packed 3D games with the
Microsoft XNA Framework

Kurt Jaegers

[PACKT] enterprise 88
PUBLISHING
professional expertise distilled

BIRMINGHAM - MUMBAI

XNA 4 3D Game Development by Example Beginner's Guide

First published: September 2012

Production Reference: 1180912

Published by Packt Publishing Ltd.
Livery Place
35 Livery Street
Birmingham B3 2PB, UK.

ISBN 978-1-84968-708-9

www.packtpub.com

Cover Image by Sandeep Babu (sandyjb@gmail.com)

Credits

Author
Kurt Jaegers

Reviewers
Kenneth Dahl Pedersen

Michael Schuld

Newton Sheikh

Pedro Daniel Güida Vázquez

Acquisition Editor
Dilip Venkatesh

Lead Technical Editor
Ankita Shashi

Technical Editors
Prashant Salvi

Ankita Shashi

Copy Editor
Alfida Paiva

Project Coordinator
Joel Goveya

Proofreaders
Aaron Nash

Chris Smith

Indexer
Tejal Soni

Graphics
Aditi Gajjar

Production Coordinator
Arvindkumar Gupta

Cover Work
Arvindkumar Gupta

About the Author

Kurt Jaegers is an Oracle Database Administrator and Windows Network Administrator, as well as a long-time hobbyist game developer. He has built games for everything from the Commodore 64 to the Xbox 360. He is the owner of `xnaresources.com`, and the author of *XNA 4.0 Game Development by Example: Beginner's Guide* (C# edition) and *XNA 4.0 Game Development by Example: Beginner's Guide – Visual Basic Edition*, both of which were published by Packt Publishing.

As always, I would like to thank my wife Linda for proofreading my original drafts. I would also like to thank the visitors to my website and the readers of my first two XNA books for their support, encouragement, and thought provoking questions. Finally, I would like to thank the team at Packt Publishing. This is my third book with them, and the experience has always been wonderful.

About the Reviewers

Kenneth Dahl Pedersen now aged 35, has been programming since he got his first computer at age 6, starting on the Commodore 64 with small programs that could do next to nothing. It quickly evolved when he migrated to the much more powerful Amiga 500, developing some demos and light applications, and finally culminated when he got his first PC.

Since then, game development has held his interest in a vice grip and Kenneth has since then studied numerous programming languages and APIs for that purpose, his repertoire includes C/C++, OpenGL, DirectX, C#, WPF, WCF, MDX, and XNA.

With the appearance of readily available high-end engines, such as Unreal Development Kit, Kenneth had found another interest to keep him well sated in his thirst for game development knowledge. UnrealScript provided another mountain top to climb.

Kenneth has an education as a Systems Analyst and Developer. Originally from Denmark, where he still works, he now lives in Sweden with his wife and baby daughter.

Other than his wife and daughter, he uses his spare time for game development, seeking new knowledge, and dabbling in 3D visual arts in applications such as 3D Studio Max and ZBrush. And of course, Kenneth is an avid gamer – after all, you cannot make a game if you don't enjoy playing them!

First of all, I would like to thank my wife, Nina, for the patience she's shown while I was doing this review—I have probably not been as helpful around the house as I should have been while this has been going on.

My beautiful daughter, Nadia, for always giving me a reason to smile and laugh.

Michael Schuld started his foray into game development using Managed DirectX v9; after playing with the framework for a few months, he decided there wasn't enough beginner content out in the world to help those people who are new to game development.

To fix this problem, he immediately set out writing a tutorial series that he kept up to date with the change from Managed DirectX to XNA and all the updates to the XNA Framework since then. Along with these tutorials, he has hosted a popular XNA Game Development forum and has helped hundreds of programmers new to game development get their feet wet. The site and tutorials have been listed by Microsoft and GameInformer as one of a select list of community resources for anyone wanting to learn the XNA Framework.

More recently, he has expanded his work into DirectX v11 and reviewing books in the game development arena. His recent work, tutorials, and reviews can all be found on `http://www.thehazymind.com`.

I would like to thank David Bonner, Charles Humphrey, and Michael Quandt for their early interest and assistance with my tutorial series, both in reviewing the content for ease of use and helping out with the forums. I'm glad to have you guys around to keep things from getting too crazy.

Newton Sheikh, is a software engineer working on Cloud applications for Windows Azure platform. Newton has been working with .NET technologies for the last 4 years and loves programming both in C# and VB. Newton's hobbies include web development and web designing. He is a casual game programmer for Android and Windows. When not programming, Newton loves to hang out with his friends.

Newton made a very humble start of his career with a company named Inyxa LLC based in Faridabad, India. Currently Newton is working with Hanu Softwares in Gurgaon, India.

Pedro Daniel Güida Vázquez is an Economist, System Analyst, Professor, and Microsoft MVP for DirectX and XNA, which are some of the accomplishments obtained throughout his life. Owner of Pulsar Coders, an indie company that develops videogames for many platforms, he enjoys working daily on everything related to videogame development. His skills cover many areas in the field, both technical and artistic, and he is always looking for interesting challenges to extend his personal and professional goals. You can find a comprehensive bio of Pedro at `http://www.linkedin.com/in/pedroguida`.

Pedro has worked on *XNA 4.0 Game Development by Example: Beginner's Guide – Visual Basic Edition* (Book) and *XNA Game Development Video Training Screencast* (Video tutorial), both of which are endeavors by Packt Publishing.

www.PacktPub.com

Support files, eBooks, discount offers and more

You might want to visit www.PacktPub.com for support files and downloads related to your book.

Did you know that Packt offers eBook versions of every book published, with PDF and ePub files available? You can upgrade to the eBook version at www.PacktPub.com and as a print book customer, you are entitled to a discount on the eBook copy. Get in touch with us at service@packtpub.com for more details.

At www.PacktPub.com, you can also read a collection of free technical articles, sign up for a range of free newsletters and receive exclusive discounts and offers on Packt books and eBooks.

http://PacktLib.PacktPub.com

Do you need instant solutions to your IT questions? PacktLib is Packt's online digital book library. Here, you can access, read and search across Packt's entire library of books.

Why Subscribe?

- ◆ Fully searchable across every book published by Packt
- ◆ Copy and paste, print and bookmark content
- ◆ On demand and accessible via web browser

Free Access for Packt account holders

If you have an account with Packt at www.PacktPub.com, you can use this to access PacktLib today and view nine entirely free books. Simply use your login credentials for immediate access.

Instant Updates on New Packt Books

Get notified! Find out when new books are published by following @PacktEnterprise on Twitter, or the Packt Enterprise Facebook page.

Table of Contents

Preface

Microsoft's XNA Framework provides C# developers with a robust and efficient method of utilizing the DirectX and Direct3D **Application Programming Interfaces (APIs)** in order to build 3D games for the Windows, Xbox 360, and Windows Phone platforms.

This book will present a series of video games, utilizing the XNA Framework to create 3D environments and objects. The games we build in this book will be targeted to the Windows platform, though they can be compiled to run on both the Xbox 360 and Windows Phone with minor changes to accommodate input methods on those devices.

Each of the games presented will build on the 3D concepts of the previous games, and finally wrapping up with a game built around the Game State Management system sample code available from the Microsoft XNA website.

What this book covers

Chapter 1, Introduction to XNA, begins by installing the Windows Phone Development Tools package that includes the Version 4.0 release of the XNA tools. We will examine the basic building blocks of an XNA game and create a 2D mini game called Speller to establish a baseline of 2D techniques that will be needed while building 3D games later.

Chapter 2, Cube Chaser – A Flat 3D World, introduces basic 3D concepts such as cameras and projections. We will build a floor for our 3D maze using colored triangles and allow the player to walk around on it.

Chapter 3, Cube Chaser – It's A-Mazing!, explores the generation of a random maze layout using the Depth-first search method. We will construct walls based on the generated maze and restrict player movement within those walls.

Chapter 4, Cube Chaser – Finding Your Way, guides us through the construction of the cube we will be chasing, including mapping textures to the faces of an object. We will randomly position the cube and rotate it to perform a simple animation. We will take a closer look at matrix math in order to understand just what is happening when we move, rotate, and scale objects.

Chapter 5, Tank Battles – A War-torn Land, embarks on the building of a tank combat game. In this chapter we will build a new type of 3D camera and generate a terrain based on a heightmap image. We will explore the fundamentals of **High Level Shader Language** (**HLSL**) used to create shader effects that describe the surfaces of the objects we will be rendering.

Chapter 6, Tank Battles – The Big Guns, adds 3D models to our game, importing a tank model and positioning it appropriately on the game's terrain. We also delve into bone-based animation for 3D models, allowing the tank's turret and cannon to be moved by the player.

Chapter 7, Tank Battles – Shooting Things, combines our existing 3D elements with a 2D interface, allowing us to accept input from the user via onscreen buttons. We will create and track shots fired by the players and implement billboard-based particle explosions.

Chapter 8, Tank Battles – Ending the War, wraps up the Tank Battles game by incorporating a simple game flow structure to surround game play and establishing a sequence of turns between two players, modifying the state of our user interface elements appropriately. We will determine the result of fired shots, allowing players to score hits on the enemy tank and win the game. Additionally, we will return to HLSL to implement lighting and multitexturing effects on our terrain to improve the graphical quality of the game.

Chapter 9, Mars Runner, begins a new game – a side-scrolling, jumping game on the surface of Mars. We will work with the Game State Management sample code provided by Microsoft to build the structure of our game. The backdrop for Mars Runner will be implemented as a 3D skybox that surrounds the stationary camera. Finally, we will revisit the heightmap-based terrain by generating terrain tiles that can be joined together to create a track for the player's rover to drive on.

Chapter 10, Mars Runner – Reaching the Finish Line, completes the Mars Runner game by enhancing our handling of 3D models and adding both the player's Mars rover and an enemy alien saucer to the game. We allow both the player and the enemy to fire shots at each other and use bounding box collision detection to determine when one of the entities has been hit. To finish up, we will implement a basic sound effect system, allowing us to play audio clips based on the events taking place in the game.

What you need for this book

In order to install and use the Microsoft XNA 4.0 tools, you will need a Windows PC with either Microsoft Windows Vista or Microsoft Windows 7, and a video card supporting DirectX 9 or later. Shader Model 1.1 is required for XNA, but it is highly recommended that your video card support Shader Model 2.0 or later, as many of the XNA samples available online require 2.0 support.

Who this book is for

If you are an aspiring game developer, looking to get started with XNA, or to expand your 2D XNA knowledge into the 3D realm, this book is for you. A basic knowledge of C# is helpful to kick start your game development, but is not essential.

Conventions

In this book, you will find several headings appearing frequently.

To give clear instructions of how to complete a procedure or task, we use:

Time for action – heading

1. Action 1
2. Action 2
3. Action 3

Instructions often need some extra explanation so that they make sense, so they are followed with:

What just happened?

This heading explains the working of tasks or instructions that you have just completed.

You will also find some other learning aids in the book, including:

Pop quiz – heading

These are short multiple-choice questions intended to help you test your own understanding.

Have a go hero – heading

These practical challenges give you ideas for experimenting with what you have learned.

You will also find a number of styles of text that distinguish between different kinds of information. Here are some examples of these styles, and an explanation of their meaning.

Code words in text are shown as follows: " You may notice that we used the Unix command `rm` to remove the `Drush` directory rather than the DOS `del` command."

A block of code is set as follows:

```
# * Fine Tuning
#
key_buffer = 16M
key_buffer_size = 32M
max_allowed_packet = 16M
thread_stack = 512K
thread_cache_size = 8
max_connections = 300
```

When we wish to draw your attention to a particular part of a code block, the relevant lines or items are set in bold:

```
# * Fine Tuning
#
key_buffer = 16M
key_buffer_size = 32M
max_allowed_packet = 16M
thread_stack = 512K
thread_cache_size = 8
max_connections = 300
```

Any command-line input or output is written as follows:

```
cd /ProgramData/Propeople
rm -r Drush
git clone --branch master http://git.drupal.org/project/drush.git
```

New terms and **important words** are shown in bold. Words that you see on the screen, in menus or dialog boxes for example, appear in the text like this: "On the **Select Destination Location** screen, click on **Next** to accept the default destination.".

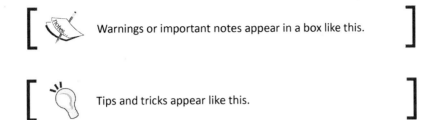

Warnings or important notes appear in a box like this.

Tips and tricks appear like this.

Reader feedback

Feedback from our readers is always welcome. Let us know what you think about this book—what you liked or may have disliked. Reader feedback is important for us to develop titles that you really get the most out of.

To send us general feedback, simply send an e-mail to feedback@packtpub.com, and mention the book title through the subject of your message.

If there is a topic that you have expertise in and you are interested in either writing or contributing to a book, see our author guide on www.packtpub.com/authors.

Customer support

Now that you are the proud owner of a Packt book, we have a number of things to help you to get the most from your purchase.

Downloading the example code

You can download the example code files for all Packt books you have purchased from your account at http://www.packtpub.com. If you purchased this book elsewhere, you can visit http://www.packtpub.com/support and register to have the files e-mailed directly to you.

Errata

Although we have taken every care to ensure the accuracy of our content, mistakes do happen. If you find a mistake in one of our books—maybe a mistake in the text or the code—we would be grateful if you would report this to us. By doing so, you can save other readers from frustration and help us improve subsequent versions of this book. If you find any errata, please report them by visiting http://www.packtpub.com/support, selecting your book, clicking on the **errata submission form** link, and entering the details of your errata. Once your errata are verified, your submission will be accepted and the errata will be uploaded to our website, or added to any list of existing errata, under the Errata section of that title.

Piracy

Piracy of copyright material on the Internet is an ongoing problem across all media. At Packt, we take the protection of our copyright and licenses very seriously. If you come across any illegal copies of our works, in any form, on the Internet, please provide us with the location address or website name immediately so that we can pursue a remedy.

Please contact us at copyright@packtpub.com with a link to the suspected pirated material.

We appreciate your help in protecting our authors, and our ability to bring you valuable content.

Questions

You can contact us at questions@packtpub.com if you are having a problem with any aspect of the book, and we will do our best to address it.

1
Introduction to XNA

Microsoft's XNA Framework provides a powerful set of tools for building both 2D and 3D games for Windows, the Xbox 360, and the Windows Phone platforms. As an extension of the Visual Studio development environment, XNA provides developers with a set of free tools for these environments.

The XNA project templates include an integrated game loop, easy to use (and fast) methods to display graphics, full support for 3D models, and simple access to multiple types of input devices.

In this introductory chapter, we will do the following:

- Review the system requirements for XNA development
- Install the Windows Phone Tools SDK, which includes Visual Studio Express and the XNA 4.0 extensions
- Examine the basic structure of an XNA game by building a simple 2D game
- Explore a fast-paced rundown of 2D techniques that will provide a foundation for moving forward into 3D with XNA

Starting out a book on 3D game development by building a 2D game may seem like an odd approach, but most 3D games use a number of 2D techniques and resources, even if only to display a readable user interface to the player.

If you already have an understanding of 2D game development in XNA, you may want to glance over this chapter and proceed to *Chapter 2, Cube Chaser – A Flat 3D World*, where we begin building our first 3D game.

System requirements

In order to develop games using XNA Game Studio, you will need a computer capable of running both Visual Studio 2010 and the XNA Framework extensions. The general requirements are as follows:

Component	Minimum requirements	Notes
Operating System	Windows Vista SP2 or Windows 7 (except Starter Edition)	Windows XP is not supported.
Graphics Card	Shader Model 1.1 support DirectX 9.0 support	Microsoft recommends Shader Model 2.0 support as it is required for many of the XNA Starter Kits and code samples. The projects in this book also require Shader Model 2.0 support.
Development Platform	Visual Studio 2010 or Visual Studio 2010 Express	Visual Studio 2010 Express is installed along with the XNA Framework.
Optional		
Windows Phone	Windows Phone Development Tools, DirectX 10 or later, compatible video card	The Windows Phone SDK includes a Windows Phone emulator for testing.
Xbox Live	Xbox Live Silver membership XNA Creator's Club Premium membership	Xbox Live Silver is free. The XNA Creator's Club Premium membership costs $49 for 4 months or $99 for 1 year.

Installing the Windows Phone SDK

Originally developed as a separate product, XNA is now incorporated in the Windows Phone SDK. You can still develop games for Windows and the Xbox 360 using the tools installed by the Windows Phone SDK.

If you have an existing version of Visual Studio 2010 on your PC, the XNA Framework templates and tools will be integrated into that installation as well as the Visual Studio 2010 Express for Windows Phone installation that is part of the Windows Phone SDK, which we are going to install now.

Time for action – installing Windows Phone SDK

To install Windows Phone SDK , perform the following steps:

1. Visit `http://create.msdn.com/en-us/home/getting_started` and download the latest version of the Windows Phone SDK package. Run the setup wizard and allow the installation package to complete.

2. Open Visual Studio 2010 Express. Click on the **Help** menu and select **Register Product**. Click on the **Register Now** link to go to the Visual Studio Express registration page. After you have completed the registration process, return to Visual Studio 2010 Express and enter the registration number into the registration dialog box.

3. Close Visual Studio 2010 Express.

4. Launch Visual Studio 2010 Express, and the **Integrated Development Environment (IDE)** will be displayed as shown in the following screenshot:

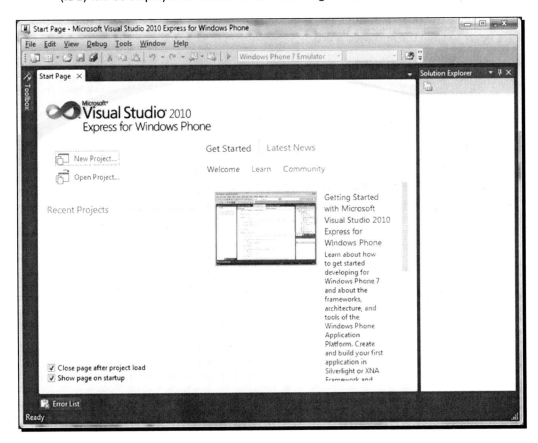

What just happened?

You have now successfully installed the Windows Phone SDK, which includes Visual Studio 2010 Express, the XNA Extensions for Visual Studio, and the Redistributable Font Pack provided by Microsoft for XNA developers.

Speller – Our first XNA game

If you have never used XNA before, it would be helpful to review a number of concepts before you dive into 3D game design. In most 3D games, there will be at least some 2D content for user interfaces, **Heads-up display (HUD)** overlays, text alerts, and so on. In addition, many 3D game constructions are really evolutions of 2D game concepts.

In order to provide both an overview of the XNA game template and to build a foundation for moving forward into 3D development, we will construct a simple game called Speller. In Speller, the player controls a small square using the keyboard. During each round we will generate a random set of letters, including the letters needed to spell a particular word. The player's job is to navigate through the forest of letters and hit only the correct ones in the right order to spell the indicated word.

By building this game, we will be:

- Performing initialization when our game is executed
- Adding graphical assets to the game and loading them at run time
- Displaying 2D images with the `SpriteBatch` class
- Drawing text to the screen with the `SpriteFont` class
- Colorizing images and fonts
- Handling keyboard input and calculating player movement adjusted for the frame rate
- Bounding box collision detection
- Keeping and displaying the score
- Generating random numbers

That is quite a bit of ground to cover in a very small game, so we had better get started!

Time for action – creating an XNA project

To create an XNA project, perform the following steps:

1. In the Visual Studio window, open the **File** menu and select **New Project...**.
2. Under **Project Type**, make sure **C#** is selected as the language and that the **XNA Game Studio 4.0** category is selected.
3. Under **Templates**, select **Windows Game (4.0)**.
4. Name the project `Speller` (this will automatically update the **Solution Name**).
5. Click on **OK**.

The Speller game's `Game1.cs` file, when opened in Visual Studio, would look like the following screenshot:

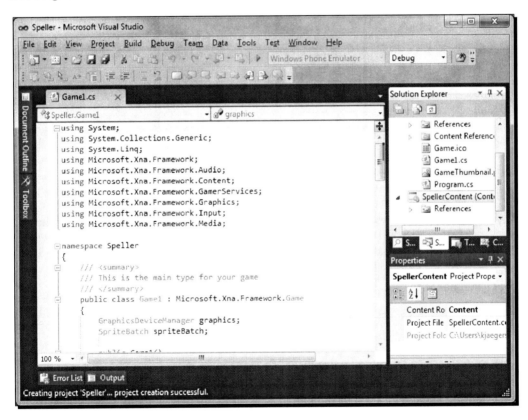

What just happened?

We now have the skeleton of a project upon which we can build the Speller game. Each of the major XNA methods is declared, usually with no additional code except the execution of the method's base. We will examine each area of the XNA game template as we create the pieces necessary for Speller.

Managing content

Two separate projects get created when you start a new XNA Game Studio project in Visual Studio. The first is your actual game project, and the second is a special type of project called a content project. This is shown in the following screenshot:

Any non-code pieces of your game, including graphical resources, sounds, fonts, and any number of other item types (you can define your own content interpreters to read things such as level maps) are added to the content project. This project gets built along with the code in your primary project and the two are combined into a single location with everything your game needs to run.

When the content project is built, each item is examined by a content importer—a bit of code that interprets the raw data of the content file, a .jpg image for example, and converts it into a format that can be passed into a content processor. The content processor's job is to convert this file into a managed code object that can be stored on a disk and read directly into memory by XNA's ContentManager class. These compiled binary files carry the .xnb file extension and are located, by default, in a subdirectory of your game's executable folder called Content.

ContentManager

Though its primary job is to load the content resources into memory at runtime, `ContentManager` does more than that. Each instance of `ContentManager` maintains a library of all of the content that has been loaded. If multiple requests to load the same content file are sent to a `ContentManager` instance, it will only load the resource from the disk the first time. The remaining requests are supplied with a reference to the item that already exists in memory.

Out of the box, XNA contains importers/processors for 3D meshes, images, fonts, audio, shaders, and XML data. We will create the content used for Speller with an image editor and the tools built into XNA Game Studio.

Time for action – creating content assets

To create content assets, perform the following steps:

1. Open Microsoft Paint, or your favorite image creation program, and create a new 16 x 16 image. Fill the image with white color and save the file to a temporary location as SQUARE.BMP.

2. Switch back to Visual Studio and right-click on the **SpellerContent (Content)** project in **Solution Explorer**.

3. Select **Add | Existing Item...** from the pop-up menu and browse to the SQUARE.BMP file. Select it and click on **Add** to add it to the content project.

4. Again, right-click on the content project in **Solution Explorer** and this time select **Add | New Item...**.

5. In the **Add New Item** window, select **Sprite Font** from the window's center pane.

6. Enter Segoe14.spritefont as the name of the file and click on **Add**.

7. Close the XML document that appears after Sprite Font has been added to the project.

What just happened?

We have now added both an image and a font to our content project. We will see how we load these assets into the game at runtime and how we can use them during gameplay.

Alternatives when adding content

You can also drag-and-drop files directly from Windows Explorer into the Solution Manager pane in Visual Studio to add them to your content project. If you have the full version of Visual Studio, you can add a new bitmap object by selecting **Add | New Item...** from the project's pop-up menu and selecting **Bitmap** as the type. The free version of Visual Studio does not support creating bitmaps from within Visual Studio.

The `SpriteFont` file that we created in step 6 and the XML document mentioned in step 7 actually load an XML template that describes how the content pipeline should create the resulting `.xnb` file. In this case, the default values for the `SpriteFont` template are sufficient for our game. This resulted in the Segoe UI Mono font (added to your system when the Windows Phone SDK is installed), with a value of 14 points being used. As we will only be using the standard A to Z character set, we do not need to make any changes to this template for Speller.

Member variables

Just after the `Game1` class declaration in the `Game1.cs` file there are two class member declarations:

```
GraphicsDeviceManager graphics;
SpriteBatch spriteBatch;
```

These two members will provide access to the system's video hardware (`graphics`) and an instance of a class that can be used to draw 2D images and text (`spriteBatch`). We can add our own member variables here for things we need to keep track of while our game is running.

Time for action – declaring new member variables

Just after the `graphics` and `spriteBatch` declarations, add the following code snippet to include the new members:

```
SpriteFont letterFont;
Texture2D playerSquare;

Vector2 playerPosition;
Vector2 moveDirection;
int playerScore;

Random rand = new Random();

string currentWord = "NONE";
int currentLetterIndex = 99;
```

```
class GameLetter
{
    public string Letter;
    public Vector2 Position;
    public bool WasHit;
}
List<GameLetter> letters = new List<GameLetter>();
const float playerSpeed = 200.0f;
```

What just happened?

We have declared all of the member variables we will need for the Speller game. The `letterFont` member will hold the sprite font object that we added to the content project earlier, and work in conjunction with the predefined `spriteBatch` object to draw text on the screen.

The square image that will represent the player will be stored in the `Texture2D` member called `playerSquare`. We can use the `Texture2D` objects to hold graphics that we wish to draw to the screen using the `SpriteBatch` class.

The `playerPosition` `Vector2` value will be used to hold the positions of the player, while `moveDirection` stores a vector pointing in the direction that the player is currently moving. Each time the player picks up a correct letter, `playerScore` will be incremented. Hitting an incorrect letter will cost the player one point.

An instance of the `Random` class, `rand`, will be used to select which word to use in each round and to place letters on the screen in random locations.

In order to keep track of which word the player is currently working on, we store that word in the `currentWord` variable, and track the number of letters that have been spelled in that word in `currentLetterIndex`.

The letters that are being displayed on the screen need several pieces of information to keep track of them. First, we need to know which letter is being displayed; next, we need to know the position the letter should occupy on the screen. Finally we need some way for our code to recognize that after we have hit an incorrect letter, we lose some of our score for it, but that we may spend several game update frames in contact with that letter and should not lose some of our score more than once for the infraction.

> **Downloading the example code**
>
> You can download the example code files for all Packt books you have purchased from your account at http://www.packtpub.com. If you purchased this book elsewhere, you can visit http://www.packtpub.com/support and register to have the files e-mailed directly to you.

All three pieces of information are wrapped into a child class of the Game1 class called GameLetter. If we were not intentionally keeping everything in Speller in the Game1 class, we would most likely create a separate code file for the GameLetter class for organizational purposes. Since Speller will be very straightforward, we will leave it inside Game1 for now.

As the GameLetter class defines a letter, we need a way to store all of the letters currently on the screen, so we have declared letters as a .NET List collection object. A List is similar to an array in that it can store a number of values of the same type, but it has the advantage that we can add and remove items from it dynamically via the Add() and RemoveAt() methods.

Finally, we declare the playerSpeed variable, which will indicate how fast the player's cube moves around the screen in response to the player's input. This value is stored in pixels per second, so in our case, one second of movement will move the character 200 pixels across the screen.

The Game1 constructor

The Game1 class has a simple constructor with no parameters. An instance of this class will be created by the shell contained in the Program.cs file within the project when the game is launched.

The Program.cs file

When your XNA game starts, the Main() method in the Program.cs file is what actually gets executed. This method creates an instance of your Game1 class and calls the Run() method, which performs the initialization we will discuss shortly. It then begins executing the game loop, updating and drawing your game repeatedly until the program exits. In many games, we will not have to worry about Program.cs, but there are some instances (combining XNA and Windows Forms, for example) when it is necessary to make changes here.

By default, the constructor has created an instance of the GraphicsDeviceManager class to store in the graphics member, and has established the base directory for the Content object, which is an instance of the ContentManager class.

When we build our project, all of the items in the content project are translated into a format specific to XNA, with the .xnb file extension. These are then copied to the Content folder in the same directory as our game's executable file.

Our Speller game will not need to make any changes to the class constructor, so we will simply move on to the next method that is called when our game starts.

Initialization

Once the instance of the `Game1` class has been created and the constructor has been executed, the `Initialize()` method is executed. This is the only time during our game's execution that this method will execute, and it is responsible for setting up anything in our class that does not require the use of content assets.

The default `Initialize()` method is empty and simply calls the base class' `Initialize()` method before exiting.

Time for action – customizing the Initialize() method

Add the following code snippet to the `Initialize()` method before `base:Initialize()`:

```
    playerScore = 0;
```

What just happened?

The only initialization we need to do is set the player's score to zero. Even this initialization is not strictly necessary, as zero is the default value for an `int` variable, but it is a good practice not to assume that this work will have been done for us.

Initialize() versus LoadContent()

In practice, much of a game's initialization actually takes place in the `LoadContent()` method, which we will discuss next, instead of the `Initialize()` method. This is because many times the items we want to initialize require content assets in order to be properly created. One common use for the `Initialize()` method is to set the initial display area (resolution) and switch into full screen mode.

Loading content

After the `Initialize()` method has run, the `LoadContent()` method is called. Here, we initialize any items in our game that require the content assets we included in the content project.

Time for action – creating a square texture

Add the following code snippet to the `LoadContent()` method:

```
letterFont = Content.Load<SpriteFont>("Segoe14");
playerSquare = Content.Load<Texture2D>("Square");

CheckForNewWord();
```

What just happened?

The default `Content` object can be used to load any type of asset from our content project into an appropriate instance in memory. The type identifier in angle brackets after the `Load()` method name identifies the type of content we will be loading, while the parameter passed to the `Load()` method specifies the asset name of the content.

Asset names can be set via the **Properties** window in Visual Studio, but would default to the name of the content file, path included, without an extension. Since all of the content objects will be translated into `.xnb` files by the content pipeline, there is no need to specify the format that the file was in before it was processed.

In our case, both of our content items are in the root of the content project's file structure. It is possible (and recommended) to create subdirectories to organize your content assets, in which case you would need to specify the relative path as part of the asset name. For example, if the `Segoe14` sprite font was located in a folder off the root of the content project called `Fonts`, the default asset name would be `Fonts\Segoe14`.

Special characters in asset names

If you do organize your assets into folders (and you should!) your asset names will include the backslash character (\) in them. Because C# interprets this as an escape sequence in a string, we need to specify the name in the `Content.Load()` call as either `"Fonts\\Segoe14"` or `@"Fonts\Segoe14"`. Two backslashes are treated as a single backslash by C#. Prefacing a string with the @ symbol lets C# know that we are not using escape sequences in the string so we can use single backslash characters. A string prefaced with the @ symbol is called a verbatim string literal.

The last thing our `LoadContent()` method does is call the (as yet undefined) `checkForNewWord()` method. We will construct this method towards the end of this chapter in order to generate a new word both at the beginning of the game and when the player has completed spelling the current word.

Updating

Our game will now enter an endless loop in which the Update() and Draw() methods are called repeatedly until we exit the application. By default, this loop attempts to run 60 times per second on the Windows and Xbox platforms, and 30 times per second on the Windows Phone platform.

The Update() method is used to process all of our game logic, such as checking for and reacting to player input, updating the positions of objects in the game world, and detecting collisions. The Update() method has a single parameter, gameTime, which identifies how much real time has passed since the last call to Update(). We can use this to scale movements smoothly over time to reduce stuttering that would occur if we make the assumption that our update will always run at a consistent frame rate, and code on other system events impacted by the update cycle.

Time for action – customizing the Update() method

Add the following code snippet to the Update() method before base.Update():

```
Vector2 moveDir = Vector2.Zero;
KeyboardState keyState = Keyboard.GetState();

if (keyState.IsKeyDown(Keys.Up))
    moveDir += new Vector2(0, -1);

if (keyState.IsKeyDown(Keys.Down))
    moveDir += new Vector2(0, 1);

if (keyState.IsKeyDown(Keys.Left))
    moveDir += new Vector2(-1, 0);

if (keyState.IsKeyDown(Keys.Right))
    moveDir += new Vector2(1, 0);

if (moveDir != Vector2.Zero)
{
    moveDir.Normalize();
    moveDirection = moveDir;
}

playerPosition += (moveDirection * playerSpeed *
    (float)gameTime.ElapsedGameTime.TotalSeconds);

playerPosition = new Vector2(
```

```
    MathHelper.Clamp(
        playerPosition.X,
        0,
        this.Window.ClientBounds.Width - 16),
    MathHelper.Clamp(
        playerPosition.Y,
        0,
        this.Window.ClientBounds.Height - 16));

CheckCollisions();

CheckForNewWord();
```

What just happened?

During each frame, we will begin by assuming that the player is not pressing any movement keys. We create a `Vector2` value called `moveDir` and set it to the predefined value of `Vector2.Zero`, meaning that both the x and y components of the vector will be zero.

In order to read the keyboard's input to determine if the player is pressing a key, we use the `Keyboard.GetState()` method to capture a snapshot of the current state of all the keys on the keyboard. We store this in the `keyState` variable, which we then use in a series of `if` statements to determine if the up, down, left, or right arrow keys are pressed. If any of them are pressed, we modify the value of `moveDir` by adding the appropriate vector component to its current value.

After all the four keys have been checked, we will check to see if the value is still `Vector2.Zero`. If it is, we will skip updating the `moveDirection` variable. If there is a non-zero value in `moveDir`, however, we will use the `Normalize()` method of the `Vector2` class to divide the vector by its length, resulting in a vector pointing in the same direction with a length of one unit. We store this updated direction in the `moveDirection` variable, which is maintained between frames.

When we have accounted for all of the possible inputs, we update the player's position by multiplying the `moveDirection` by `playerSpeed` and the amount of time that has elapsed since `Update()` was last called. The result of this multiplication is added to the `playerPosition` vector, resulting in the new position for the player.

Before we can assume that the new position is ok, we need to make sure that the player stays on the screen. We do this by using `MathHelper.Clamp()` on both the X and Y components of the `playerPosition` vector. `Clamp()` allows us to specify a desired value and a range. If the value is outside the range, it will be changed to the upper or lower limit of the range, depending on which side of the range it is on. By limiting the range between zero and the size of the screen (minus the size of the player), we can ensure that the player's sprite never leaves the screen.

Finally, we call two functions that we have not yet implemented: CheckCollisions() and CheckForNewWord(). We discussed CheckForNewWord() in the LoadContent() section, but CheckCollisions() is new. We will use this method to determine when the player collides with a letter and how to respond to that collision (increase or decrease the player's score, advance the spelling of the current word, and so on).

The Draw() method

The last of the predefined methods in the XNA game template is Draw(). This method is called once after each call to Update() and is responsible for the game state for the current frame. By default, all that the Draw() method does is clears the display and sets it to the CornflowerBlue color.

Time for action – drawing Speller

To draw the visual components of our Speller game, perform the following steps:

1. Alter the GraphicsDevice.Clear(Color.CornflowerBlue) call and replace Color.CornflowerBlue with Color.Black to set the background color.

2. Add the following code after the call to clear the display:

```
spriteBatch.Begin();
spriteBatch.Draw(playerSquare, playerPosition, Color.White);

foreach (GameLetter letter in letters)
{
    Color letterColor = Color.White;

    if (letter.WasHit)
        letterColor = Color.Red;

    spriteBatch.DrawString(
        letterFont,
        letter.Letter,
        letter.Position,
        letterColor);
}

spriteBatch.DrawString(
    letterFont,
    "Spell: ",
    new Vector2(
        this.Window.ClientBounds.Width / 2 - 100,
```

```
            this.Window.ClientBounds.Height - 25),
        Color.White);

    string beforeWord = currentWord.Substring(0, currentLetterIndex);
    string currentLetter = currentWord.Substring(currentLetterIndex,
    1);
    string afterWord = "";

    if (currentWord.Length > currentLetterIndex)
        afterWord = currentWord.Substring(
        currentLetterIndex + 1);

    spriteBatch.DrawString(
        letterFont,
        beforeWord,
        new Vector2(
            this.Window.ClientBounds.Width / 2,
            this.Window.ClientBounds.Height - 25),
        Color.Green);

    spriteBatch.DrawString(
        letterFont,
        currentLetter,
        new Vector2(
            this.Window.ClientBounds.Width / 2 +
                letterFont.MeasureString(beforeWord).X,
            this.Window.ClientBounds.Height - 25),
        Color.Yellow);

    spriteBatch.DrawString(
        letterFont,
        afterWord,
        new Vector2(
          this.Window.ClientBounds.Width / 2 +
            letterFont.MeasureString(beforeWord+currentLetterIndex)
.X,
          this.Window.ClientBounds.Height - 25),
        Color.LightBlue);

    spriteBatch.DrawString(
        letterFont,
        "Score: " + playerScore.ToString(),
        Vector2.Zero,
        Color.White);

    spriteBatch.End();
```

What just happened?

When using the `SpriteBatch` class, any calls to draw graphics or text must be wrapped in calls to `Begin()` and `End()`. `SpriteBatch.Begin()` prepares the rendering system for drawing 2D graphics and sets up a specialized render state. This is necessary because all 2D graphics in XNA are actually drawn in 3D, with the projection and orientation configurations in the render state to display the 2D images properly.

In our case, the only graphical image we are drawing is the square that represents the player. We draw this with a simple call to `SpriteBatch.Draw()`, which requires the texture we will use, the location where the texture will be drawn on the screen (relative to the upper-left corner of the display area), and a tint color. Because our square image is white, we could set any color we wish here and the player's square would take on that color when displayed. We will use that to our advantage in just a moment when we draw the text of the word the player is trying to spell.

After the player has been drawn, we loop through each of the letters in the `letters` list and use the `SpriteBatch.DrawString()` method to draw the letter at its position, using the `letterFont` we created earlier. Normally, we will draw the letters in white, but if the player runs into this letter (and it is not the letter they are supposed to hit) we will draw it in red.

Next, we need to display the word that the player is attempting to spell. We display the text **Spell:** near the bottom center of the display, using the bounds of the current window to determine the location to draw.

In order to colorize the word properly, we need to split the word into different parts as what the player has already spelled, the current letter they are targeting, and the letters after the current letter. We do this using the `Substring()` method of the string class, and then draw these three components with different color tints. We utilize the `MeasureString()` method of `letterFont` to determine how much space each of these components occupies on the screen so that we can position the subsequent strings properly.

Finally, we display the player's score at the upper-left corner of the screen.

Helper methods

All that remains to finish the Speller game is to create our two missing methods, `CheckForNewWord()` and `CheckCollisions()`. We will actually break these down into other helper functions as well.

Time for action – words and letters

To implement the `CheckForNewWord()` and its helper methods, we will perform the following steps:

1. Add the `PickAWord()` method to the end of the `Game1` class, after `Draw()`:

```
private string PickAWord()
{
    switch (rand.Next(15))
    {
        case 0: return "CAT";
        case 1: return "DOG";
        case 2: return "MILK";
        case 3: return "SUN";
        case 4: return "SKY";
        case 5: return "RAIN";
        case 6: return "SNOW";
        case 7: return "FAR";
        case 8: return "NEAR";
        case 9: return "FRIEND";
        case 10: return "GAME";
        case 11: return "XNA";
        case 12: return "PLAY";
        case 13: return "RUN";
        case 14: return "FUN";
    }

    return "BUG";
}
```

2. Add the `FillLetters()` method to the `Game1` class, after `PickAWord()`:

```
private void FillLetters(string word)
{
  Rectangle safeArea = new Rectangle(
    this.Window.ClientBounds.Width / 2 - playerSquare.Width,
    this.Window.ClientBounds.Height / 2 - playerSquare.Height,
    playerSquare.Width * 2,
    playerSquare.Height * 2);

  string alphabet = "ABCDEFGHIJKLMNOPQRSTUVWXYZ";

  List<Vector2> locations = new List<Vector2>();
```

```
for (int x=25;
     x < this.Window.ClientBounds.Width - 50;
     x += 50)
{
  for (int y=25;
       y < this.Window.ClientBounds.Height - 50;
       y += 50)
  {
    Rectangle locationRect = new Rectangle(
      x,
      y,
      (int)letterFont.MeasureString("W").X,
      (int)letterFont.MeasureString("W").Y);

    if (!safeArea.Intersects(locationRect))
    {
      locations.Add(new Vector2(x, y));
    }
  }
}

letters.Clear();
for (int x = 0; x < 20; x++)
{
  GameLetter thisLetter = new GameLetter();

  if (x < word.Length)
      thisLetter.Letter = word.Substring(x, 1);
  else
      thisLetter.Letter = alphabet.Substring(
          rand.Next(0,26),1);

      int location = rand.Next(0,locations.Count);
      thisLetter.Position = locations[location];
      thisLetter.WasHit = false;
      locations.RemoveAt(location);

      letters.Add(thisLetter);
  }

}
```

3. Add the `CheckForNewWord()` method to the end of the `Game1` class, after `FillLetters()`:

```
private void CheckForNewWord()
{
    if (currentLetterIndex >= currentWord.Length)
    {
        playerPosition = new Vector2(
            this.Window.ClientBounds.Width / 2,
            this.Window.ClientBounds.Height / 2);
        currentWord = PickAWord();
        currentLetterIndex = 0;
        FillLetters(currentWord);
    }
}
```

What just happened?

In step 1, we generate a random number using the `Next()` method of the `Random` class. Given an integer value, `Next()` will return an integer between zero and that number minus one, meaning we will have a return value from zero to fourteen. Using a `select` statement, we return the randomly determined word. Note that we should never hit the last return statement in the function, so if we are ever asked to spell the word BUG, we know something is wrong.

The `FillLetters()` method is used to populate the `letters` list with letters and their locations on the screen. We could simply generate random locations for each letter, but then this would leave us with the potential for letters overlapping each other, requiring a check as each letter is generated to ensure this does not happen.

Instead, we will generate a list of potential letter positions by building the `locations` list. This list will contain each of the possible places on the screen where we will put a letter by spacing through a grid and adding entries every 25 pixels in the x and y directions. The exception is that we define an area in the center of the screen where the player will start and we will not place letters. This allows the player to start each round without being in contact with any of the game letters.

Once we have our list of locations, we clear the `letters` list and generate 20 letters. We start with the letters required to spell the target word, pulling letters from the `currentWord` string until we reach the end. After that, the letters will come from the `alphabet` string randomly. Each letter is assigned one of the locations from the `locations` list, and that location is then removed from the list so we will not have two letters on top of each other.

Lastly, the `CheckForNewWord()` method checks to see if `currentLetterIndex` is larger than the length of `currentWord`. If it is, the player's position is reset to the center of the screen and a new word is generated using `PickAWord()`. `currentLetterIndex` is reset, and the `letters` list is rebuilt using the `FillLetters()` method.

Time for action – completing the Speller project

To complete the Speller project we need to add the `CheckCollosions()` method by performing the following steps:

1. Add the `CheckCollisions()` method to the `Game1` class after `CheckForNewWord()`:

```
private void CheckCollisions()
{
    for (int x = letters.Count - 1; x >= 0; x--)
    {
        if (new Rectangle(
            (int)letters[x].Position.X,
            (int)letters[x].Position.Y,
            (int)letterFont.MeasureString(
                letters[x].Letter).X,
            (int)letterFont.MeasureString(
                letters[x].Letter).Y).Intersects(
                    new Rectangle(
                        (int)playerPosition.X,
                        (int)playerPosition.Y,
                        playerSquare.Width,
                        playerSquare.Height)))
        {
            if (letters[x].Letter ==
                currentWord.Substring(currentLetterIndex, 1))
            {
                playerScore += 1;
                letters.RemoveAt(x);
                currentLetterIndex++;
            }
            else
            {
                if (!letters[x].WasHit)
                {
                    playerScore -= 1;
                    letters[x].WasHit = true;
                }
            }
```

```
                }
            }
        else
        {
                letters[x].WasHit = false;
            }
        }
    }
}
```

2. Execute the Speller project and play! The following screenshot shows how our game will look when we execute it:

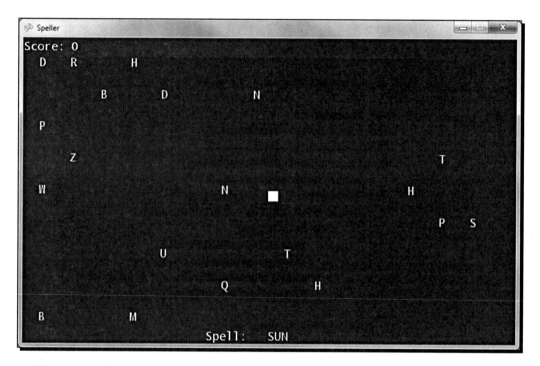

What just happened?

CheckCollisions() loops backward through the letters list, looking for letters that the player has collided with. Going backwards is necessary because we will (potentially) be removing items from the list, which cannot be done in a foreach loop. If we were moving forward through the list, we would disrupt our loop by deleting the current item, which would cause it to skip over the next items in the list. Moving backwards through the list allows us to remove items without adjusting our loop's logic.

In order to determine if we have collided with a letter, we build two rectangles. The first rectangle represents the position and size of the letter we are checking against, by using the letter's `Position` value and the size of the letter calculated with `MeasureString()`. The second rectangle represents the area occupied by the player's sprite.

The `Intersects()` method of the `Rectangle` class will return true if these two rectangles overlap at any point. If they do, we know we have hit a letter and need to take action.

If the letter impacted is the next letter in the word that the player is spelling, we increment the player's score and remove the letter from the list. We also advance `currentLetterIndex` so that when `Update()` next calls `CheckForNewWord()`, we will know if this word has been completed.

If the letter is not the player's current target, we check the letter's `WasHit` value. If it is false, we have not run into this letter, so we reduce the player's score and mark `WasHit` to true. If `WasHit` is already true, we simply do nothing so as not to deduct from the player's score multiple times while the player passes over an incorrect letter.

When the rectangles do not intersect, we know we are not currently in contact with this letter, so we set its `WasHit` variable to `false`. This has the effect that once we leave an incorrect letter, it becomes re-enabled for future collisions (and point deductions).

Have a go hero

Speller is a pretty simple game, but could be enhanced to make a more full-fledged game, by including the following, depending on your level of experience with 2D XNA development:

- Beginner: Raise the difficulty by increasing the speed of the player's square as they complete each word.

- Intermediate: Record the words with a microphone and play those recordings when a new word is generated. Instead of displaying the entire word during the `update()` method, display only the letters that have been spelled so far. This would turn the game into more of an educational kid's game with the player having to spell out the words they hear.

Summary

As a quick-fire introduction to a number of essential XNA topics, Speller covers quite a bit of ground. We have a functional game that accepts player input, draws graphics and text to the screen, generates a random playfield of letters, and detects player collision with them. We got an overview of the structure of an XNA game and the basic `Update()`/`Draw()` game loop.

As we will see, many of these concepts translate into a 3D environment with very little need for modification, other than the need to keep track of positions and movement with an extra dimension attached. We will utilize the `Vector3` objects instead of the `Vector2` objects, and we will still rely on a 2D plane for much of the layout of our game world.

Additionally, although much of the work in the following chapters will take place with 3D drawing commands and constructs, we will still be returning to the 2D `SpriteBatch` and `SpriteFont` classes to construct interface elements and convey textual information to the player.

2
Cube Chaser – A Flat 3D World

Our first 3D game will feature a very straight forward design: the player is trapped in a randomly generated maze, and must seek out the great green cube! Every time the player reaches this goal, they are awarded points for how quickly they found the cube and it is relocated to a different portion of the maze.

While simple in design, building Cube Chaser will cover a number of important topics related to 3D game development. In this chapter, we will look at:

◆ Building an FPS (First Person Shooter) style camera

◆ Drawing surfaces using triangles in the 3D world

◆ Generating a floor as a base for our maze

◆ Detecting input and allowing first-person movement through the maze

Designing the game

Cube Chaser will take place in a randomly generated 3D maze. We will use triangle lists to build the floor and walls of the maze and instruct the graphics card to draw them to the screen.

The maze itself is actually a 2D construction, with the walls being rendered in 3D. The floor of the maze will be laid out along the X-Z plane, with the walls extending upwards along the positive Y axis. The player will be able to move in the X and Z plane, but will be restricted to a single, pre-defined elevation along the Y axis.

3D coordinates

You may have noticed in the previous statement that the player will move along the X-Z plane. If you have spent any time developing 2D games, you will likely be used to working with X-Y coordinates, with X running across the screen from left to right and Y running down the screen from top to bottom.

When we move into 3D, we no longer have a fixed viewing angle on our action. In a 2D game, we typically describe actions in the X-Y plane for a side-scrolling game, overhead shooter, or a puzzle game. Since there are only two dimensions to deal with, the relationship between objects on the screen is the same type of relationship they would have if you drew them on a piece of paper. The only time we even really consider a third dimension in a 2D game, we refer to it as the Z-Order, or the order in which the sprites will be drawn to make some appear on top of others.

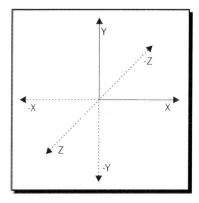

Knowing that we have three axes to deal with, X, Y, and Z, the next step is to determine how coordinates along each axis relate to the others. XNA uses a right-handed coordinate system, meaning that you can try to contort your hand in various directions to have your palm, fingers, and thumb pointing along the positive directions for each axis. Without spraining anything, what it really means is that if you were standing in the 3D world at a point where you could see the positive Y axis shooting up into the sky and the positive X axis running off to the right as in the previous diagram, the positive Z axis would be pointing towards you.

Left-handed and right-handed coordinates

XNA uses a right-handed coordinate system. If you hold your hands with your palms facing up, and curl your fingers 90 degrees up from your palm, your palm points along the positive X axis, and your fingers point along the positive Y axis. If you point your thumb out away from your hand, the thumb points along the positive Z axis, relative to X and Y. Which hand you use determines which direction is positive along the Z axis. The coordinate system in XNA is based on the right-handed rule.

Creating the project

We will begin the construction of Cube Chaser by creating a new XNA 4.0 Windows Game in Visual Studio.

Time for action – creating the Cube Chaser project

1. Open Visual Studio 2010 and select **File | New | Project...** from the menu bar.

2. Open the **Visual C#** tree in the **Installed Templates** portion of the **New Project** window, and open the **XNA Game Studio 4.0** tree under it.

3. Select the **Windows Game (4.0)** project template from the central portion of the window.

4. Under **Name**, enter `Cube Chaser` and click the **Ok** button.

5. After Visual Studio has created the solution, right-click on the `Game1.cs` file in the **Solution Explorer** window and select **Rename**.

6. Change the name of the file to `CubeChaserGame.cs`. When asked if you wish to update the references to the file, click **Yes**.

What just happened?

We now have the shell for our Cube Chaser game. We could have left our main game class as `Game1` as we did for the Speller game, but giving the class a more descriptive name helps to keep our code as self-documenting as possible.

Our view of the world

Before we can place objects and geometry into our virtual representation of a 3D world, we need to come up with a way to describe to XNA how we are going to control the viewpoint of the player. In many 2D games, a simple `Vector2` value is often enough to cover the requirements of the camera – assuming the 2D game needed a camera at all. The camera viewing a 2D world might only need to know how far across and down the game world the current view should be located. Other aspects of the view, such as the distance from which the player is viewing the action, may be fixed due to the size of the pre-drawn sprites representing the game environment and objects.

In contrast, we need a bit more information to define the camera in a 3D game. The fact that we need a third coordinate (the Z coordinate) should not be surprising; since we have moved from 2D to 3D, it only stands to reason that we need three coordinates to define a point. What may be less obvious, however, is that we also need a way to identify what direction the camera is pointing in. Two cameras in the same position will have very different views if they are pointed in opposite directions.

We will build the `Camera` class in several stages, adding more detail with each visit to the code file.

Time for action – beginning the Camera class

1. Add a new class to the Cube Chaser project by right-clicking on the project in **Solution Explorer** and selecting **Add | Class...**.

2. Ensure that the **Visual C# | Code** is selected under **Installed Templates** and select the **Class** template.

3. Enter `Camera.cs` as the name of the class file.

4. Add the following `using` directive to the top of the `Camera.cs` file:

   ```
   using Microsoft.Xna.Framework;
   ```

5. Add the following fields and properties to the `Camera` class:

   ```
   #region Fields
   private Vector3 position = Vector3.Zero;
   private float rotation;
   #endregion

   #region Properties
   public Matrix Projection { get; private set; }
   #endregion
   ```

6. Add a constructor for the `Camera` class:

   ```
   #region Constructor
   public Camera(
       Vector3 position,
       float rotation,
       float aspectRatio,
       float nearClip,
       float farClip)
   {
       Projection = Matrix.CreatePerspectiveFieldOfView(
           MathHelper.PiOver4,
           aspectRatio,
           nearClip,
           farClip);
       MoveTo(position, rotation);
   }
   #endregion
   ```

What just happened?

We have now put together some of the basic information our `Camera` class will track, including the position of the camera and the angle it is facing.

What is an FPS (First Person Shooter) camera?

When working with cameras in 3D, there are several different kinds of cameras we might want to deal with. An FPS camera, so named because it is the style of camera used in First Person Shooter games, it is a camera that is placed in the location of the character's eyes, resulting in a first-person view. As the player moves, the camera moves and rotates directly with the player. Other types of cameras include chase cameras, which follow along behind the player, and arc-ball cameras, which circle around a fixed point in 3D space. We will implement an arc-ball camera in *Chapter 5, Tank Battles – A War-Torn Land*.

Additionally, we have defined a matrix, called `Projection`, which we will create based on the values passed into the constructor for the `Camera` class. It is defined as a property that can be obtained from outside our code, but can only be set within the `Camera` class itself.

What is a matrix?

The short answer is that a matrix is a two-dimensional array of numbers used to transform points in 3D space. The long answer to this question is presented in *Chapter 4, Cube Chaser – Finding Your Way*, where we will dive into details about what a matrix is and the "magic" behind how they work. For now, we can define a matrix as a construct that we can use to manipulate points by applying different effects to them.

We have not yet defined the `MoveTo()` method, which will allow us to specify the camera position and rotation in a single call. We need a few more elements in our class before we can implement `MoveTo()`.

Also, note that we have enclosed sections of our code in `#region...#endregion` directives. These tell the Visual Studio IDE that these sections of the code can be collapsed as a unit to hide the details while we work on other sections of the code. We will use these regions throughout the book to keep our code organized.

The Projection matrix

On a physical camera, you might have a selection of various lenses with different properties – a wide angled lens for wide shots, or a telephoto lens for zooming in close. The `Projection` matrix is the way we describe such properties to the XNA rendering system. The `Projection` matrix describes to the graphics card how to translate (or project) 3D objects onto the 2D viewing area of the screen. The following image illustrates the parameters used to construct the `Projection` matrix:

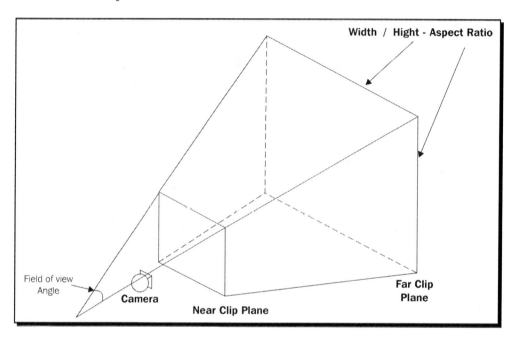

The `Matrix.CreatePerspectiveFieldOfView()` method accepts four parameters that define how our virtual camera will view the 3D scene. The first is the field of view, or viewing angle, that the camera covers. The larger this value is, the wider the angle the camera will display. In this case, we specify `MathHelper.PiOver4`, which translates to a 45 degree angle.

Angles in XNA

XNA handles all angles in radians. In a full circle there are 2*pi radians. Half of a circle is 180 degree, or pi radians. XNA provides the `MathHelper.ToRadians()` method if you wish to track angles in your code in degrees and convert them before use.

A 45 degree field of view is a fairly standard value for 3D games, and represents a realistic view angle. As the angle gets larger, you will begin to notice a fish-eye effect and the rotation of the camera will seem more and more unusual. In fact, some games have used an expanded field of view to distort the player's perspective when their character becomes disoriented or incapacitated in some way. The following image shows the impact of changing only the field of view angle while viewing the same scene:

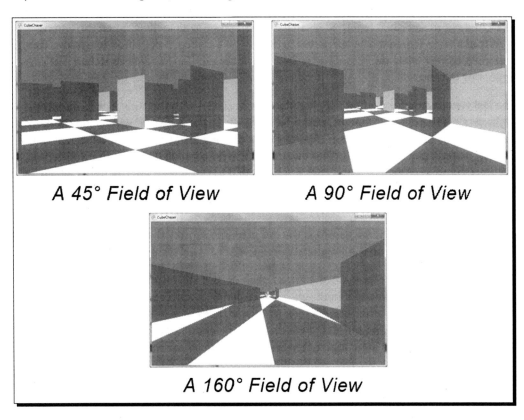

A 45° Field of View   *A 90° Field of View*

A 160° Field of View

In all three of the previous images, the player is standing in exactly the same spot in identical mazes. The only difference between each image is the field of view angle specified in the `Projection` matrix. As the viewing angle increases, objects become stretched out and distorted the further they are away from the center of the viewing area.

The second parameter, the aspect ratio, determines the shape of the viewing area. The most familiar use of aspect ratios in daily life is in televisions and monitors. A standard-definition television has a 4:3 (or 4 divided by 3, or 1.333) aspect ratio, while high-definition displays often use a 16:9 (1.777) or 16:10 (1.6) aspect ratio. Generally, the aspect ratio of your `Projection` matrix should match the aspect ratio of the viewport you are displaying your graphics in (in fact, when we define an instance of our camera, we will simply pass the viewport's aspect ratio property in for this parameter). Using a mismatched value will cause your image to be either stretched out or squashed together. A similar effect can be seen in films, when the ending credits of a wide-screen movie are scaled to display on a standard-definition television. The text looks correct while the actors and scenes in the background become stretched vertically, appearing tall and thin.

The last two parameters define clipping planes associated with the `Projection` matrix. A clipping plane defines the point, past which objects in the 3D world will no longer be displayed. Any 3D geometry closer than the near clipping distance will not be drawn to the display, nor will any geometry further away than the far clipping distance. In other words, the only things in our game world that will be drawn to the screen are the items which lie further away than the near distance, but closer than the far distance.

We need the far clipping plane to place reasonable limits on the objects we draw for performance purposes. Some games allow the player to modify the drawing distance for the far clipping plane based on the graphical horsepower of their system.

The reason for the near clipping plane is less obvious, but still important. Let's say, for example, that we are creating a multi-player, first-person shooter style game. In this case, our player is represented to other players by a 3D avatar that exists in the game world just like other players, enemies, and objects. If we define the location of the camera near the avatar's eyes, the movement and animation of the avatar may cause parts of the avatar's model to push their way in front of the camera position. By specifying a near clipping plane, we can prevent these pieces of the player's own avatar from being drawn so that the player's view is not obscured by the inside of their own head!

Looking at something

While we have a rotation value already associated with the `Camera` class, it does not mean anything to the class currently. An angle only exists in one plane in our 3D coordinate system, so we cannot simply specify an angle at which to point the camera. We need to convert the angle into a point in 3D space that lies in the direction we wish the camera to face relative to its current location.

Time for action – implementing a look-at point

1. Add the following properties to the `Fields` region of the `Camera` class:

```
private Vector3 lookAt;
private Vector3 baseCameraReference = new Vector3(0, 0, 1);
private bool needViewResync = true;
```

2. Add the following region and method to the `Camera` class:

```
#region Helper Methods
private void UpdateLookAt()
{
    Matrix rotationMatrix = Matrix.CreateRotationY(rotation);
    Vector3 lookAtOffset = Vector3.Transform(
        baseCameraReference,
        rotationMatrix);
    lookAt = position + lookAtOffset;
    needViewResync = true;
}
#endregion
```

3. Define the `MoveTo()` method that is called in the constructor. This method should be placed inside the Helper Methods region you just created:

```
public void MoveTo(Vector3 position, float rotation)
{
    this.position = position;
    this.rotation = rotation;
    UpdateLookAt();
}
```

4. Add two new public properties to the `Properties` region of the `Camera` class:

```
public Vector3 Position
{
    get
    {
        return position;
    }
    set
    {
        position = value;
        UpdateLookAt();
    }
}
```

```
public float Rotation
{
    get
    {
        return rotation;
    }
    set
    {
        rotation = value;
        UpdateLookAt();
    }
}
```

What just happened?

Just like the camera's position, the point we are going to look at is stored as a `Vector3`. In order to build this point, we need a frame of reference, indicating the direction the camera would be pointing if it were not rotated at all. We define this direction in the `baseCameraReference` field, specifying that the non-rotated camera will point along the Z axis (assuming that the camera was located at the origin point (0, 0, 0)).

The last field we added, `needViewResync`, will be used to determine when we need to rebuild the next important matrix we will be discussing – the `View` matrix. We will return to that topic in a moment.

In order to determine the point in 3D space that the camera will look towards (called the Look At point), we create a `rotation` matrix around the Y axis (which points up from the X-Z plane) equal to the current value of the rotation field. We then transform the `baseCameraReference` vector with this `rotation` matrix, resulting in a `Vector3` which points in the direction of the rotation relative to the world origin at (0, 0, 0) in 3D space.

We then build the `lookAt` point field by adding this offset vector to the camera's current position, in effect relocating the `lookAt` point from the origin to be relative to the camera position. Finally, we mark the `needViewResync` flag as true.

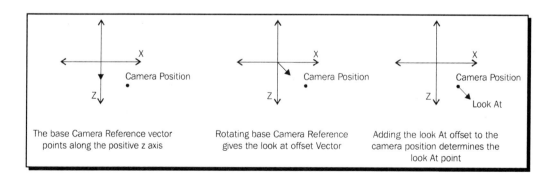

| The base Camera Reference vector points along the positive z axis | Rotating base Camera Reference gives the look at offset Vector | Adding the look At offset to the camera position determines the look At point |

The remaining code mentioned previously implements the `MoveTo()` method, and exposes public properties for the `Position` and `Rotation` values. All three of these items simply set their related fields and call the `UpdateLookAt()` method we just defined.

The View matrix

The last bit of information we need our camera to provide in order to be able to draw a scene is called the `View` matrix. This matrix defines the position and direction from which the camera views the 3D world. In other words, we combine our camera position and the point we are looking at, to create the structure that XNA needs, to interpret how we wish our camera to view the 3D scene.

Time for action – the View matrix

1. Add the following variable to the `Fields` region of the `Camera` class:

   ```
   private Matrix cachedViewMatrix;
   ```

2. Add the following property to the `Properties` region of the `Camera` class:

   ```
   public Matrix View
   {
       get
       {
           if (needViewResync)
               cachedViewMatrix = Matrix.CreateLookAt(
                   Position,
                   lookAt,
                   Vector3.Up);

           return cachedViewMatrix;
       }
   }
   ```

What just happened?

We could simply recalculate the `View` matrix every time the `Camera` class was asked for it, but doing so would incur a small performance penalty. Because we do not have a lot of action happening in Cube Chaser, this penalty would not impact our game, but we can avoid it altogether. We are building a caching mechanism into the camera code in the event our game develops to the point that this optimization is helpful. Any time the `View` matrix is calculated, we will store it in `cachedViewMatrix` and simply return that matrix if the `View` matrix is requested without the underlying camera information having been modified.

In order to create the `View` matrix, we use the convenient `Matrix.CreateLookAt()` method, which accepts the camera position, the look at point we calculated previously, and a vector indicating what direction is considered to be up for the camera. In our case, we are using the pre-defined `Vector3.Up`, which translates to (0, 1, 0), or up along the positive Y axis.

That is enough of the camera to get us started. We will return to the `Camera` class later when we implement movement. For now, let's get on with actually drawing something to the screen!

From the ground up

Even if we were to go ahead and implement the code to allow us to utilize the Camera class, there would be nothing to display at this point, as we have not defined any objects in our 3D world other than the camera, and it is invisible.

There are several different ways we could approach drawing the floor of the maze. We could draw the whole floor as a single square in a particular color. We could draw the same giant square using a texture that was repeated over the whole thing.

Both of these methods are quite valid, but we are going to take a slightly different approach. We will build a square for each cell of the maze floor, alternating the colors of the squares to create a checkerboard-like pattern. We will draw all of the floor tiles In a single operation, sending all of the geometry to the graphics card at once.

Time for action – creating the Maze classes

1. Add a new class file called `Maze.cs` to the Cube Chaser project.

2. Add the following `using` directives to the top of the `Maze.cs` class file:

```
using Microsoft.Xna.Framework;
using Microsoft.Xna.Framework.Graphics;
```

3. Add the following fields to the `Maze` class:

```
#region Fields
public const int mazeWidth = 20;
public const int mazeHeight = 20;

GraphicsDevice device;

VertexBuffer floorBuffer;

Color[] floorColors = new Color[2] { Color.White, Color.Gray };
#endregion
```

4. Add a constructor for the `Maze` class:

```
#region Constructor
public Maze(GraphicsDevice device)
{
    this.device = device;

    BuildFloorBuffer();
}
#endregion
```

5. Add the following region and helper methods to the `Maze` class:

```
#region The Floor
private void BuildFloorBuffer()
{
    List<VertexPositionColor> vertexList =
        new List<VertexPositionColor>();

    int counter = 0;

    for (int x = 0; x < mazeWidth; x++)
    {
        counter++;
        for (int z = 0; z < mazeHeight; z++)
        {
            counter++;
            foreach (VertexPositionColor vertex in
                FloorTile(x, z, floorColors[counter % 2]))
            {
                vertexList.Add(vertex);
            }
        }
    }

    floorBuffer = new VertexBuffer(
        device,
        VertexPositionColor.VertexDeclaration,
        vertexList.Count,
        BufferUsage.WriteOnly);

    floorBuffer.SetData<VertexPositionColor>(vertexList.
ToArray());
}

private List<VertexPositionColor> FloorTile(
```

```
        int xOffset,
        int zOffset,
        Color tileColor)
{

    List<VertexPositionColor> vList =
        new List<VertexPositionColor>();

    vList.Add(new VertexPositionColor(
        new Vector3(0 + xOffset, 0, 0 + zOffset), tileColor));
    vList.Add(new VertexPositionColor(
        new Vector3(1 + xOffset, 0, 0 + zOffset), tileColor));
    vList.Add(new VertexPositionColor(
        new Vector3(0 + xOffset, 0, 1 + zOffset), tileColor));

    vList.Add(new VertexPositionColor(
        new Vector3(1 + xOffset, 0, 0 + zOffset), tileColor));
    vList.Add(new VertexPositionColor(
        new Vector3(1 + xOffset, 0, 1 + zOffset), tileColor));
    vList.Add(new VertexPositionColor(
        new Vector3(0 + xOffset, 0, 1 + zOffset), tileColor));

    return vList;
}
#endregion
```

What just happened?

So far, we have not really defined anything about the actual maze associated with the `Maze` class other than the width and height of the maze we will be generating. The goal at this point is to build the floor of the maze and then bring our `Maze` and `Camera` classes together to allow us to display something to the game screen.

After we have generated all of the triangles necessary for our floor, they will be stored in the `floorBuffer` field. This field is a `VertexBuffer`, which holds a list of 3D vertices that can be sent to the graphics card in a single push.

Drawing with triangles

While we want to draw square floor tiles, the graphics card really only works with triangles. Even the most complex 3D models are made up of thousands or millions of small triangles. Fortunately, a square can be easily created with two equally-sized right triangles placed next to each other. Even when we load and display complex 3D models they are actually composed of lots of small triangles positioned to make up the surface of the object we are displaying.

In order to fill out this `VertexBuffer`, we need to generate the points that make up the triangles for the floor. This is the job of the `BuildFloorBuffer()` method, and its helper, `FloorTile()`. `BuildFloorBuffer()` begins by defining a `List` of `VertexPositionColor` objects. The built-in vertex declarations in XNA allow for different combinations of color, texture, and normal vectors to be associated with the position of the vertex (no matter what else a vertex has, it will always have a position). As the name implies, a `VertexPositionColor` defines a vertex with a position in 3D space and an associated color.

We will determine the color of the vertices (and thus the triangles and the squares) on the floor of the maze by alternating between white and gray, picking the colors from the `floorColors` list as the vertices are built.

The vertices for each square are built by calling the `FloorTile()` method, which returns a list of `VertexPositionColor` objects. Because we need two triangles to make up a square, we need to return six `VertexPositionColor` elements. We will use a similar technique when we build the maze walls later in this chapter.

The `FloorTile()` method accepts the X and Z offsets for this tile (if we were looking down at the maze from above, the number of squares across and down the maze we are building this square for) and the color for this particular tile. It then builds a new set of `VertexPositionColor` objects by adding six new vertices, three for each triangle, to a `List` object. The order that we define the vertices, called the **winding order**, is important. The vertices of each triangle need to be specified in a clockwise direction based on the angle from which the triangle will be viewed. The graphics device considers triangles to be single-sided entities. If we were to swing our camera underneath the maze, the floor would completely disappear.

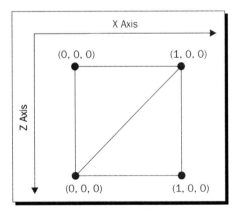

In the previous image, we can see that we need four vertices to define the two triangles which compose a single floor square. We build the first triangle from the upper-left, upper-right, and lower-left vertices, and the second triangle from the upper-right, lower-right, and lower-left vertices, in those orders.

In the `FloorTile()` method mentioned previously, we explicitly add these six points to the list of vertices that will be returned from the function, offsetting the X and Z values of each vertex by the values passed into the function. This has the effect of translating the triangles to their appropriate positions in the 3D world; otherwise they would be stacked all on top of each other near the world origin.

Drawing the floor

Now that we have defined all of the triangles that will make up the checker-boarded floor for our maze, let's go ahead and complete the code necessary to draw the floor to the screen.

Time for action – drawing the floor

1. Add the `Draw` region and the `Draw()` method to the `Maze` class:

```
#region Draw
public void Draw(Camera camera, BasicEffect effect)
{
    effect.VertexColorEnabled = true;
    effect.World = Matrix.Identity;
    effect.View = camera.View;
    effect.Projection = camera.Projection;

    foreach (EffectPass pass in effect.CurrentTechnique.Passes)
    {
        pass.Apply();
        device.SetVertexBuffer(floorBuffer);
        device.DrawPrimitives(
            PrimitiveType.TriangleList,
            0,
            floorBuffer.VertexCount / 3);
    }
}
#endregion
```

2. In the `CubeChaserGame` class, add the following declarations to the declarations area of the class:

```
Camera camera;
Maze maze;
BasicEffect effect;
```

3. In the `Initialize()` method of the `CubeChaserGame` class, initialize the camera, maze, and effect objects, placing this code before the call to `base.Initialize()`:

```
camera = new Camera(
    new Vector3(0.5f, 0.5f, 0.5f),
    0,
    GraphicsDevice.Viewport.AspectRatio,
    0.05f,
    100f);
effect = new BasicEffect(GraphicsDevice);
maze = new Maze(GraphicsDevice);
```

4. In the `Draw()` method of the `CubeChaserGame` class, add a call to draw the maze after the `GraphicsDevice.Clear()` statement:

```
maze.Draw(camera, effect);
```

5. Execute the Cube Chaser game project:

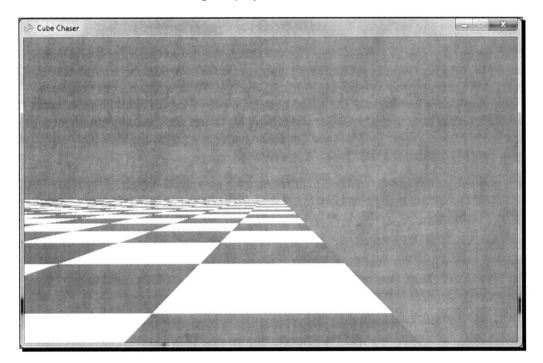

What just happened?

The `Maze` class' `Draw()` method accepts two parameters: the camera that will be used as the viewing point for drawing the maze, and an object called a `BasicEffect`. Whenever we draw anything with XNA's 3D drawing system, we need an effect associated with what we are going to display.

An effect describes to the rendering system how the pixels on the display should be constructed based on the code for each particular effect. Effects are constructed with a mini-programming language called **High Level Shader Language** (**HLSL**), and can produce a wide variety of surfaces and special effects. We will touch a bit on effects and how they work in more detail in *Chapter 5, Tank Battles – A War-Torn Land*, but for now, the `BasicEffect` class which is built into XNA contains everything we need for Cube Chaser.

In order to use our `BasicEffect`, we need to specify a few parameters that instruct it how it should view the 3D scene and what to do with the vertices and triangles we give it.

First, we set `VertexColorEnabled` to `true`, since we are going to rely on the colors we passed into our `FloorTile()` method to create the checkerboard effect for the floor.

Next, we need to specify three matrices for the effect. The first of these, the World matrix, we set to `Matrix.Identity`. This special matrix is similar to multiplying a number by one. You get the same original number as the result. The World matrix allows us to transform everything we are drawing with the effect. Because we specified the absolute coordinates we want for our floor tiles when we created them, we do not want to transform them with the World matrix. We set the View and Projection matrices equal to the View and Projection matrices that our `Camera` class has calculated for us.

Any given effect can contain multiple techniques, each potentially completely unrelated to the other techniques in the effect file. In the case of the `BasicEffect`, we are using the default technique.

Each technique can additionally be composed of multiple passes. Each pass runs sequentially, building up the final image as its particular shader effects are applied. The default technique for the `BasicEffect` class uses a single pass, but as written, our code could support more advanced techniques that iterate over multiple passes.

When the pass begins, we call the `Apply()` method to signal that the pass has begun. Next, we tell the graphics device about the vertex buffer we wish to use to draw our maze floor using the `SetVertexBuffer()` method.

Finally, we call `DrawPrimitives()` to cause the graphics device to interpret the vertex buffer and output the triangles it contains to the graphics card. We do this by specifying that we are drawing a list of triangles (`PrimitiveType.TriangleList`), beginning with the first element in the vertex buffer (element 0), and drawing a number of triangles equal to the number of vertices divided by three (because each triangle is composed of three vertices).

In order to utilize the `Draw()` method that we have added to the `Maze` class, we need to set up a few items in the `CubeChaserGame` class, including the camera we will be using, an instance of the maze itself, and the `BasicEffect` object that we will pass to the `Draw()` method.

When the camera is initialized during the `Initialize()` method, we pass it a location `(0.5f, 0.5f, 0.5f)` that will place the camera directly in the center of the upper-left corner of the maze, one half of a unit off the floor.

The second parameter for the camera constructor is the beginning rotation angle for the camera, which we specify as 0. Recall that our camera code specifies that without any rotation, our camera will be facing along the positive Z axis, looking along the side of the maze, which grows ahead and to the left of us.

The remaining camera parameters specify the aspect ratio (which we simply pass along from `GraphicsDevice.Viewport.AspectRatio`, which will correspond to the aspect ratio of the window or full screen resolution we are using), and the near and far clipping plane distances. Here, we specify that anything closer to the camera than `0.05f` units will not be drawn, and the maximum distance we will consider for drawing anything is `100f` units. Since our entire maze will be contained within a 20x20 unit area, this means we could theoretically see the entire thing from any point in the maze.

Moving around

Now that we have a floor to walk on, we need to implement the code necessary to allow the player to move about within our environment. In order to facilitate this, we will first expand on our `Camera` class to add a couple of new helper methods.

Time for action – expanding the Camera

1. In the `Helper Methods` region of the `Camera` class, add the following new methods:

```
public Vector3 PreviewMove(float scale)
{
    Matrix rotate = Matrix.CreateRotationY(rotation);
    Vector3 forward = new Vector3(0, 0, scale);
    forward = Vector3.Transform(forward, rotate);
    return (position + forward);
}

public void MoveForward(float scale)
{
    MoveTo(PreviewMove(scale), rotation);
}
```

What just happened?

`PreviewMove()` accepts a distance we wish to move along the direction that the camera is facing. It then calculates a matrix which is used to rotate a vector by the current camera rotation. Recall that an unrotated camera will always be pointing in the 0, 0, 1 direction, so we replace the 1 in this vector with the distance we wish to move, creating vector `forward`. We then apply the rotate transform to this vector, resulting in a vector that points in the direction the camera is actually facing, with a length equal to the distance we want to move the camera.

The `PreviewMove()` method is used by the `MoveForward()` method to get this vector and call `MoveTo()` to actually move the camera. The reason we split the movement process into two different methods is that we will need to check for collisions with walls later on, and we want to be able to see where we will end up if we allow the player to move forward without actually executing the move. Since we have built that ability into `PreviewMove()`, there is no reason to duplicate the code in the `MoveForward()` method.

Of course, now that our camera supports moving around the scene, we need to allow the player to actually do so.

Time for action – letting the player move

1. Add the following fields to the declarations area of the `CubeChaserGame` class:

```
float moveScale = 1.5f;
float rotateScale = MathHelper.PiOver2;
```

2. Add the following to the `Update()` method of the `CubeChaserGame` class:

```
float elapsed = (float)gameTime.ElapsedGameTime.TotalSeconds;
KeyboardState keyState = Keyboard.GetState();
float moveAmount = 0;

if (keyState.IsKeyDown(Keys.Right))
{
    camera.Rotation = MathHelper.WrapAngle(
        camera.Rotation - (rotateScale * elapsed));
}

if (keyState.IsKeyDown(Keys.Left))
{
    camera.Rotation = MathHelper.WrapAngle(
        camera.Rotation + (rotateScale * elapsed));
}

if (keyState.IsKeyDown(Keys.Up))
{
    //camera.MoveForward(moveScale * elapsed);
```

```
        moveAmount = moveScale * elapsed;
}

if (keyState.IsKeyDown(Keys.Down))
{
    //camera.MoveForward(-moveScale * elapsed);
    moveAmount = -moveScale * elapsed;
}

if (moveAmount != 0)
{
    Vector3 newLocation = camera.PreviewMove(moveAmount);
    bool moveOk = true;

    if (newLocation.X < 0 || newLocation.X > Maze.mazeWidth)
        moveOk = false;
    if (newLocation.Z < 0 || newLocation.Z > Maze.mazeHeight)
        moveOk = false;

    if (moveOk)
        camera.MoveForward(moveAmount);
}
```

3. Execute the Cube Chaser game and use the arrow keys to move around:

What just happened?

As with the movement of the player's square in Speller, we use the `gameTime` parameter that gets passed to `Update()` to scale everything we do in relation to the time that has elapsed since the last call time the game was updated.

We can directly rotate the camera in response to player input because we never need to check to see if rotation causes us a problem. The player is free to spin in any place they want without worrying about walls or the boundaries of the maze. In order to do this, we use the `MathHelper.WrapAngle()` method to constrain the newly modified angle (based on the current angle and the speed at which the camera will rotate) to one full revolution. `WrapAngle()` will handle going past 360 degrees or below 0 degrees for us and return a value that traverses this boundary without us having to do the calculations ourselves.

Movement requires a bit more work, as we do not want the player to leave the area of the maze. In this case, we use the camera's `PreviewMove()` method to predict where the camera will be if we allow the movement the player is requesting. For now, we will simply check to make sure the new movement bounds are within the maze area. If everything checks out ok, we go ahead and execute the move.

Summary

Cube Chaser is well under way! Even though it currently has no walls, we can draw the beginnings of our 3D world and move around using an FPS style camera. We have looked at the 3D coordinate system and the various components of the camera used to view the world. We now have the basic mechanism in place that we will build upon to limit the player's ability to move through walls once we have constructed them.

In the next chapter, we will continue to build the Cube Chaser game, creating the maze walls and detecting player-wall collisions.

3
Cube Chaser – It's A-Mazing!

Now that we have constructed a floor that we can render in 3D and walk around on, we need to generate the maze of walls that will be placed onto the floor and prevent the player from walking through them.

In this chapter, we will:

- ◆ Randomly generate a maze using the depth-first search method
- ◆ Use the generated maze layout to construct walls in our 3D world
- ◆ Implement player-wall collisions

Maze generation

Before we can generate the walls of our maze, we need to determine how we are going to represent the maze in memory. In order to do this, we need to decide what kind of maze we will be creating.

In some games, we may want to construct the maze by hollowing corridors and rooms out of a solid block, so that each floor tile would either be open or impassable. In the case of Cube Chaser, we want all of the floor areas of the maze to be accessible, with walls between the floor tiles providing the challenge to navigate the maze. Instead of open and closed floor tiles, each floor tile will have four walls, each of which can be passable or impassable. We will define a class that describes an individual cell of the maze along with the walls it contains.

Time for action – defining a MazeCell

1. Right-click on the Cube Chaser project in **Solution Explorer** and select **Add | Class...**.

2. Name the new class `MazeCell` and click **OK**.

3. Add the following declarations to the `MazeCell` class:

```
public bool[] Walls = new bool[4] {true, true, true, true};
public bool Visited = false;
```

What just happened?

The definition of each maze cell is very straightforward. We have an array of Boolean values for the walls of the cell. A `true` value indicates that a wall exists in that position, and a `false` value indicates that the wall is an opening. In the declaration of the array, we have provided initialization values, specifying that a newly-generated cell will have walls on all four sides. We will arbitrarily decide that the first entry in the array (index 0) is the north wall of the cell. From there, we will proceed clockwise around the cell for the remaining walls (1 is equal to east, 2 is equal to south, and 3 is equal to west) as shown in the following image:

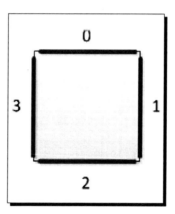

The `Visited` value, which is initially set to `false` for a newly-created `MazeCell`, will be used during the generation of the maze to control how walls are removed from the map to generate the final layout. This represents the maze generation algorithm, which we will discuss shortly, visiting the cell, not the player.

Now that we can describe a maze cell, we need to build a class to contain the maze itself.

Time for action – generating the Maze class

1. In the `Maze.cs` class file, add the following to the `Fields` region:

```
private Random rand = new Random();
public MazeCell[,] MazeCells = new MazeCell[mazeWidth,
mazeHeight];
```

2. In the `Maze` class constructor, add the following after the call to `BuildFloorBuffer()`:

```
for (int x = 0; x < mazeWidth; x++)
    for (int z = 0; z < mazeHeight; z++)
    {
        MazeCells[x, z] = new MazeCell();
    }

GenerateMaze();
```

3. Add a new region to the `Maze` class:

```
#region Maze Generation
#endregion
```

4. Add the `GenerateMaze()` method to the Maze Generation region of the `Maze` class:

```
public void GenerateMaze()
{
    for (int x = 0; x < mazeWidth; x++)
        for (int z = 0; z < mazeHeight; z++)
    {
        MazeCells[x, z].Walls[0] = true;
        MazeCells[x, z].Walls[1] = true;
        MazeCells[x, z].Walls[2] = true;
        MazeCells[x, z].Walls[3] = true;
        MazeCells[x, z].Visited = false;
    }

    MazeCells[0,0].Visited = true;
    EvaluateCell(new Vector2(0, 0));
}
```

5. Add the `EvaluateCell()` method to the Maze Generation region of the `Maze` class, as shown in the following code:

```
private void EvaluateCell(Vector2 cell)
{
```

```
List<int> neighborCells = new List<int>();
neighborCells.Add(0);
neighborCells.Add(1);
neighborCells.Add(2);
neighborCells.Add(3);

while (neighborCells.Count > 0)
{
    int pick = rand.Next(0, neighborCells.Count);
    int selectedNeighbor = neighborCells[pick];
    neighborCells.RemoveAt(pick);

    Vector2 neighbor = cell;

    switch (selectedNeighbor)
    {
        case 0: neighbor += new Vector2(0, -1);
            break;
        case 1: neighbor += new Vector2(1, 0);
            break;
        case 2: neighbor += new Vector2(0, 1);
            break;
        case 3: neighbor += new Vector2(-1, 0);
            break;
    }

    if (
        (neighbor.X >= 0) &&
        (neighbor.X < mazeWidth) &&
        (neighbor.Y >= 0) &&
        (neighbor.Y <mazeHeight)
        )
    {
        if (!MazeCells[(int)neighbor.X, (int)neighbor.Y].
Visited)
        {
            MazeCells[
                (int) neighbor.X,
                (int) neighbor.Y].Visited = true;
            MazeCells[
                (int)cell.X,
                (int)cell.Y].Walls[selectedNeighbor] = false;
            MazeCells[
                (int)neighbor.X,
```

```
                (int)neighbor.Y].Walls[
                    (selectedNeighbor + 2) % 4] = false;
                EvaluateCell(neighbor);
            }
        }

    }
}
```

What just happened?

The information we need to construct the 3D walls of the maze is stored in the `MazeCells` array, a two-dimensional array of `MazeCell` objects. By modifying the constructor, we can fill this array with `MazeCell` objects when an instance of the `Maze` class is created, ensuring we always have cells in a known starting state to work with.

When we call the `GenerateMaze()` method, it begins by setting all of the walls of the maze to `true`, meaning that each cell of the maze is completely closed off from all of the other cells in the maze. While the default setting for a newly-created `MazeCell` is to have walls on all four sides, we will be calling `GenerateMaze()` again to build a new maze when the player locates the cube, so we need to initialize the walls to a known state before we begin generation, instead of assuming that the walls will always be in the state we need them to be in.

We then select the first cell of the maze (0, 0), which will correspond to the north-west corner of our maze in the 3D world, and call the recursive `EvaluateCell()` method on it. It is `EvaluateCell()` that does the real work of generating the maze, following a randomized depth-first search pattern.

Depth-first is a search algorithm that can be used to locate nodes in a tree or graph structure. When searching using the depth-first algorithm, a node is selected as the beginning point for the search. One of the nodes connected to this point is selected to explore, and the algorithm proceeds along this branch of the structure until it reaches a dead end. At that point, the algorithm returns to the most recent node it has visited and picks a new branch to explore.

Our maze generation technique is a modification of this search pattern. We select a starting node (in our case, the (0, 0) node) and mark the cell as having been visited by our search. We then select a random neighbor cell that we have not yet visited. We remove the wall between the current cell and that neighbor. We then make that neighbor the current cell and repeat the process until we have run out of neighboring cells to visit.

`EvaluateCell()` implements this by starting off with a list of all four neighbors for the cell being evaluated. It then randomly selects one of these neighbors from the list and removes the entry from the list. In our code, we have assigned a number to each of the four directions a neighbor can lie in. A 0 represents the neighbor above, 1 is to the right, 2 is below, and 3 is to the left of the current node in relation to the layout of the 2D array. We can also think of this as north, east, south, and west for 0, 1, 2, and 3 respectively. This is the same order that we designated for the walls in a `MazeCell` object.

After selecting the appropriate neighbor and locating it in the array, we check to make sure that we are still within the array bounds and that we have not yet visited the cell. If we have, we simply do nothing.

Because our walls are one-sided, when we remove a wall from a cell, we also need to remove the corresponding wall from its neighboring cell, as illustrated in the following image:

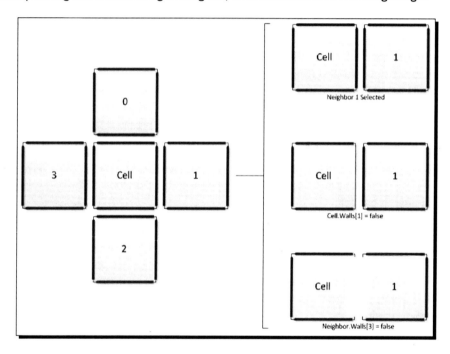

If the cell has not been visited, we mark it as visited and then set the two wall's values between the current cell and the neighbor cell to false. Recall that each cell has four walls, so even though the walls of two neighbor cells are logically shared, they exist on both sides of the boundary and we need to set both of them to `false`. For the current cell, this is straightforward. We simply use the neighbor direction and modify the corresponding `Walls[]` entry. For the neighbor cell, we need to modify the opposite wall. For example, if our neighbor value is 1, meaning the neighbor is to the east of the current cell, we need to modify the west wall of the neighbor cell.

We could accomplish this with a lookup table, where 0 matches 2, 1 matches 3, and so on. Alternatively (and the way we have implemented it here), we know that for 0 and 1 the opposing values are always simply two higher than the current value. If we were to wrap around from 3 to 0, the same would be true for values of 2 and 3. We can accomplish this by using the modulo (%) operator, specifying an upper limit of 4. Hence, (2 + 2) % 4 will result in 0, and (3 + 2) % 4 will result in 1.

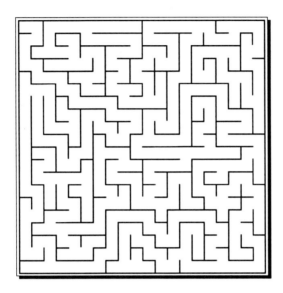

As we can see in the previous image, which is a 2D rendering of a maze generated by the depth-first maze building code, there are several advantages to the way we have generated the maze.

First, the maze is completely enclosed around the outer edges. This is because each edge node does not have a neighbor cell outside the map, so there is never a situation where those walls will be removed by the EvaluateCell() method.

Second, every node in the maze is accessible via some route. There are no closed off areas, though you may have to travel a distance out of your way to reach any given location. This means that, when it is time to place the cube, we can place it anywhere on the map and not have to worry about the player being able to reach the cube.

Finally, while the maze contains a number of small room-like areas, none of them are large enough to create wide-open spaces in the maze.

Constructing the walls

Unfortunately, we still have no visual representation of the maze we have generated. If we execute our game at this point, the `Maze` class constructor will generate the maze, but we do not yet have triangles in 3D to represent the walls that our algorithm has laid out for us.

We will build upon the technique we used to build the floor to create the triangles needed to represent the walls of the maze.

Time for action – building walls

1. Add the following to the declarations area of the `Maze` class:

```
VertexBuffer wallBuffer;
Vector3[] wallPoints = new Vector3[8];
Color[] wallColors = new Color[4] {
    Color.Red, Color.Orange, Color.Red, Color.Orange };
```

2. Add the following code to the end of the constructor in the `Maze` class to initialize the `wallPoints` array and build the walls:

```
wallPoints[0] = new Vector3(0, 1, 0);
wallPoints[1] = new Vector3(0, 1, 1);
wallPoints[2] = new Vector3(0, 0, 0);
wallPoints[3] = new Vector3(0, 0, 1);
wallPoints[4] = new Vector3(1, 1, 0);
wallPoints[5] = new Vector3(1, 1, 1);
wallPoints[6] = new Vector3(1, 0, 0);
wallPoints[7] = new Vector3(1, 0, 1);

BuildWallBuffer();
```

3. Add the `BuildWallBuffer()` method to the `Maze` class as follows:

```
#region Walls
private void BuildWallBuffer()
{
    List<VertexPositionColor> wallVertexList = new
List<VertexPositionColor>();

    for (int x = 0; x < mazeWidth; x++)
    {
        for (int z = 0; z < mazeHeight; z++)
        {
            foreach (VertexPositionColor vertex
                in BuildMazeWall(x, z))
```

```
            {
                wallVertexList.Add(vertex);
            }
        }
    }

    wallBuffer = new VertexBuffer(
        device,
        VertexPositionColor.VertexDeclaration,
        wallVertexList.Count,
        BufferUsage.WriteOnly);

    wallBuffer.SetData<VertexPositionColor>(
        wallVertexList.ToArray());
}
#endregion
```

4. Add the `BuildMazeWall()` method to the `Walls` region of the `Maze` class, shown as follows:

```
private List<VertexPositionColor> BuildMazeWall(int x, int z)
{
    List<VertexPositionColor> triangles = new
        List<VertexPositionColor>();

    if (MazeCells[x, z].Walls[0])
    {
        triangles.Add(CalcPoint(0, x, z, wallColors[0]));
        triangles.Add(CalcPoint(4, x, z, wallColors[0]));
        triangles.Add(CalcPoint(2, x, z, wallColors[0]));
        triangles.Add(CalcPoint(4, x, z, wallColors[0]));
        triangles.Add(CalcPoint(6, x, z, wallColors[0]));
        triangles.Add(CalcPoint(2, x, z, wallColors[0]));
    }

    if (MazeCells[x, z].Walls[1])
    {
        triangles.Add(CalcPoint(4, x, z, wallColors[1]));
        triangles.Add(CalcPoint(5, x, z, wallColors[1]));
        triangles.Add(CalcPoint(6, x, z, wallColors[1]));
        triangles.Add(CalcPoint(5, x, z, wallColors[1]));
        triangles.Add(CalcPoint(7, x, z, wallColors[1]));
        triangles.Add(CalcPoint(6, x, z, wallColors[1]));
    }
```

```
if (MazeCells[x, z].Walls[2])
{
    triangles.Add(CalcPoint(5, x, z, wallColors[2]));
    triangles.Add(CalcPoint(1, x, z, wallColors[2]));
    triangles.Add(CalcPoint(7, x, z, wallColors[2]));
    triangles.Add(CalcPoint(1, x, z, wallColors[2]));
    triangles.Add(CalcPoint(3, x, z, wallColors[2]));
    triangles.Add(CalcPoint(7, x, z, wallColors[2]));
}

if (MazeCells[x, z].Walls[3])
{
    triangles.Add(CalcPoint(1, x, z, wallColors[3]));
    triangles.Add(CalcPoint(0, x, z, wallColors[3]));
    triangles.Add(CalcPoint(3, x, z, wallColors[3]));
    triangles.Add(CalcPoint(0, x, z, wallColors[3]));
    triangles.Add(CalcPoint(2, x, z, wallColors[3]));
    triangles.Add(CalcPoint(3, x, z, wallColors[3]));
}

    return triangles;
}
```

5. Add the `calcPoint()` method to the `Walls` region of the `Maze` class:

```
private VertexPositionColor CalcPoint(
    int wallPoint, int xOffset, int zOffset, Color color)
{
    return new VertexPositionColor(
        wallPoints[wallPoint] + new Vector3(xOffset, 0, zOffset),
        color);
}
```

What just happened?

We begin by establishing a list of points that define a standard block inside our game world. We need eight points to define the corners of a cube, and we store these in the `wallPoints` array that we declared previously. We will create walls for the maze by using these eight points to create triangles and then offsetting their locations to move them to the appropriate position within the maze, as shown in the following diagram:

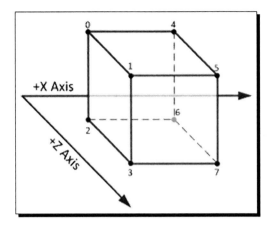

In this diagram, we can see that any wall in the maze can be defined using four of the eight points from a cube. When we define the `wallPoints` array, we fill in the coordinates corresponding to each of the points in the same order as the labeled points in the preceding illustration. The north wall will use points **0**, **2**, **4**, and **6**, for example.

When we construct the triangles that make up our walls, it is important to remember that we need to wind the triangles in a clockwise direction, as we would see them standing inside the cube.

For this reason, the north wall of the cube, comprised of point **0**, **2**, **4**, and **6**, are defined in the `BuildMazeWall()` method in the order **0**, **4**, **2**, and **4**, **6**, **2**. The reverse of this point is also true. An observer standing outside the cube would not see the wall we just built at all because the vertices of the triangles would be in counter-clockwise order from that vantage point.

This is the reason we define walls on all four sides of a cell instead of simply defining walls along two adjacent directions. Our walls are only visible from one direction, so we need to create wall triangles on both sides of the boundary between two cells when a wall exists at that location.

`BuildWallBuffer()` loops through each of the cells in our maze and calls `BuildMazeWall()` in order to accumulate a list of triangles that are then stored in the `wallBuffer`, just like we did when building the floor of the maze.

The `CalcPoint()` method does the work of looking up the points that will comprise each wall segment and building the actual `VertexPositionColor` element that will be added to `wallBuffer`. Again, just like building the floor, we use fixed points relative to each other as the basis for our vertices and offset them by the location of the wall segment within the maze.

Time for action – drawing the walls

1. In the `Draw()` method of the `Maze` class, after the existing call to `device.DrawPrimitives()`, add the following lines of code:

```
device.SetVertexBuffer(wallBuffer);
device.DrawPrimitives(
    PrimitiveType.TriangleList,
    0,
    wallBuffer.VertexCount / 3);
```

2. Execute your game and wander around in the maze:

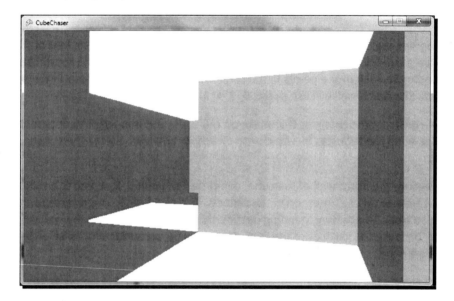

What just happened?

Since the result of all of our wall generation code is to create another vertex buffer, all we need to do to draw the walls is to pass the buffer along to the graphics device, just like we did with the floor buffer.

You will notice, however, that you can walk right through all of the walls in the maze, which makes finding your way around a bit less than challenging.

Solid walls

Giving our maze walls the ability to stop players from walking through them can be accomplished in several different ways. The simplest, brute force method would be to create a list of the bounding boxes (cubes in 3D space that represent the wall edges) for all of the walls in the maze and check to see that our camera location never crosses into one of these solid areas.

For a small map like we are using here, this method would work, but as our map grows larger we would end up making a lot more bounding box checks than we would ever need. In fact, we really only ever need to check four boxes – the four surrounding our current location – to determine if we have run into a wall.

Time for action – bouncing off the walls

1. Add the `BuildBoundingBox()` method to the `Walls` region of the `Maze` class as follows:

```
private BoundingBox BuildBoundingBox(
    int x,
    int z,
    int point1,
    int point2)
{
    BoundingBox thisBox = new BoundingBox(
        wallPoints[point1],
        wallPoints[point2]);
    thisBox.Min.X += x;
    thisBox.Min.Z += z;
    thisBox.Max.X += x;
    thisBox.Max.Z += z;

    thisBox.Min.X -= 0.1f;
    thisBox.Min.Z -= 0.1f;
    thisBox.Max.X += 0.1f;
    thisBox.Max.Z += 0.1f;

    return thisBox;
}
```

2. Add the `GetBoundsForCell()` method to the `Walls` region of the `Maze` class:

```
public List<BoundingBox> GetBoundsForCell(int x, int z)
{
    List<BoundingBox> boxes = new List<BoundingBox>();

    if (MazeCells[x, z].Walls[0])
        boxes.Add(BuildBoundingBox(x, z, 2, 4));

    if (MazeCells[x, z].Walls[1])
        boxes.Add(BuildBoundingBox(x, z, 6, 5));

    if (MazeCells[x, z].Walls[2])
        boxes.Add(BuildBoundingBox(x, z, 3, 5));

    if (MazeCells[x, z].Walls[3])
        boxes.Add(BuildBoundingBox(x, z, 2, 1));

    return boxes;
}
```

3. In the `Update()` method of the `CubeChaserGame` class, add the following code snippet right before the line that reads `if (moveOk)`, after the X and Z components of `newLocation` have been checked for residing within the size of the maze:

```
foreach (BoundingBox box in
    maze.GetBoundsForCell((int)newLocation.X, (int)newLocation.Z))
{
    if (box.Contains(newLocation) == ContainmentType.Contains)
        moveOk = false;
}
```

4. Execute your game and wander around in the maze. Notice that you are no longer able to walk through the walls.

What just happened?

The `BuildBoundingBox()` helper method accepts a location and two points from the `wallPoints` array. It initially constructs a box using the two given points, constructing the basic boundary.

Using the location passed into the method by the x and z variables, the bounding box is offset from the world origin in the same way that we moved the triangle vertices that make up the visible walls. We add the location to the base values for the points to get the offset wall locations.

Finally, a small padding factor is added to each end of the X and Z components of the box, pushing the boundary out away from the wall itself by 0.1f units. Recall that we have a near clipping plane defined in our Camera of 0.05f, so if we allow the camera too close to the wall, we will be stopped by the bounding box, but the wall will not be drawn to the screen because it will be inside the near clipping plane.

When the time comes to actually check for wall collisions, we call a second method, `GetBoundsForCell()`, which uses `BuildBoundingBox()` up to four times, depending on which of the walls exist for the location passed into the method. In the `CubeChaserGame.Update()` method, we call `GetBoundsForCell()` and check against the bounding boxes it returns, to decide if we should disallow the movement the player is trying to make.

Have a go hero

The maze generated by the DFS system is a classic maze, with tightly restrictive corridors and dead ends aplenty. Try opening up the maze design by removing random walls after the maze has been generated but before the 3D geometry has been built. This will create rooms within the maze and allow for more open views and multiple paths through the labyrinth. Wander the maze and note the larger open spaces and determine if you wish to remove more walls to create larger or more frequent open areas.

Summary

We have generated a random maze and translated its walls into 3D geometry. In addition, we have added the ability for Cube Chaser to enforce the solidity of the walls of the maze.

In the next chapter, we will implement the cube the player is chasing, allow for tracking the player's score, and generate new cubes as the player collects them.

4
Cube Chaser – Finding Your Way

We are nearing completion of the Cube Chaser game, with just a few more features to complete to make it playable. Our goal now is to implement the cube that the player is chasing.

In this chapter, we will:

- ◆ Randomly place the goal cube within the maze
- ◆ Draw the cube, making it rotate slowly in place while the player searches for it
- ◆ Detect player-to-cube collisions to determine when the player has scored points

In addition to completing the Cube Chaser game, we will take a more in-depth look at the matrices we use to manipulate objects in 3D.

The cube

With our maze in place, we can now turn our attention to creating the cube that the player will be chasing in Cube Chaser. We will continue to use triangles built by hand to represent our cube, but this time instead of giving the triangles solid colors, we will see how to map a texture image onto the faces of the cube.

A texture is a two-dimensional bitmap image that is projected onto a 3D object in order to give the object the desired appearance. By using a texture instead of a vertex color, we can give the cube surface details. In the case of our cube, we will use a circuit board image, but we could just as easily apply a photograph or any other type of image as the cube's texture.

In order to create the cube, we will add the texture to our game's content project and build the cube's vertices.

Time for action – placing the cube

1. From the book's companion website, download the `7089_04_GRAPHICSPACK.ZIP` file and extract the `circuitboard.png` file to a temporary location.

2. Back in Visual Studio, right-click on the content project (listed as **Cube ChaserContent (Content)**) in **Solution Explorer** and select **Add | Existing Item….**

3. Browse to the `circuitboard.png` file you just extracted, select it, and click **Add**:

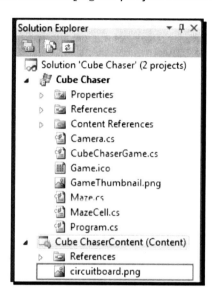

4. Add a new class file called `Cube.cs` to the Cube Chaser project.

5. Add the following `using` directives to the top of the class file:

```
using Microsoft.Xna.Framework;
using Microsoft.Xna.Framework.Graphics;
```

6. Add the following fields to your new `Cube` class:

```
#region Fields
private GraphicsDevice device;
private Texture2D texture;

private Vector3 location;

private VertexBuffer cubeVertexBuffer;
private List<VertexPositionTexture> vertices = new
    List<VertexPositionTexture>();
#endregion
```

7. Add a constructor to the Cube class:

```
#region Constructor
public Cube(
    GraphicsDevice graphicsDevice,
    Vector3 playerLocation,
    float minDistance,
    Texture2D texture)
{
    device=graphicsDevice;
    this.texture = texture;

    PositionCube(playerLocation, minDistance);

    // Create the cube's vertical faces
    BuildFace(new Vector3(0, 0, 0), new Vector3(0, 1, 1));
    BuildFace(new Vector3(0, 0, 1), new Vector3(1, 1, 1));
    BuildFace(new Vector3(1, 0, 1), new Vector3(1, 1, 0));
    BuildFace(new Vector3(1, 0, 0), new Vector3(0, 1, 0));

    // Create the cube's horizontal faces
    BuildFaceHorizontal(new Vector3(0, 1, 0), new Vector3(1, 1,
1));
    BuildFaceHorizontal(new Vector3(0, 0, 1), new Vector3(1, 0,
0));

    cubeVertexBuffer = new VertexBuffer(
        device,
        VertexPositionTexture.VertexDeclaration,
        vertices.Count,
        BufferUsage.WriteOnly);

    cubeVertexBuffer.SetData<VertexPositionTexture>(
        vertices.ToArray());
}
#endregion
```

8. Add the BuildFace() helper method to the Cube class as follows:

```
#region Helper Methods
private void BuildFace(Vector3 p1, Vector3 p2)
{
    vertices.Add(BuildVertex(p1.X, p1.Y, p1.Z, 1, 0));
    vertices.Add(BuildVertex(p1.X, p2.Y, p1.Z, 1, 1));
    vertices.Add(BuildVertex(p2.X, p2.Y, p2.Z, 0, 1));
    vertices.Add(BuildVertex(p2.X, p2.Y, p2.Z, 0, 1));
```

```
        vertices.Add(BuildVertex(p2.X, p1.Y, p2.Z, 0, 0));
        vertices.Add(BuildVertex(p1.X, p1.Y, p1.Z, 1, 0));
}
#endregion
```

9. Add `BuildFaceHorizontal()` to the Helper Methods region of the `Cube` class, shown as follows:

```
private void BuildFaceHorizontal(Vector3 p1, Vector3 p2)
{
        vertices.Add(BuildVertex(p1.X, p1.Y, p1.Z, 0, 1));
        vertices.Add(BuildVertex(p2.X, p1.Y, p1.Z, 1, 1));
        vertices.Add(BuildVertex(p2.X, p2.Y, p2.Z, 1, 0));
        vertices.Add(BuildVertex(p1.X, p1.Y, p1.Z, 0, 1));
        vertices.Add(BuildVertex(p2.X, p2.Y, p2.Z, 1, 0));
        vertices.Add(BuildVertex(p1.X, p1.Y, p2.Z, 0, 0));
}
```

10. Add the `BuildVertex()` method to the Helper Methods region of the `Cube` class:

```
private VertexPositionTexture BuildVertex(
        float x,
        float y,
        float z,
        float u,
        float v)
{
            return new VertexPositionTexture(
            new Vector3(x, y, z),
            new Vector2(u,v));
}
```

11. Add a temporary `PositionCube()` method to the Helper Methods region of the `Cube` class:

```
public void PositionCube(
        Vector3 playerLocation,
        float minDistance)
{
            location = new Vector3(1.5f, 0.5f, 1.5f);
}
```

12. Add the `Draw()` method to the `Cube` class:

```
#region Draw
public void Draw(Camera camera, BasicEffect effect)
{
        effect.VertexColorEnabled = false;
```

```
effect.TextureEnabled = true;
effect.Texture = texture;

Matrix center = Matrix.CreateTranslation(
    new Vector3(-0.5f, -0.5f, -0.5f));
Matrix scale = Matrix.CreateScale(0.5f);
Matrix translate = Matrix.CreateTranslation(location);

effect.World = center * scale * translate;
effect.View = camera.View;
effect.Projection = camera.Projection;

foreach (EffectPass pass in effect.CurrentTechnique.Passes)
{
    pass.Apply();
    device.SetVertexBuffer(cubeVertexBuffer);
    device.DrawPrimitives(
        PrimitiveType.TriangleList,
        0,
        cubeVertexBuffer.VertexCount / 3);
}
}
#endregion
```

13. In the fields area of the `CubeChaserGame` class, add a declaration for an instance of the `Cube` class as follows:

```
private Cube cube;
```

14. In the `LoadContent()` method of the `CubeChaserGame` class, initialize this instance of `Cube`:

```
cube = new Cube(
    this.GraphicsDevice,
    camera.Position,
    10f,
    Content.Load<Texture2D>("circuitboard"));
```

15. Modify the `Draw()` method of the `CubeChaserGame` class by commenting out the line that draws the maze by placing two slashes in front of it:

```
//maze.Draw(camera, effect);
```

16. Right after this commented out line, add a line to draw the cube:

```
cube.Draw(camera, effect);
```

17. Execute your game and turn slightly left to face the cube. Note that you may not be able to move directly to the cube, as even though we are not drawing the walls of the maze, they are still there for collision purposes:

What just happened?

We have covered quite a bit of ground with the previous code, so let's break it down step-by-step.

In steps 1 through 3, we are adding a new texture image to the content project of our game. We used both textures and fonts as content objects in *Chapter 1, Introduction to XNA*, but have not found it necessary to revisit them until now because we have been drawing with solid colors for the walls and floor of our maze.

Next, in steps 4 through 6, we create the basic cube class, adding the declarations we need to be able to display the cube. We will actually add two more items to this list in the next section, but for now, we need to cache the graphics device for our game and store the texture we will use to draw the faces of the cube.

Additionally, we have a location within the world that we wish the cube to be placed, as well as the now familiar list of vertices and a vertex buffer to hold them, meaning we know that we will be drawing with triangles again.

While creating the constructor in step 7, we store the `GraphicsDevice` and `Texture2D` objects that we receive from the caller and call `PositionCube()`. Glancing down at step 11, we can see that, for now, we are simply setting the location of the cube to a hard-coded value of (1.5f, 0.5f, 1.5f), meaning that the center of the cube will be in the center of the square at 1 unit along the positive X and Z axis, and 0.5 units above the floor of the maze, shown as follows:

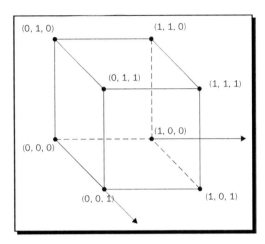

The constructor then calls `BuildFace()` four times and `BuildFaceHorizontal()` twice, giving the method's pairs of points on each call. In the previous diagram, we can see that these points correspond to the opposite corners of each face of a cube that is positioned with one point at the world origin and extending 1 unit along each axis. We only need to specify these opposite corners to build the two triangles for our cube faces, because we are using a perfect cube and can determine the position of the other vertices needed to build the triangle from the components of these points.

For instance, the western face of the previous cube is defined by the points (**0, 0, 0**) and (**0, 1, 1**). We know that we need the point above the origin, and can calculate it by taking the X and Z component of the first point and the Y component of the second. We can calculate the final point for the square by taking the X and Z component from the second point, and Y from the first. Note that this will work for the vertical faces of the cube, but the same would not hold true for the top or bottom of the cube. For this reason, we also have `buildFaceHorizontal()`, which adjusts the previous procedure slightly to account for the points being in the same vertical position.

After all of the faces have been built, the vertex buffer itself is populated with these points.

We implement the logic to build faces in steps 9 and 10, building six vertices for each face and adding them to the vertices list. In addition to the points with which to build the triangles, we are also passing two float values to the `BuildVertex()` method that are either 0 or 1, and correspond to that method's u and v parameters.

So what are u and v? In step 11, we implement `BuildVertex()` to build a new type of vertex called a `VertexPositionTexture`. For our walls and floor, we specified a position and a color for each vertex. For the cube, we want to place the circuit board texture onto the faces of the cube, so we no longer need to specify a color, but need some way to specify how the parts of the texture image are mapped onto the faces of the cube.

A texture is simply a two-dimensional image, so we might be tempted to use X and Y coordinates to reference the parts of the texture. Because we are working in 3D, however, X and Y already have meanings within our coordinate system. Since the texture will not be aligned on the X-Y plane, referencing positions on the texture as X-Y coordinates would be potentially confusing.

For this reason, coordinates on a texture are referred to with u and v instead of x and y. The u coordinate references the horizontal position within the texture, while the v coordinate represents the vertical position. Why u and v in particular? Simply because they are the letters before x, y, and z!

Another important distinction when mapping textures to 3D objects is we do not reference the size of the texture in pixels to determine u/v coordinates. The `circuitboard.png` image we are using for the cube is 512 x 512 pixels in size, but if we were using an image that had multiple resolution levels in it (called **mipmaps**) there might be a 256 x 256 version of this texture, a 64 x 64 version, and so on.

Mipmaps (or MIP maps)

When using large textures in 3D, on-the-fly sampling of these textures by the graphics card can produce poor results as objects get further and further away from the viewer. Mipmaps help resolve this problem by pre-building lower detail textures with slower scaling algorithms that produce better results. If you want to try this with the cube, select the `circuitboard.png` file in **Solution Explorer**, click on the little triangle next to **Content Processor** in the properties pane, and change **Generate Mipmaps** from **false** to **true**. Rerun your game and notice the smoother appearance of the cube.

To allow for these multiple texture sizes, the u-v coordinates range from 0, 0 (upper-left corner of the texture) to 1, and 1 (lower-right corner of the texture). This means that a u-v coordinate of (0.5, 0.5) would be halfway through the texture, or at (256, 256) in the case of our circuit board.

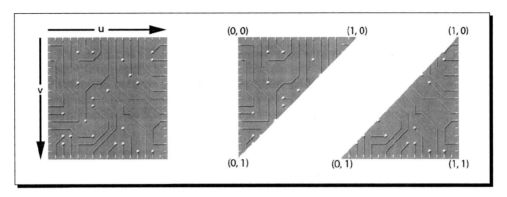

When we construct the previous faces, we are specifying that the first point we pass into the `BuildFace()` method is the lower-left corner of the face, while the second point is the upper-right corner, relative to the way the texture should be mapped onto the face. Looking at the first triangle created for the face, we see that the first vertex has u-v coordinates of (**0, 1**), or the lower-left corner of the texture. The second vertex, located directly above the first, has u-v coordinates of (**0, 0**) – the upper-left corner of the texture. Finally, the last vertex of the triangle corresponds to the upper-right corner of the texture, and has u-v coordinates of (**1, 0**).

In *step 12*, it is finally time to draw the cube to the screen, and most of this code should look familiar. We are still drawing with a vertex buffer as we have in the past, but with a couple of important changes.

First, since we are going to be using textures instead of colors, we set `VertexColorEnabled` to `false` and `TextureEnabled` to `true` on our `BasicEffect` instance. We then supply the texture we will be drawing to the `Effect`.

Next, we generate three different matrices. All of these will be combined to form the `World` matrix parameter of the effect instance, but each has a different function.

Remember that we specified the points of our cube relative to the origin point, with one corner of the cube at the origin. Any manipulation we make to the vertices in the cube are relative to the origin, so we create the center matrix to translate the cube from its default location by -0.5f units in each direction. This has the effect of moving it so that the center of the cube is at the origin of the 3D world.

Next we use `Matrix.CreateScale()` to shrink the cube by 50 percent. If we did not resize the cube, it would occupy an entire square within our maze and look like it was an oddly-textured maze wall.

Finally, we build a matrix called `location` by simply passing the `location` field to the `CreateTranslation()` method. This will enable us to push our cube out from the origin to where it is supposed to be in the world.

Centering and scaling

Why not just create the cube centered around the origin and at the right size in the first place? This is a good point, as it would allow us to skip the centering and scaling described previously. We have opted to implement the cube as we have in order to illustrate the origin-centric nature of transforms and the importance of the order in which matrix operations are performed.

All of these matrices are then applied to `effect.World`, in the order in which we want them to happen. The order is critical. We can build a single matrix that will incorporate all of the movement, scaling, and rotation we wish to perform on a set of vertices as long as we multiply them in the order in which we want them to happen. In this case, we center the cube first, then scale it, and finally move it out to its destination within the world.

The remainder of our drawing code is identical to the code we use to draw the walls and floor of the maze, with the exception that we specify the new vertex format during the `DrawPrimitives()` call.

Wrapping up with steps 13 through 16, we make the necessary changes to the `CubeChaserGame` class to draw the cube (and temporarily hide the maze) so we can see the results of our efforts.

Rotating the cube

The cube is nice (and if you have enabled mipmaps, it looks pretty good sitting there in the middle of nowhere) but we can give it a bit more character by making it rotate slowly while waiting for the player to pick it up.

Time for action – rotating the cube

1. Add the following declaration to the `Fields` region of the `Cube` class:

```
private float rotation = 0f;
private float zrotation = 0f;
```

2. Add an `Update()` method to the `Cube` class as follows:

```
#region Update
public void Update(GameTime gameTime)
{
    rotation = MathHelper.WrapAngle(rotation + 0.05f);
    zrotation = MathHelper.WrapAngle(zrotation + 0.025f);
}
#endregion
```

3. In the `Draw()` method of the `Cube` class, add two new items to the list of the generated matrices:

```
Matrix rot = Matrix.CreateRotationY(rotation);
Matrix zrot = Matrix.CreateRotationZ(zrotation);
```

4. Still in the `Draw()` method, replace the current line that sets `effect.World` with the following:

```
effect.World = center * rot * zrot * scale * translate;
```

5. In the `Update()` method of the `CubeChaserGame` class, add the following line right before the existing call to `base.Update(gameTime)`:

```
cube.Update(gameTime);
```

6. Execute your game and turn to face the cube:

What just happened?

Just like translation and scaling, rotation can be accomplished with a matrix. Here we create two different rotations, one to spin the cube around the Y axis, and a second to rotate it around the Z axis. By combining these two rotations, we can create a more interesting rotation effect than if we simply had the cube spinning around a single axis. We have now used matrices for three types of transformation effects, but so far we have not really answered the following question: What in the world is a matrix, anyway?

Matrices – big scary math things?

You knew we could not avoid it forever, right? It is time to talk briefly about matrices and matrix math. Don't worry! It is not nearly as scary as it sounds at first.

A matrix is really nothing more than a grid of numbers. Mathematically, a matrix can have any number of rows and columns, but in XNA we use 4 by 4 matrices, meaning the matrix has four rows of four columns. Each of these columns contains a number. The XNA Matrix class defines these values as floats, and assigns them names of M11 through M44 (the first number being the row, the second being the column; so M23 is the second row, third column). We will also use 1 by 4 matrices, or matrices with one column and four rows. We have already used them, in fact, though you may not immediately recognize them as 1 by 4 matrices because of the way they are declared in our code. More on that in a moment.

We have used the identity matrix before, and it looks like this:

$$\begin{bmatrix} 1 & 0 & 0 & 0 \\ 0 & 1 & 0 & 0 \\ 0 & 0 & 1 & 0 \\ 0 & 0 & 0 & 1 \end{bmatrix}$$

When we multiply two matrices together, we work across each row of the first matrix, multiplying the values in the row by the descending columns of the second matrix and then adding all of these values together to get the resulting value in the new matrix. That sounds awfully confusing, but the following diagram, which shows a 4 by 4 matrix multiplied by a 1 by 4 matrix, should help:

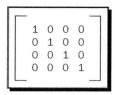

The shape of the two matrices being multiplied together will determine the shape of the resultant matrix. The number of rows in the resultant matrix will match the number of rows in the first matrix being multiplied. The number of columns in the resultant matrix will match the number of columns in the second matrix of the multiplication. As you can see in the previous diagram, the result matrix has four rows (matching the first matrix) and one column (matching the second matrix). The second matrix must have the same number of rows as the first matrix has columns in order to be valid for multiplication.

So how does this relate to matrices and vectors in XNA? We represent all of our vertices as Vector3s which specify a location in 3D space. This would seem to pose a problem, since we want to multiply a 4 by 4 matrix by a 1 by 3 vector. We can resolve this problem by pretending there is a fourth component of the `Vector3` that has a value of 1. This is how we end up with the 1 by 4 matrices we talked about previously.

Now, when we want to multiply a `Vector3` by a matrix, we simply need to follow the multiplication pattern, summing up all of the results into a final value:

$$\begin{bmatrix} 1 & 0 & 0 & 0 \\ 0 & 1 & 0 & 0 \\ 0 & 0 & 1 & 0 \\ 0 & 0 & 0 & 1 \end{bmatrix} * \begin{bmatrix} X \\ Y \\ Z \\ 1 \end{bmatrix} = \begin{bmatrix} (1*X) + (0*Y) + (0*Z) + (0*1) \\ (0*X) + (1*Y) + (0*Z) + (0*1) \\ (0*X) + (0*Y) + (1*Z) + (0*1) \\ (0*X) + (0*Y) + (0*Z) + (1*1) \end{bmatrix} = \begin{bmatrix} X \\ Y \\ Z \\ 1 \end{bmatrix}$$

Here we can see that the identity matrix really works just like multiplying a simple number by 1. The result you get out of the multiplication is the same as the value you put into the multiplication.

The translation matrix

In our code so far, we have used several matrices other than the identity matrix. Let's look at a translation matrix. For a **translation matrix**, the X, Y, and Z components of the translation are placed in the fourth column of the matrix, with a 1 filling in the last value. If we wish to translate a point 5 units along the X axis, and 3 units along the Z axis, while leaving the Y axis unchanged, we would create the matrix as follows:

```
Matrix.CreateTranslation(5, 0, 3)
```

The resulting matrix would look as follows:

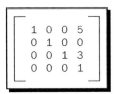

$$\begin{bmatrix} 1 & 0 & 0 & 5 \\ 0 & 1 & 0 & 0 \\ 0 & 0 & 1 & 3 \\ 0 & 0 & 0 & 1 \end{bmatrix}$$

To apply this matrix as a transformation to a 3D point (the `Vector3` of (2, 3, 4) in this case), we would follow the pattern and get the following:

$$
\begin{bmatrix} 1 & 0 & 0 & 5 \\ 0 & 1 & 0 & 0 \\ 0 & 0 & 1 & 3 \\ 0 & 0 & 0 & 1 \end{bmatrix} * \begin{bmatrix} 2 \\ 3 \\ 4 \\ 1 \end{bmatrix} = \begin{bmatrix} (1*2) + (0*3) + (0*4) + (5*1) \\ (0*2) + (1*3) + (0*4) + (0*1) \\ (0*2) + (0*3) + (1*4) + (3*1) \\ (0*2) + (0*3) + (0*4) + (1*1) \end{bmatrix} = \begin{bmatrix} 7 \\ 3 \\ 7 \\ 1 \end{bmatrix}
$$

Since translation is a fairly straightforward transformation, we can easily check the math here and see that, indeed, moving (2, 3, 4) by (5, 0, 3) will result in (7, 3, 7).

Transformations

There are a few terms we have been using that should be clarified here. A **transformation** refers to the altering of the values of a set of vertices, and these transformations can be of three different types: scaling, rotation, and translation. **Scaling** is used to alter the overall size of the set of vertices, **rotation** moves the vertices around an axis, and **translation** moves the vertices by a fixed given distance in a three-dimensional direction.

The rotation matrix

As we saw previously, in a translation matrix the components of the translation are contained in the right-most column of the matrix. When a rotation matrix is created, the values in the matrix and where they are placed are determined by the axis the rotation is around. You will remember that in our code to rotate the cube, we create a rotation around the Y axis to make the cube spin horizontally.

The matrices created by `Matrix.CreateRotationX()`, `Matrix.CreateRotationY()`, and `Matrix.CreateRotationZ()` look as follows, where theta (Ɵ) is the angle specified when the matrix is created:

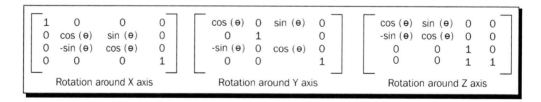

The values for sine and cosine will always be numbers between -1 and 1. Just as with our translation points, we can use matrix multiplication to apply these transforms to points within our world.

When we rotate the cube, we first translate it so that the center of the cube is located at the world origin point (0, 0, 0) because all rotation is relative to the origin. If we were simply to rotate the cube without centering it first, it would end up orbiting around the origin instead of spinning in place.

The scale matrix

The final type of matrix we need to look at is also the simplest. A **scale matrix** simply duplicates the same scalar value diagonally down and to the right by three places as shown in the following image:

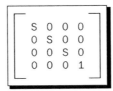

We can see right away that the identity matrix is the same as a scaling matrix with the scale value set to 1. This makes sense, as scaling something to 1.0 times its size leaves you with an object of the same size as you started with.

Combining matrices

One nice feature of matrices, which we have used in the previous code, is that if we multiply them together, the resulting matrix contains all of the transformations that the component matrices contained.

The order is critical however. When working with simple numbers, multiplication is commutative, meaning that the order in which the operations are performed does not matter. If we multiply 2 * 5, we get 10. The same is true for 5 * 2.

Matrix multiplication, however, is non-commutative. Matrix A * matrix B gives a different result than matrix B * matrix A, as we can see in the following image. Here we are multiplying two 2 x 2 matrices following the pattern shown previously. Changing the order that two matrices are multiplied in completely changes the result:

$$\begin{bmatrix} 1 & 2 \\ 3 & 4 \end{bmatrix} * \begin{bmatrix} 5 & 6 \\ 7 & 8 \end{bmatrix} = \begin{bmatrix} 19 & 22 \\ 43 & 50 \end{bmatrix}$$

$$\begin{bmatrix} 5 & 6 \\ 7 & 8 \end{bmatrix} * \begin{bmatrix} 1 & 2 \\ 3 & 4 \end{bmatrix} = \begin{bmatrix} 23 & 34 \\ 31 & 46 \end{bmatrix}$$

Another way to think of the requirement that matrices be combined in a particular order is to imagine that you have driving directions that say to drive 10 miles (translation) and then turn left (rotation). If you turn left first and then drive 10 miles, you will end up in a completely different place because the order in which you do the operations is critical to the outcome.

What does it all mean?

The important point to take away from all of this is that we specify groups of vertices in our world using vectors and use transformations, represented by matrices, to position them appropriately. Even the view and projection matrices we calculate for our camera are doing nothing more than altering the positions of the vertices that are shown on the display. In effect, you can think of your display as a fixed point in 3D space, around which the entire game world is rotated, scaled, skewed, and otherwise coerced so that what you are intended to see falls within the display area of your monitor.

It is also important to note that the cube itself, as we have defined the vertices, is not really located at the point we place it in the game world. We have defined a cube that has one corner at the origin (0, 0, 0) and the opposite corner at (1, 1, 1). We never compute and store a translated version of the cube. It always has the same vertices. Only when the cube is drawn do we apply our transformations, in order to move the visual representation of the cube into the position we wish for it to appear in.

All of this matrix calculation and applying transformations during every draw cycle may seem like an awful lot of work for our game to be performing. Fortunately, modern video cards are purpose-built to be very good at working with matrices. While it might take us some time to figure out what is going on with our matrices, the video card hardware will make short work of them, displaying the results very, very quickly.

Positioning the cube

Now that we have looked at matrix math, let's return to Cube Chaser and position the cube somewhere in the maze other than right next to the starting point.

Time for action – randomly positioning the cube

1. Add the following declaration to the Fields region of the Cube class:

```
private Random rand = new Random();
```

2. Replace the current PositionCube() method in the Cube class with the following:

```
public void PositionCube(Vector3 playerLocation, float
minDistance)
```

```
{
    Vector3 newLocation;

    do
    {
        newLocation = new Vector3(
            rand.Next(0, Maze.mazeWidth) + 0.5f,
            0.5f,
            rand.Next(0, Maze.mazeHeight) + 0.5f);
    }
    while (
        Vector3.Distance(playerLocation, newLocation) <
minDistance);

    location = newLocation;
}
```

3. In the `Draw()` method of the `Maze` class, add the following to the top of the method to make sure we have the correct current settings for our effect, now that we are also using textures:

```
effect.TextureEnabled = false;
```

4. In the `Draw()` method of the `CubeChaserGame` class, uncomment the line that draws the maze by removing the two slashes (//) from the front of the line.

5. Execute the game and search the maze for the cube. Note that if you have implemented the random removal of some of the walls from the maze to create rooms, finding the cube will be much easier than in the fully restricted maze:

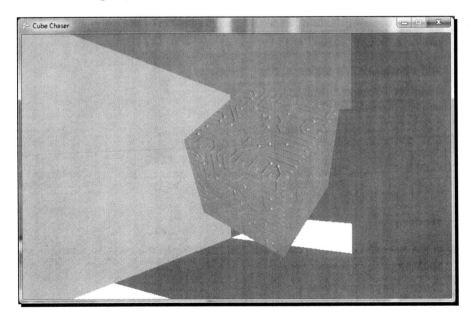

What just happened?

When generating a position for the cube, we generate random X and Z coordinates, and add 0.5f to them (to elevate the cube to the center of the square it is located in). We keep generating coordinates until the cube is at a reasonable distance away from the player's current position, as determined by the `minDistance` parameter, so that the cube cannot appear right on top of the player.

Also note that we needed to go back and update the `Maze` class to turn off `TextureEnabled` for our effect. If we do not do this, we will get an error from Visual Studio after the first frame is drawn, saying that the vertex definition we are using does not contain all of the necessary elements. This is because our effect, along with its parameters, persists between frames. When we started using textures to draw the cube, we enabled textures on the effect. Since the `Maze` class uses `VertexPositionColor` as its vertex declaration, it does not contain the texture coordinates that the effect expects to find when `TextureEnabled` is `true`.

Catching the cube

We need to implement the ability to actually collect the cube by running into it. We could accomplish this with a bounding box the same way we check for walls, but since our cube will be spinning in mid-air, a bounding sphere would be a more appropriate shape.

Time for action – catching the cube

1. Add the following declaration to the `Fields` region of the `Cube` class:

   ```
   private const float collisionRadius = 0.25f;
   ```

2. Add a `Properties` region of the `Cube` class:

   ```
   #region Properties
   public BoundingSphere Bounds
   {
       get
       {
           return new BoundingSphere(location, collisionRadius);
       }
   }
   #endregion
   ```

3. In the `CubeChaserGame` class, add the following to the class declarations area to hold the player's current score:

   ```
   float lastScoreTime = 0f;
   int score = 0;
   ```

4. In the `Update()` method of the `CubeChaserGame` class, add the following code right before the call to `cube.Update()`:

```
if (cube.Bounds.Contains(camera.Position) ==
    ContainmentType.Contains)
{
    cube.PositionCube(camera.Position, 5f);
    float thisTime = (float)gameTime.TotalGameTime.TotalSeconds;
    float scoreTime = thisTime - lastScoreTime;
    score += 1000;
    if (scoreTime < 120)
    {
        score += (120 - (int)scoreTime) * 100;
    }
    lastScoreTime = thisTime;
}
```

5. In the `Draw()` method of the `CubeChaserGame` class, add the following code at the end of the method, right before the call to `base.Draw()`:

```
this.Window.Title = score.ToString();
```

6. Run the Cube Chaser game and go hunting for the cube. When you have located it, move into the cube to increase your score and reposition the cube within the maze. Notice that your current score is displayed in the title bar of the game's window, as shown in the following screenshot:

What just happened?

In *step 1*, we specify how close the player needs to get to the cube in order to collect it. In this case, we use 0.25f units, or one quarter of the width of one of our floor tiles. Since our cube is half the size of a tile and located in the center of the tile horizontally and vertically, this means our player will have to actually run into the cube in order to grab it. The Bounds property uses this radius, along with the location of the cube, to return a BoundingSphere object, which we can use to determine if a given point lies within the area of the sphere.

After establishing variables to hold the time the player last recovered the cube and the player's score, we check against the Bounds property to see if it contains the camera's current position. Since we have not defined a separate player avatar, the camera position also represents the player's position within the world.

If Bounds contains the camera's location, we have collected the cube. We relocate it somewhere else in the maze and store the time at which we found the cube. We automatically add 1000 points to the player's score, and then check to see if it has been less than two minutes since the player last found the cube. If it has, we award an extra 100 points for every second under two minutes that the player spent searching.

Finally, since we have not yet delved into mixing 2D and 3D in the same project, we use the window title area of the game's window to display the player's current score.

Have a go hero!

The Cube Chaser game, while playable, could use some improving! There are many different things we could implement, based on your level of familiarity with XNA, which are as follows:

- Modify the code that generates the maze walls to use a texture instead of the plain color walls we are currently using. Adding textured walls will give the maze a bit more visual appeal, as it will be easier to identify wall corners and distances based on the scaling of the textured image.

- Increase the height of the maze walls a bit (perhaps to 1.5 units in height) and add a textured ceiling. Keep the winding order of the triangles used to build the ceiling in mind so that you can see it from underneath!

- If you are familiar with 2D game development in XNA, or if you come back to this section after completing *Chapter 8, Tank Battles – Ending the War*, refactor the Cube Chaser code and build a game state management structure around the Cube Chaser game, including a title screen and conditions for losing the game (such as not finding the cube for 5 minutes, decreasing the time limit slightly as each cube is found). Alternatively, implement Cube Chaser as screens in a Game State Management sample project as discussed in *Chapter 9, Mars Runner* and *Chapter 10, Mars Runner – Reaching the Finish Line*.

◆   Build a game state system via one of the two previous methods, but include a
      3D-rendered version of the spinning cube on the title screen.

Summary

While not a blockbuster, the Cube Chaser game demonstrates the fundamentals of
building 3D objects with triangles and displaying them on the screen. We have also
covered important 3D concepts such as cameras, view, and projections matrices, and
gotten an introduction to matrix math and how it allows us to position and display the
components of our 3D world.

Over the course of the next four chapters, we will be looking at a new game that combines
both triangle-based drawing techniques with externally generated 3D models, and including
2D components in our 3D games.

5
Tank Battles – A War-torn Land

In Tank Battles, we will create a 3D version of a classic game, in which the player controls a stationary tank doing battle against a computer-controlled tank, by alternating turns while firing shots at each other.

The player can adjust the direction, elevation, and power applied to their shots to zero in on the settings necessary to hit the enemy target, but they need to do so before the enemy does the same to them.

We will build tank battles over four chapters, and in this initial chapter, we will look at:

- Implementing an arc-ball camera
- Generating terrain based on a height map image
- Applying textures to our generated terrain geometry

Along the way, we will also take a look at the basics of **HLSL** (**High Level Shader Language**), the programming language used to instruct the graphics card on how to render our 3D world.

Creating the project

We will, of course, begin by creating a new XNA 4.0 Windows Game project for Tank Battles.

Time for action – creating the Tank Battles project

1. Download the `7089_05_GRAPHICSPACK.ZIP` file from the book's website and extract the files it contains to a temporary folder.
2. Open Visual Studio 2010 and select **File | New Project...** from the menu bar.

3. Open the **Visual C#** tree in the **Installed Templates** portion of the **New Project** window, and open the **XNA Game Studio 4.0** tree under it.

4. Select the **Windows Game (4.0)** project template from the central portion of the window.

5. Under **Name**, enter **Tank Battles** and click the **OK** button.

6. After Visual Studio has created the solution, right-click on the `Game1.cs` file in the **Solution Explorer** window and select **Rename**.

7. Change the name of the file to `TankBattlesGame.cs`. If you are asked if you wish to update references to the file, click **Yes**.

8. Right-click on the **Tank BattlesContent (Content)** project and select **Add | New Folder** and create a new folder named **Textures**.

9. Add a second new folder to the content project called **Effects**.

10. Add a third new folder to the content project called **Models**.

11. Add a fourth new folder to the content project called **Fonts**.

12. Copy all of the PNG files from the temporary folder you extracted them to in step 1 into the **Textures** folder created in step 8. You can do this by dragging the files directly from **Windows Explorer** into the folder inside **Solution Explorer** in Visual Studio. This will automatically include them in the content project, as shown in the following screenshot:

What just happened?

Just as we did with Cube Chaser, we have created an empty XNA game project for Tank Battles and renamed the default `Game1.cs` file to something more meaningful. We have also created four folders to hold various content items we will be using in Tank Battles. We will make use of the **Textures** and **Effects** folders in this chapter, and save **Models** and **Fonts** for later.

An arc-ball camera

While building Cube Chaser, we implemented an **FPS** or **First Person Shooter** style camera. For Tank Battles, we want to take a different approach. The player will not be moving around on the terrain from a first person perspective, but will instead hover over the playfield, with the ability to rotate the camera around while focusing on the center of the game area.

Imagine a dome covering the play area, with the camera being able to slide along the dome to any position while still pointing inward at the center of the action. This kind of camera is known as an **arc-ball camera**, and acts as if the camera rides around on a ball surrounding the target point, as seen in the following image:

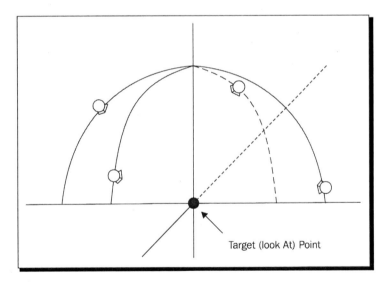

No matter where the camera is placed on the surface of the dome, it rotates to face the target point in the center. In order to implement our arc-ball camera, we will construct a class similar to the camera we created in Cube Chaser, but with modified controls for positioning the camera to maintain its position on the dome and view of the target point.

Time for action – the ArcBallCamera class – part 1

1. Add a new class to the **Tank Battles** project by right-clicking on the project in **Solution Explorer** and selecting **Add | Class…**.

2. Ensure that **Visual C# | Code** is selected under **Installed Templates** and select the **Class** template.

3. Enter `ArcBallCamera.cs` as the name of the class file.

4. Add the following `using` directive to the top of the `ArcBallCamera.cs` file:

    ```
    using Microsoft.Xna.Framework;
    ```

5. Add the following fields to the `ArcBallCamera` class:

    ```
    #region Fields
    private Vector3 cameraPosition = Vector3.Zero;
    private Vector3 targetPosition = Vector3.Zero;

    private float elevation;
    private float rotation;

    private float minDistance;
    private float maxDistance;
    private float viewDistance = 12f;

    private Vector3 baseCameraReference = new Vector3(0, 0, 1);
    private bool needViewResync = true;

    private Matrix cachedViewMatrix;
    #endregion
    ```

6. Add the following properties to the `ArcBallCamera` class:

    ```
    #region Properties
    public Matrix Projection { get; private set; }

    public Vector3 Target
    {
        get { return targetPosition; }
        set
        {
            targetPosition = value;
            needViewResync = true;
        }
    }
    ```

```
public Vector3 Position
{
    get
    {
        return cameraPosition;
    }
}

public float Elevation
{
    get { return elevation; }
    set
    {
        elevation = MathHelper.Clamp(
            value,
            MathHelper.ToRadians(-70),
            MathHelper.ToRadians(-10));
        needViewResync = true;
    }
}

public float Rotation
{
    get { return rotation; }
    set
    {
        rotation = MathHelper.WrapAngle(value);
        needViewResync = true;
    }
}

public float ViewDistance
{
    get { return viewDistance; }
    set
    {
        viewDistance = MathHelper.Clamp(
            value,
            minDistance,
            maxDistance);
    }
}
#endregion
```

What just happened?

The basics of the `ArcBallCamera` may at first appear similar to the FPS camera from Cube Chaser, and in fact, in some cases that is true. We are still going to track the position of the camera. We will need to provide `Projection` and `View` matrices. Finally, we will use the same caching mechanism for the `View` matrix that we did with the `Camera` class in Cube Chaser.

There are, though, some important differences even in those few pieces. First of all, notice that the `Position` property is read-only. We cannot directly set the position of the camera because, by definition, its position must be fixed along the ball. Instead, we will allow an external code to specify an elevation angle and a rotation angle, which we will use to calculate the position of the camera.

The `Elevation` and `Rotation` properties contain constraints in their set code that limit the values that can be stored in the internal fields. In the case of `Rotation`, we are using `MathHelper.WrapAngle()` to keep the value of the angle within one full circle of rotation.

`Elevation` requires somewhat more detailed restrictions. Remember that, by default, everything we draw is one-sided. If we were to allow the camera to move too close to, or below the horizon, we would be unable to see the triangles that will make up our game's terrain. An angle of 0 degrees would be looking straight along the X-Z plane, while an angle of -90 degrees will allow us to look straight down on the X Z plane. To prevent either side-on or directly top-down viewing, both of which would look a bit strange, we use `MathHelper.Clamp()` to keep the value of the elevation angle between `-70` and `-10` degrees, padding the viewing angle a bit on either end. There is nothing magical about these figures; they were just what looked good via experimentation.

The `minDistance`, `maxDistance`, and `viewDistance` fields, along with the `ViewDistance` property, control how far back from the target point the camera will be placed. This allows us to define the radius of the ball that the camera rides on. It will also allow us to move the camera closer to the playfield to view details, or move further back to gain a wider perspective on the battle.

One property that you might notice is missing from what we have implemented so far is the `View` matrix. This is because, of all of the aspects of our camera, it is the `View` matrix that differs most from what we did with our FPS camera in Cube Chaser. Let's go ahead and add a constructor for the `ArcBallCamera` and then finish up by adding the property to return the `View` matrix.

Time for action – finishing the ArcBallCamera class

1. Add the `Constructor` region to the `ArcBallCamera` class as follows:

```
#region Constructor
public ArcBallCamera(
    Vector3 targetPosition,
    float initialElevation,
    float initialRotation,
    float minDistance,
    float maxDistance,
    float initialDistance,
    float aspectRatio,
    float nearClip,
    float farClip)
{
    Target = targetPosition;
    Elevation = initialElevation;
    Rotation = initialRotation;
    this.minDistance = minDistance;
    this.maxDistance = maxDistance;
    ViewDistance = initialDistance;

    Projection = Matrix.CreatePerspectiveFieldOfView(
        MathHelper.PiOver4,
        aspectRatio,
        nearClip,
        farClip);

    needViewResync = true;
}
#endregion
```

2. Add the `View` property to the `Properties` region of the `ArcBallCamera` class:

```
public Matrix View
{
    get
    {
        if (needViewResync)
        {
            Matrix transformMatrix = Matrix.CreateFromYawPitchRoll(
                rotation,
                elevation,
                0f);
```

```
                cameraPosition = Vector3.Transform(
                    baseCameraReference,
                    transformMatrix);
                cameraPosition *= viewDistance;
                cameraPosition += targetPosition;

                cachedViewMatrix = Matrix.CreateLookAt(
                    cameraPosition,
                    targetPosition,
                    Vector3.Up);
            }

        return cachedViewMatrix;
        }
    }
```

What just happened?

The constructor for the `ArcBallCamera` just passes the parameters given to it along to the various class fields, sets up the `Projection` matrix just like we did with the FPS camera in Cube Chaser, and sets the `needViewResync` flag to `true`. This flag indicates that one of the components that make up the `View` matrix has changed, and that the `View` matrix will need to be recalculated the next time it is requested.

In addition to calculating and returning a `View` matrix, the `View` property has the additional job of determining the camera position based on the `Elevation` and `Rotation` fields whenever the view needs to be resynced.

We start off by using `Matrix.CreateFromYawPitchRoll()` to build a matrix using the camera's `Rotation` field as the Yaw, and `Elevation` as the Pitch. We leave the Roll parameter as zero to keep the camera oriented vertically.

As we can see in the following image, **Yaw**, **Pitch**, and **Roll** are simply names for rotation around a specific axis:

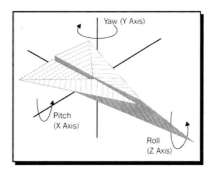

YawPitchRoll versus CreateRotation

In Cube Chaser, we used `Matrix.CreateRotationX()` and `Matrix.CreateRotationZ()` in order to calculate rotation matrices. This would work here as well, but we would need to be careful to combine the rotations in the correct order. We would need to use `Matrix.CreateRotationX(elevation)` first and multiply it by `Matrix.CreateRotationY(rotation)` in order to produce the same matrix created by `Matrix.CreateFromYawPitchRoll()`.

Let's assume for a moment that the point we are focused on is the world origin (0, 0, 0). Recall that with our FPS camera, we used `baseCameraReference` to point along a default viewing direction. In the case of the `ArcBallCamera` class, `baseCameraReference` has a similar purpose, and even has the same value (0, 0, 1). This time, however, instead of representing the direction we are looking in, it represents the position we would be looking from if we were looking at the origin, assuming zero values for both `Rotation` and `Elevation`. In other words, if we have not rotated or elevated our camera, the camera would be sitting at zero on the X and Y axis, one unit along the positive Z axis:

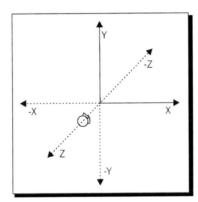

In order to determine the actual position of the camera, we first transform the `baseCameraReference` with the matrix we built using the `elevation` and `rotation` values. This leaves the camera in the appropriate direction relative to the origin, but exactly one unit away. To pull the camera out to the appropriate viewing distance, we multiply this position by the `viewDistance` field.

Our camera would now be in the correct position if the point we wanted to look at is the world origin. In order to move it to focus on the point we wish to view, we simply need to add the target position to the position we have so far worked out for our camera.

Finally, we once again use `Matrix.CreateLookAt()`, specifying the position we just calculated for our camera along with the fixed target position we wish to look at.

Building the playfield

Now that we have a fancy new style of camera, we need something to actually point it at. For Tank Battles, we are going to use height maps to generate terrain for the playfield.

Height maps

What is a height map anyway? A **height map** is nothing more than a 2D image that we will use to represent the height of each vertex that makes up our terrain. To generate the height maps included in the `resources` file for this chapter, the Clouds effect of Paint. NET (available at no cost at `http://www.getpaint.net`) was used on empty images of 128x128 pixels. The size of the height map image will determine the number of nodes present in the terrain when we convert the height map into vertices:

The Clouds filter of programs like Paint.NET and Photoshop produce smoothly transitioning gradients with some degree of randomization applied to them. The previous image contains a few of these randomly generated images as an example. Their smooth transition between light and dark levels makes them perfect for quick height maps because they will create realistically transitioning terrain levels.

Height maps can also be created by hand, by darkening and lightening areas of a grayscale image to create valleys (darker areas) and mountains (lighter areas). Any area of the same color will have the same elevation in the generated terrain.

Generating the terrain

The process of generating the terrain for Tank Battles is somewhat similar to creating the floor of the maze in Cube Chaser. When we built the floor, we created a number of triangles to represent the floor tiles, always placing them along the X-Z plane (in other words, with a 0 as the Y coordinate of the `Vector3` describing the vertex). We will do nearly the same thing with the terrain for Tank Battles, with a couple of important changes.

First, we will use both a vertex buffer and an index buffer. We are already familiar with a vertex buffer – it supplies the location of the vertices we wish the graphics card to use, to the effect that it will render the 3D geometry for us. In Cube Chaser, we supplied the vertex buffer with vertices in groups of three to form individual triangles. For our terrain in Tank Battles, though, we will simply build a grid of vertices to supply to the graphics card in our vertex buffer. While we will create them in a specific order, we will not be relying on the vertex buffer to also provide information about the triangles themselves.

Instead, we will use an index buffer, which will supply the indices of the vertices in the vertex buffer that we will use to draw each triangle. In other words, the vertex buffer holds the locations of the points, while the index buffer stores the list of points that make up each triangle we will draw.

Why the split? Remember that it takes two triangles to make up a single square. That square contains four vertices (upper-left, upper-right, lower-left, and lower-right). In order to define those two triangles, we need to specify six vertices. We ended up duplicating the upper-right and lower-left vertices for each square of the floor in Cube Chaser. Neighboring squares also shared two vertices. In fact, many of our vertices were part of six different triangles, and therefore repeated six times in our vertex buffer. We can cut down considerably on the number of vertices we need to specify by leaving out the duplicates and specifying indices instead.

The second major difference between the floor in Cube Chaser and the terrain in Tank Battles, of course, is that we will not be leaving the Y coordinate as a zero! We will use the color value of each pixel on the height map to determine the elevation of that vertex in the terrain.

Time for action – generating the terrain

1. Add a new class to the **Tank Battles** project by right-clicking on the project in **Solution Explorer** and selecting **Add | Class...**.

2. Ensure that the **Visual C# | Code** is selected under **Installed Templates** and select the **Class** template.

3. Enter `Terrain.cs` as the name of the class file.

4. Add the following `using` directive to the top of the `Terrain.cs` file:

```
using Microsoft.Xna.Framework;
using Microsoft.Xna.Framework.Graphics;
```

5. Add the following fields to the `Terrain` class:

```
#region Fields
private VertexBuffer vertexBuffer;
private IndexBuffer indexBuffer;

private GraphicsDevice device;
```

```
private Texture2D terrainTexture;
private float textureScale;
private float[,] heights;
#endregion
```

6. Add a constructor to the `Terrain` class:

```
#region Constructor
public Terrain(
    GraphicsDevice graphicsDevice,
    Texture2D heightMap,
    Texture2D terrainTexture,
    float textureScale,
    int terrainWidth,
    int terrainHeight,
    float heightScale)
{
    device = graphicsDevice;
    this.terrainTexture = terrainTexture;
    this.textureScale = textureScale;

    ReadHeightMap(
        heightMap,
        terrainWidth,
        terrainHeight,
        heightScale);

    BuildVertexBuffer(
        terrainWidth,
        terrainHeight,
        heightScale);

    BuildIndexBuffer(
        terrainWidth,
        terrainHeight);
}
#endregion
```

What just happened?

We now have the shell of our `Terrain` class, so let's look at the components we have now before we move on to filling out the rest of the class.

As described previously, we will now be using both a `VertexBuffer` and an `IndexBuffer` to describe to the graphics card what we wish to draw. The fields of the `Terrain` class also include a texture to use for the terrain, and a two-dimensional array of float values that will store the heights read from the height map image.

The `Terrain` class constructor stores the graphics device and textures passed to it, and then calls three helper methods: `ReadHeightMap()`, `BuildVertexBuffer()`, and `BuildIndexbuffer()`. We will add each of these methods to the class individually, discussing the code after each one.

Height data

The bitmaps we will be using are grayscale images, so the red, green, and blue values of each pixel are identical. The lighter the pixel on the image, the higher each of these values will be. A fully black pixel has an RGB value of 0, 0, 0, while a fully white pixel has a value of 255, 255, 255.

The goal of our `ReadHeightMap()` method is to examine each pixel of the height map and translate the color values into the `heights` array which we will use in `BuildVertexBuffer()`.

Time for action – adding the ReadHeightMap() method

1. Add the `Height Map` region to the `Terrain` class, shown as follows:

```
#region Height Map
private void ReadHeightMap(
    Texture2D heightMap,
    int terrainWidth,
    int terrainHeight,
    float heightScale)
{
    float min = float.MaxValue;
    float max = float.MinValue;

    heights = new float[terrainWidth, terrainHeight];

    Color[] heightMapData = new Color[
        heightMap.Width * heightMap.Height];
```

```
        heightMap.GetData(heightMapData);
        for (int x = 0; x < terrainWidth; x++)
            for (int z = 0; z < terrainHeight; z++)
            {
                byte height = heightMapData[x + z * terrainWidth].R;
                heights[x, z] = (float)height / 255f;

                max = MathHelper.Max(max, heights[x, z]);
                min = MathHelper.Min(min, heights[x, z]);
            }

        float range = (max - min);

        for (int x = 0; x < terrainWidth; x++)
            for (int z = 0; z < terrainHeight; z++)
            {
                heights[x, z] =
                    ((heights[x, z] - min) / range) * heightScale;
            }
    }
    #endregion
```

What just happened?

We begin by declaring min and max to allow us to track both the highest and lowest point in the height data we retrieve from the height map. We set min to float.MaxValue, and max to float.MinValue, ensuring that the values in our height map will replace them immediately.

Next, we create the two-dimensional array of floats that will hold the height of each vertex in the terrain we will generate later.

In order to read the color values from the height map, we use the GetData() method of the Texture2D class to copy the colors into an array of Color objects. This array has the same number of elements as the image has pixels (width * height). To read each value, we use a pair of for loops to iterate through the height and width of the image.

As we loop, we read the value of the red component (R) from the heightMapData array and store it in the height variable. We then place the value into the heights array, after dividing it by 255. Since we know that the R property of the Color type is a byte, we know that the value returned will be between 0 and 255. By dividing this value by 255, we end up with a float value between 0 (the lowest possible valley) and 1 (the highest mountaintop).

Why red?

In a grayscale image, the red, green, and blue values are all the same, so we simply choose one to read for our height map data. Either of the others would have produced identical results. You could store additional information in your height map; for instance, the location of trees to be placed on the landscape, by using the other color channels without impacting the height generation.

With each run through the loop, we check to see if we need to update min, max, or both. Finally, when the loop has been completed, we loop through the heights array we just filled in. This time, we subtract the min value from each height, and divide the value by the spread between min and max, and then multiply the result by the desired height scale. The purpose of all of this manipulation is to place the lowest point in our terrain at zero on the Y axis, while scaling the rest of the terrain so that the highest point matches the heightScale value passed to the constructor.

Building vertices

Building the vertices for our terrain is actually a simpler process than building the floor of the maze in Cube Chaser, because we are not worried about connecting the vertices to each other to form triangles at this point. We are simply going to create a grid of vertices and store them in the vertex buffer.

Time for action – adding the BuildVertexBuffer() method

1. Add the Vertex Buffer region to the Terrain class as follows:

```
#region Vertex Buffer
private void BuildVertexBuffer(
    int width,
    int height,
    float heightScale)
{
    VertexPositionNormalTexture[] vertices =
        new VertexPositionNormalTexture [width*height];

    for (int x=0; x<width; x++)
        for (int z=0; z<height; z++)
        {
            vertices[x + (z*width)].Position =
                new Vector3(x, heights[x,z], z);
        }

    vertexBuffer = new VertexBuffer(
```

```
        device,
        typeof(VertexPositionNormalTexture),
        vertices.Length,
        BufferUsage.WriteOnly);

    vertexBuffer.SetData(vertices);
}
#endregion
```

What just happened?

After creating an empty array of `VertexPositionNormalTexture`
objects, we loop through the width and height of our terrain, creating a new
`VertexPositionNormalTexture` for each vertex. The X and Z coordinates of the vertex
are directly equal to the current position within our loops. Each vertex will be one unit away
from its neighboring vertices along the X and Z axes. If the vertices were rendered as points
and viewed from directly above, they would appear as a simple grid of evenly-spaced dots.

The Y coordinate of the vertex is retrieved from the `heights` array that we filled in with the
`ReadHeightMap()` method.

Once we have the array of vertices created, we add it to the vertex buffer in the same way
we did with the floor tiles in Cube Chaser. Namely, we create the `VertexBuffer` to be
of the appropriate size and then use the `SetData()` method to copy the contents of the
`vertices` array into the buffer.

Building the indices

The last thing we need to do to build the structure of our terrain is to fill out the index buffer
that will instruct the graphics card on how to use the vertex buffer to create triangles.

Time for action – the buildIndexBuffer() method

1. Add the `Index Buffer` region to the `Terrain` class:

```
#region Index Buffer
private void BuildIndexBuffer(int width, int height)
{
    int indexCount = (width-1) * (height-1) * 6;
    short[] indices = new short[indexCount];
    int counter = 0;

    for (short z = 0; z < height - 1; z++)
        for (short x = 0; x < height - 1; x++)
        {
```

```
                  short upperLeft = (short)(x + (z * width));
                  short upperRight = (short)(upperLeft + 1);
                  short lowerLeft = (short)(upperLeft + width);
                  short lowerRight = (short)(upperLeft + width + 1);

                  indices[counter++] = upperLeft;
                  indices[counter++] = lowerRight;
                  indices[counter++] = lowerLeft;
                  indices[counter++] = upperLeft;
                  indices[counter++] = upperRight;
                  indices[counter++] = lowerRight;
            }

      indexBuffer = new IndexBuffer(
            device,
            IndexElementSize.SixteenBits,
            indices.Length,
            BufferUsage.WriteOnly);
      indexBuffer.SetData(indices);
    }
    #endregion
```

What just happened?

We will still create our triangles in pairs, as that makes creating the whole set a simple matter of looping through the terrain just like we did when creating the vertices. We want to stop one vertex before the end in both directions. If we have, say 10 vertices, there would only be nine lines needed to connect them. The same is true for generating the triangles for our terrain.

Since we still need three points to define a triangle and two triangles per square, we need six indices per terrain square, so the total number of indices we are going to create is calculated and used to create the indices array. You may have noticed that this array is of type short, which we have not yet used.

The reason for this is that the Reach graphics profile (the default for XNA 4.0) does not support 32-bit index elements. The short type is 16-bits, which we specify when creating the indexBuffer at the bottom of the method. Otherwise, we set the index buffer the same way we set the vertex buffer – creating the space to hold the values and then using SetData() to copy them in.

Let's see the terrain already!

We have done quite a bit of background work with nothing to show for it so far. Let's change that by adding enough code to allow us to at least see what we have created so far. We will also get a sneak peek of HLSL!

Time for action – drawing the terrain

1. In **Solution Explorer**, right-click on the **Effects** folder in the content project. Select **Add | New Item...**.

2. In the central pane of the **Add New Item** window, select **Effect File**.

3. Name the file `Terrain.fx` and click **Add**.

4. If you wish, browse through the `template effect` file that opens when it is added to the project, and then close the file.

5. Add the `Draw` region to the `Terrain` class:

```
#region Draw
public void Draw(
    ArcBallCamera camera,
    Effect effect)
{
    effect.CurrentTechnique = effect.Techniques["Technique1"];
    effect.Parameters["World"].SetValue(Matrix.Identity);
    effect.Parameters["View"].SetValue(camera.View);
    effect.Parameters["Projection"].SetValue(camera.Projection);

    foreach (EffectPass pass in effect.CurrentTechnique.Passes)
    {
        pass.Apply();
        device.SetVertexBuffer(vertexBuffer);
        device.Indices = indexBuffer;
        device.DrawIndexedPrimitives(
            PrimitiveType.TriangleList,
            0,
            0,
            vertexBuffer.VertexCount,
            0,
            indexBuffer.IndexCount / 3);
    }
}
#endregion
```

6. In the `TankBattlesGame` class, add the following declarations right after the declarations for `GraphicsDeviceManager` and `SpriteBatch`:

```
ArcBallCamera camera;
Terrain terrain;
Effect effect;
```

7. In the `Initialize()` method of the `TankBattlesGame` class, initialize the camera:

```
camera = new ArcBallCamera(
    new Vector3(64f, 16f, 64f),
    MathHelper.ToRadians(-30),
    0f,
    32f,
    192f,
    128f,
    GraphicsDevice.Viewport.AspectRatio,
    0.1f,
    512f);
```

8. In the `LoadContent()` method of the `TankBattlesGame` class, initialize the terrain and load the effect file:

```
terrain = new Terrain(
    GraphicsDevice,
    Content.Load<Texture2D>(@"Textures\HeightMap_02"),
    Content.Load<Texture2D>(@"Textures\Grass"),
    32f,
    128,
    128,
    30f);

effect = Content.Load<Effect>(@"Effects/Terrain");
```

9. In the `Draw()` method of the `TankBattlesGame` class, add the following line after the graphics device has been cleared:

```
terrain.Draw(camera, effect);
```

10. Execute the game and view the bright red hill-like blob floating in the middle of nowhere!

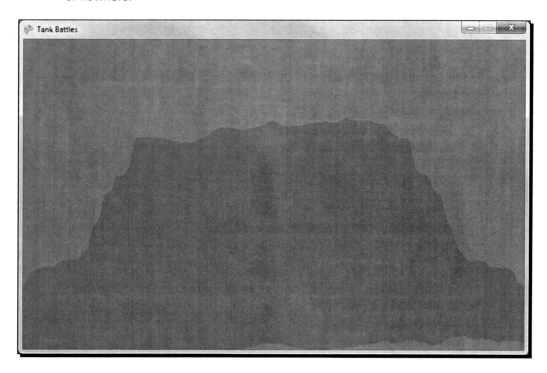

What just happened?

While we could have gone ahead and used a `BasicEffect` like we did in Cube Chaser, we have instead created our own effect file that we will examine more closely later in this chapter. Everything that we will do in this chapter could have been handled by `BasicEffect`, but when we add new features to our terrain (like multi-texturing in Chapter 8, *Tank Battles – Ending the War*), we will need to use the extra power available to us by creating our own effect in order to implement them, so we might as well start off on the right foot in the first place.

The usage of our custom effect is not too different from using the `BasicEffect`, except that we have to specify a technique (if you browsed through the `Terrain.fx` file, you should have seen a technique called `Technique1` near the bottom of the file). We also need to use a different format for specifying the parameters we are going to pass to the effect. While `BasicEffect` declares things such as `Texture`, `World`, and `View` for us, our effect may not use them or may call them different things depending on what we are trying to achieve. For this reason, we use the `Parameters` collection of the effect along with the `SetValue()` method to set the parameters we are passing to the effect.

The remainder of the `Draw()` method should be familiar – it works the same way the draw method for the maze did in Cube Chaser after the parameters have been set.

When we initialize the camera in the `Initialize()` method of the `TankBattleGame` class, we specify that it is looking at (64, 16, 64). If we glance ahead to the declaration of our terrain, we find that the terrain is declared as 128 units of length and width, with the X and Z spacing set to `1.0f`. This means that the look at point for the camera will be the center of the terrain, 16 units above the X-Z plane.

The camera is elevated -30 degrees and rotated 0 degrees around the Y axis. It will have a minimum view distance of 32 units and a maximum of 192 units, with an initial value of 128 units. The remaining parameters are identical to the FPS camera we created for Cube Chaser.

When declaring the terrain itself in `LoadContent()`, we pass it a height map and a texture to use (though we are not currently displaying the texture). We will look at the `textureScale` parameter a bit later in this chapter (the value is set to `32f` here). Like the texture itself, this value is currently unused by our code.

As we saw before, the terrain is 128x128 units with a spacing of 1 in both the X and Z directions. Finally, we specify a scaling factor of 30, meaning that the highest point in the terrain should be at `30f` on the Y axis. The lowest point on the terrain will be at `0f`, and the values in between will be scaled appropriately to fit within that range.

But, why is it red? We are using `VertexPositionNormalTexture` as our vertex declaration, but we have not specified a texture, or texture coordinates, so the `Technique1` of the `Terrain` effect just uses default values. The result is that the pixels in our terrain end up showing as solid red.

Adding texture – a gentle introduction to HLSL

We have already specified the texture we want to use for the terrain in the `LoadContent()` event, so now we just need to adjust our code to take the texture into account. Since we are not using a `BasicEffect` for rendering, we will need to expand the code in the `Terrain.fx` file in order to utilize the texture we pass to the `Terrain` class.

While a full discussion of the intricacies of High Level Shader Language (HLSL) is well beyond the scope of this book – entire books can and have been written about writing shaders – we can certainly cover enough of the basics to allow us to generate all of the effects we will need for Tank Battles.

Originally developed by Microsoft and NVIDIA for Direct3D, HLSL is a programming language designed for the creation of shaders. We can work with both vertex shaders, which convert the vertex information for our triangles into pixels to be rendered to the display, and pixel shaders, which describe the characteristics of each pixel, such as its color and transparency level. The conversion of our 3D geometry to the 2D screen is called **Rasterization**.

Shader models and other shader types

DirectX defines a series of specification versions for developing shaders called **shader models**. Each successive model builds on the capabilities of the model before it. XNA supports shader models 1 through 3, and the default effect file specifies 2.0 as the target shader model (in the technique at the bottom of the file, the Vertex and Pixel shaders are compiled with `vs_2_0` and `ps_2_0` as their specified shader models).

Newer shader models include support for new types of shaders, namely the geometry shader in shader model 4, useful for things like point sprites and particle effects as it allows the shader to create additional primitives to be rendered into the scene, and compute shaders in shader model 5 which do not necessarily involve graphics at all and allows general code to be executed on the graphics card to take advantage of the high-speed nature of the hardware. Since these shader models are associated with DirectX 10 and 11, while XNA is designed around DirectX 9, these are not available to us in XNA.

For our own `Terrain.fx` file, we will need to make changes to both the vertex and pixel shaders that are built into the default effect file, as well as adding our own parameters to the effect. We will cover each of the areas of the effect code we need to modify as their own separate short section.

Declaring variables

Just like we would in a C# program, we can define effect-wide variables for our HLSL code to use. We generally place these variables at the top of the effect file. The default file contains three fields already, and we will add two new declarations to this area.

Time for action – HLSL declarations

1. Update the declarations area of the `Terrain.fx` file (at the very top of the file) to include a declaration for the texture we will be passing to the effect. The section should now read:

```
float4x4 World;
float4x4 View;
float4x4 Projection;

texture terrainTexture1;

sampler2D textureSampler = sampler_state {
  Texture = (terrainTexture1);
  AddressU = Wrap;
  AddressV = Wrap;
};
```

What just happened?

At the top of the default file that is generated when we add a new effect to our project, three variables of the type `float4x4` are declared for us. These variables have familiar names, `World`, `View`, and `Projection`. If you think back to our discussion on matrices, an XNA matrix is a 4 by 4 array of float values, so the HLSL type `float4x4` corresponds to an XNA matrix. In fact, these are the variables in the effect file that we set when we use the `Parameters[].SetValue()` method in our draw code.

We add the `terrainTexture1` variable here, declaring it as type texture. Since HLSL is designed specifically for working with the graphics card, texture is one of the built-in data types that the language understands. The texture type corresponds to a `Texture2D` in XNA.

In order for our HLSL functions to read portions of our texture to map them to the display (a process called **sampling**) we need to define a `sampler2D`. It explains to HLSL how it should handle providing information about the texture to functions in our HLSL code. In this case, we are specifying that we want the sampler to use `terrainTexture1` as the source for texture information. By specifying `AddressU` and `AddressV` as `Wrap`, we indicate that, if we specify values greater than 1 or less than 0 for texture coordinates, the texture will wrap around and start sampling from the other side, allowing the texture to be tiled onto a surface.

Texture address modes

The `AddressU` and `AddressV` settings are known as texture address modes. There are two other settings we can use in addition to wrapping the texture. **Clamp mode** will use the nearest edge texture value for texture coordinates outside the 0 to 1 range. A texture coordinate less than 0 will be assumed to be 0. The **mirror mode** works similarly to the wrap mode, in that the texture will be tiled as values increase, however, it will be mirrored for each odd increment of the texture coordinate. Coordinates from 0 to 1 will appear normally, while 1 to 2 will appear reversed, or mirrored. Coordinates from 2 to 3 will sample normally again, and so on.

The vertex shader structures

Our HLSL code needs some way to pass information about vertices around to the vertex and pixel shader functions. In order to do this, two structures are defined in the default effect file. These default structures do not include the information necessary for mapping a texture to our surfaces, so we will need to modify the definitions of the structures to include this information.

Time for action – Vertex Shader Input and Output definition

1. Modify the declaration for the `VertexShaderInput struct` by adding an entry for a texture coordinate. The new `struct` should be as follows:

```
struct VertexShaderInput
{
    float4 Position : POSITION0;
    float2 TextureCoordinate : TEXCOORD0;
};
```

2. Similarly, modify the declaration for the `VertexShaderOutput` function in the same way:

```
struct VertexShaderOutput
{
    float4 Position : POSITION0;
    float2 TextureCoordinate : TEXCOORD0;
};
```

What just happened?

The `VertexShaderInput` structure is passed to our vertex shader function, which we will be modifying in the next section. The return value of the vertex shader is a `VertexShaderOutput` structure. This is similar to what we would do with C# to define the type of data we are passing into a function and specifying what type of information it returns.

The default shader code already has the `Position` field, which is declared as a `float4`. Once again, thinking back to our discussion on matrices in Chapter 4, *Cube Chaser – Finding your Way*, recall that a `Vector3` contains three float types, but that for the purposes of matrix math, we assume that there are four values and that the last value is a one. Thus, when we specify a position as a `Vector3` in XNA, it will be translated to a `float4` in our shader code.

When we add the `TextureCoordinate` field, we specify that it is a `float2`, which matches nicely with the `Vector2` type in XNA. Recall that our texture coordinates are specified as U and V offsets into our texture image, and we store them as `Vector2` values in the vertex buffer. These `Vector2` values will be placed in the `TextureCoordinate` field automatically by the effect when it is processed.

That leaves the question of exactly how these values get placed. After all, if you look through the rest of the HLSL code, even if you are not sure exactly what it does, the values of the `VertexShaderInput` are never set anywhere. In reality, this is happening for us behind the scenes. Notice that the `Position` field has: POSITION0 tacked onto the end of the line. Similarly, the `TextureCoordinate` field has the cryptic: TEXCOORD0 trailing it.

These identifiers are called **semantics**, and indicate to HLSL what type of data our variables contain. We could just as easily call our `TextureCoordinate` "Fred" and as long as we specified the `TEXCOORD0` semantic, it would still be used in the same way by the shader.

While these semantics allow us to specify what gets fed into our input structure, they are also used to indicate what comes out in our output structure. In our code, both `Position` and `TextureCoordinate` are identical in the input and output structures, but they do not necessarily need to be that way. As long as the two semantics we are using are included in both structures, it really does not matter what we call the fields internally.

The vertex shader

The **vertex shader** converts the vertex information about our triangles into pixels to be displayed to the screen. We need to modify the default vertex shader in order to include support for texture mapping, even though we are not going to reference the texture at all in the function.

Time for action – the vertex shader

1. Modify the default code for the `VertexShaderFunction` function to include setting texture coordinates:

```
VertexShaderOutput VertexShaderFunction(VertexShaderInput input)
{
    VertexShaderOutput output;

    float4 worldPosition = mul(input.Position, World);
    float4 viewPosition = mul(worldPosition, View);
    output.Position = mul(viewPosition, Projection);

      output.TextureCoordinate = input.TextureCoordinate;

    return output;
}
```

What just happened?

Similar to a C# function, an HLSL function declaration begins with a return type, followed by the function name and the parameters it takes inside the parenthesis. The first line of the function declares a variable to hold the output value that will be returned at the end of the function.

The next three lines use the `World`, `View`, and `Projection` matrices to transform the input position of the vertex to position them properly for display on the screen. As we can see, the first step is to multiply the position by the `World` matrix. In our case, the `World` matrix has always been equal to the identity matrix, so the resulting world position will be equal to the input position.

Next, the world position is multiplied by the `View` matrix, which is set based on the position of the camera. The resulting view position represents the vertex transformed into its appropriate location relative to the camera.

Finally, the view position is multiplied by the `Projection` matrix. This accounts for the properties of the camera that we specified when we created it, such as the field of view and the aspect ratio. The value we get from this multiplication is the final position of this vertex, so it is stored in the `Position` field of the output structure.

Our addition to the code is to simply copy the `TextureCoordinate` field from the input structure to the output structure. We are not manipulating the texture coordinate at all in the vertex shader; we just need to pass the information along so that things further down the rendering pipeline can use it.

The pixel shader

The output of the vertex shader gets sent to the pixel shader, which is responsible for determining the characteristics of the pixel that will be rendered. We will now replace the default pixel shader with a new code to sample from our texture, according to the texture coordinate passed in via the `VertexShaderOutput` structure.

Time for action – the pixel shader

1. Examine the code of the `PixelShaderFunction`, in particular the line that reads `return float4(1, 0, 0, 1)`.

2. Modify the code for the `PixelShaderFunction`, replacing the contents with the following:

```
float4 PixelShaderFunction(VertexShaderOutput input) : COLOR0
{
        return tex2D(textureSampler, input.TextureCoordinate);
}
```

What just happened?

In *step 1*, we see that the default pixel shader function is quite simple. All it does is return a `float4` value of (1, 0, 0, 1). But what does this mean? Note the `COLOR0` at the end of the declaration for the pixel shader function. This is another semantic that indicates that this function returns the color of the pixel that will be sent to the display.

If we interpret the `float4` value as a color, in the order Red, Green, Blue, Alpha, we see that the default pixel shader simply returns a non-transparent red. Ah ha! This is why our terrain is currently rendering as a large red blob!

Our replacement function uses the `tex2D` HLSL method, passing it our texture sampler and the `TextureCoordinate` that gets passed to the pixel shader (note that the input of the pixel shader is of type `VertexShaderOutput`). The `tex2D` method uses the sampler to look up the color of the desired location on the texture and returns it to be used for that particular pixel.

Techniques and passes

We do not need to modify the last part of the default effect file, which declares the `Technique1` technique and a single pass inside it. More complicated shaders can have many different techniques, and each technique may contain multiple passes. In the default pass, the built-in `VertexShader` and `PixelShader` values are set to the functions that we modified previously. Any number of different shader functions can be included in the effect file.

We are almost ready to render our terrain with a texture. All we need to do now is modify the drawing code so that we use the new features we have added to our shader, and modify the code that builds our vertices to include texture coordinates.

Time for action – utilizing Terrain.fx

1. In the `Terrain.cs` class file, add the following to the `Draw()` method, right after setting `CurrentTechnique` for the effect:

```
effect.Parameters["terrainTexture1"].SetValue(terrainTexture);
```

2. In the `BuildVertexBuffer()` method of the `Terrain` class, add the following right after the position of the vertex is set inside the loop:

```
vertices[x + (z * width)].TextureCoordinate =
    new Vector2((float)x / textureScale, (float)z / textureScale);
```

3.   Execute the program and view the textured terrain, as shown in the following screenshot:

What just happened?

We now have a simple grass texture mapped to our terrain. It is still a bit difficult to make out the features of the landscape, but they are certainly more visible than when the whole thing was just a red blob. We will come back to improving the look of our terrain in Chapter 8, *Tank Battles – Ending the War*.

Moving the camera

Before we move on to loading 3D models, let's see how we can rotate our view around the terrain we are now rendering in the center of the screen. We will implement mouse-based camera rotation similar to what you might see in a first-person shooter game, where you hold down the right mouse button to activate camera movement mode.

Time for action – moving the camera with the mouse

1. In the `TankBattlesGame` class, add five fields to the declarations area:

```
Point screenCenter;
Point saveMousePoint;
bool moveMode = false;
float scrollRate = 1.0f;
MouseState previousMouse;
```

2. In the `Initialize()` method of the `TankBattlesGame` class, add the following before the call to `base.Initialize()`:

```
screenCenter.X = this.Window.ClientBounds.Width / 2;
screenCenter.Y = this.Window.ClientBounds.Height / 2;

this.IsMouseVisible = true;

previousMouse = Mouse.GetState();
Mouse.SetPosition(screenCenter.X, screenCenter.Y);
```

3. In the `Update()` method of the `TankBattlesGame` class, add the following before the call to `base.Update()`:

```
if (this.IsActive) {

  MouseState mouse = Mouse.GetState();

  if (moveMode)
  {
      camera.Rotation += MathHelper.ToRadians(
          (mouse.X - screenCenter.X) / 2f);
      camera.Elevation += MathHelper.ToRadians(
          (mouse.Y - screenCenter.Y) / 2f);

      Mouse.SetPosition(screenCenter.X, screenCenter.Y);
  }

  if (mouse.RightButton == ButtonState.Pressed)
  {
      if (!moveMode &&
          previousMouse.RightButton == ButtonState.Released)
      {
          if (graphics.GraphicsDevice.Viewport.Bounds.Contains(
              new Point(mouse.X, mouse.Y)))
          {
```

```
                    moveMode = true;
                    saveMousePoint.X = mouse.X;
                    saveMousePoint.Y = mouse.Y;
                    Mouse.SetPosition(screenCenter.X, screenCenter.Y);
                    this.IsMouseVisible = false;
                }
            }
        }
        else
        {
            if (moveMode)
            {
                moveMode = false;
                Mouse.SetPosition(saveMousePoint.X, saveMousePoint.Y);
                this.IsMouseVisible = true;
            }
        }

        if (mouse.ScrollWheelValue - previousMouse.ScrollWheelValue !=
0)
        {
            float wheelChange = mouse.ScrollWheelValue -
                previousMouse.ScrollWheelValue;

            camera.ViewDistance -= (wheelChange / 120) * scrollRate;
        }

    previousMouse = mouse;
}
```

4. Execute the game and hold down the right mouse button to rotate your view and change elevation by moving the mouse. Use the mouse scroll wheel to zoom in and out.

What just happened?

When the user wishes to rotate the camera, we need to know how far the mouse has travelled during each frame of game time. We begin by establishing the center of the game window, which we will use to evaluate how far the mouse has travelled. We establish that, when launched, the game will not be in the camera moving mode by setting moveMode to false.

During the Update() method, we start off by checking that the game is the active window on the computer via this.IsActive. If some other window is active, we do not want to steal the mouse cursor when the user is trying to do something in another program.

Assuming we are active, we then need to decide if we should move the camera during this frame. We track a Boolean value that determines if we are currently moving the camera or not based on the state of the right mouse button.

When the movement mode is initiated, we move the mouse cursor to the center of the window and hide it. Even when hidden, the mouse still tracks its current position. This is important to us because, during each frame, while we are in move mode, we will follow these steps to determine how to move the camera:

1. Compare the current mouse position to the center of the screen.
2. Add half the distance the mouse has travelled horizontally to the camera's rotation.
3. Add half the distance the mouse has travelled vertically to the camera's elevation.
4. Move the mouse cursor to the center of the window.

Because we treat the center of the screen as the starting point for our movement, if the mouse moves left, the value for the horizontal movement (X) will be negative. The same is true for the vertical position (Y) if the mouse moves upward. We divide these values by 2 simply to present a reasonable movement rate for the camera. If you wish to slow down the camera rotation, the divisor in both of these statements just needs to be increased.

Remember that both the `Rotation` and `Elevation` properties of the `Camera` class take care of things like wrapping angles and limiting the elevation for us, so we do not need to worry about that in our code that uses the camera.

When the user leaves movement mode (by releasing the right mouse button), we reset the mouse cursor back to the center of the screen and make the cursor visible again.

The other method the user can use to manipulate the camera is to zoom in and out using the mouse's scroll wheel. The `ScrollWheelValue` property of the `Mouse` class keeps track of how far the scroll wheel has moved since your game started. This value starts at zero when the game launches and is updated every time the scroll wheel is moved. Every click of the scroll wheel changes the value by 120 in either the positive (scrolling up) or negative (scrolling down) direction.

We compare the current and previous value of the scroll wheel and divide the result by 120 which gives the number of stops the wheel has moved in the last frame. We have set a `scrollRate` of 1.0f, meaning we will simply use the resultant value as the amount we modify the camera's `ViewDistance` by during the frame. If we want to scroll faster, we would increase `scrollRate`. To allow for finer (and slower) zooming, we could decrease `scrollRate`.

Just as with the `Elevation` and `Rotation` properties, the `ViewDistance` property takes care of making sure the values are in the allowed range for us, so we do not need to perform those checks in our `Update()` method. We simply supply our intent to the property and let it decide what to do with it.

Summary

As we begin Tank Battles, we have covered quite a bit of ground! We implemented a basic arc-ball camera that we can rotate around our game world, read a bitmap image to create a three-dimensional terrain map, and implemented HLSL code to texture the terrain.

In Chapter 6, *Tank Battles – The Big Guns*, we will look at adding a 3D tank model to our game and positioning it within the game world.

6
Tank Battles – The Big Guns

Now that we have a landscape for our tanks to fight on, it is time to bring them into the mix. Our tanks will be 3D models created externally to XNA in one of several different 3D modeling packages.

In this chapter, we will cover all that is necessary to get our tanks into the game and placed in the game world, including:

- Adding models to our game's content project and loading them into the game
- Drawing the tank model to the screen
- Animating the various components of the tank model
- Matching the elevation of the tank to its position on the generated terrain
- Adding a second tank and positioning both tanks appropriately on the map

Adding the tank model

For tank battles, we will be using a 3D model available for download from the App Hub website (`http://create.msdn.com`) in the **Simple Animation CODE SAMPLE** available at `http://xbox.create.msdn.com/en-US/education/catalog/sample/simple_animation`.

Our first step will be to add the model to our content project in order to bring it into the game.

Time for action – adding the tank model

We can add the tank model to our project by following these steps:

1. Download the `7089_06_GRAPHICSPACK.ZIP` file from the book's website and extract the contents to a temporary folder.

2. Select the `.fbx` file and the two `.tga` files from the archive and copy them to the Windows clipboard.

3. Switch to Visual Studio and expand the **Tank BattlesContent (Content)** project.

4. Right-click on the **Models** folder and select **Paste** to copy the files on the clipboard into the folder.

5. Right-click on `engine_diff_tex.tga` inside the **Models** folder and select **Exclude From Project**.

6. Right click on `turret_alt_diff_tex.tga` inside the **Models** folder and select **Exclude From Project**.

What just happened?

Adding a model to our game is like adding any other type of content, though there are a couple of pitfalls to watch out for.

Our model includes two image files (the `.tga` files – an image format commonly associated with 3D graphics files because the format is not encumbered by patents) that will provide texture maps for the tank's surfaces. Unlike the other textures we have used, we do not want to include them as part of our content project. Why not?

The content processor for models will parse the `.fbx` file (an Autodesk file format used by several 3D modeling packages) at compile time and look for the textures it references in the directory the model is in. It will automatically process these into `.xnb` files that are placed in the output folder—**Models**, for our game.

If we were to also include these textures in our content project, the standard texture processor would convert the image just like it does with the textures we normally use. When the model processor comes along and tries to convert the texture, an .xnb file with the same name will already exist in the **Models** folder, causing compile time errors.

Incidentally, even though the images associated with our model are not included in our content project directly, they still get built by the content pipeline and stored in the output directory as `.xnb` files. They can be loaded just like any other `Texture2D` object with the `Content.Load()` method.

Free 3D modeling software

There are a number of freely available 3D modeling packages downloadable on the Web that you can use to create your own 3D content. Some of these include:

◆ **Blender**: A free, open source 3D modeling and animation package. Feature rich, and very powerful. Blender can be found at `http://www.blender.org`.

◆ **Wings 3D**: Free, open source 3D modeling package. Does not support animation, but includes many useful modeling features. Wings 3D can be found at `http://wings3d.com`.

◆ **Softimage Mod Tool**: A modeling and animation package from Autodesk. The Softimage Mod Tool is available freely for non-commercial use. A version with a commercial-friendly license is also available to XNA Creator's Club members at `http://usa.autodesk.com/adsk/servlet/pc/item?id=13571257&siteID=123112`.

Building tanks

Now that the model is part of our project, we need to create a class that will manage everything about a tank. While we could simply load the model in our `TankBattlesGame` class, we need more than one tank, and duplicating all of the items necessary to handle both tanks does not make sense.

Time for action – building the Tank class

We can build the `Tank` class using the following steps:

1. Add a new class file called `Tank.cs` to the `Tank Battles` project.

2. Add the following `using` directives to the top of the `Tank.cs` class file:

```
using Microsoft.Xna.Framework;
using Microsoft.Xna.Framework.Graphics;
```

3. Add the following fields to the `Tank` class:

```
#region Fields
private Model model;
private GraphicsDevice device;

private Vector3 position;
private float tankRotation;
private float turretRotation;
```

```
        private float gunElevation;

        private Matrix baseTurretTransform;
        private Matrix baseGunTransform;
        private Matrix[] boneTransforms;
        #endregion
```

4. Add the following properties to the `Tank` class:

```
#region Properties
public Vector3 Position
{
    get
    {
        return position;
    }
    set
    {
        position = value;
    }
}


public float TankRotation
{
    get
    {
        return tankRotation;
    }
    set
    {
        tankRotation = MathHelper.WrapAngle(value);
    }
}


public float TurretRotation
{
    get
    {
        return turretRotation;
    }
    set
    {
        turretRotation = MathHelper.WrapAngle(value);
    }
```

```
    }

    public float GunElevation
    {
        get
        {
            return gunElevation;
        }
        set
        {
            gunElevation = MathHelper.Clamp(
                value,
                MathHelper.ToRadians(-90),
                MathHelper.ToRadians(0));
        }
    }
    #endregion
```

5. Add a constructor to the `Tank` class, as follows:

```
#region Constructor
public Tank(GraphicsDevice device, Model model, Vector3 position)
{
    this.device = device;
    this.model = model;
    Position = position;
    boneTransforms = new Matrix[model.Bones.Count];
}
#endregion
```

6. Add the `Draw()` method to the `Tank` class, as follows:

```
#region Draw
public void Draw(ArcBallCamera camera)
{
    model.Root.Transform = Matrix.Identity *
        Matrix.CreateScale(0.005f) *
        Matrix.CreateRotationY(TankRotation) *
        Matrix.CreateTranslation(Position);

    model.CopyAbsoluteBoneTransformsTo(boneTransforms);

    foreach (ModelMesh mesh in model.Meshes)
    {
        foreach (BasicEffect basicEffect in mesh.Effects)
        {
```

```
            basicEffect.World = boneTransforms[mesh.ParentBone.
    Index];
            basicEffect.View = camera.View;
            basicEffect.Projection = camera.Projection;

            basicEffect.EnableDefaultLighting();
        }

        mesh.Draw();
    }
}
#endregion
```

7. In the declarations area of the `TankBattlesGame` class, add a new `List` object to hold a list of `Tank` objects, as follows:

```
List<Tank> tanks = new List<Tank>();
```

8. Create a temporary tank so we can see it in action by adding the following to the end of the `LoadContent()` method of the `TankBattlesGame` class:

```
tanks.Add(
    new Tank(
        GraphicsDevice,
        Content.Load<Model>(@"Models\tank"),
        new Vector3(61, 40, 61)));
```

9. In the `Draw()` method of the `TankBattlesGame` class, add a loop to draw all of the Tank objects in the tank's list after the terrain has been drawn, as follows:

```
foreach (Tank tank in tanks)
{
    tank.Draw(camera);
}
```

10. Execute the game. Use your mouse to rotate and zoom in on the tank floating above the top of the central mountain in the scene, as shown in the following screenshot:

What just happened?

The Tank class stores the model that will be used to draw the tank in the model field. Just as with our terrain, we need a reference to the game's GraphicsDevice in order to draw our model when necessary.

In addition to this information, we have fields (and corresponding properties) to represent the position of the tank, and the rotation angle of three components of the model. The first, TankRotation, determines the angle at which the entire tank is rotated.

As the turret of the tank can rotate independently of the direction in which the tank itself is facing, we store the rotation angle of the turret in TurretRotation. Both TankRotation and TurretRotation contain code in their property setters to wrap their angles around if we go past a full circle in either direction.

The last angle we want to track is the elevation angle of the gun attached to the turret. This angle can range from 0 degrees (pointing straight out from the side of the turret) to -90 degrees (pointing straight up). This angle is stored in the GunElevation property.

The last field added in step 3 is called boneTransforms, and is an array of matrices. We further define this array while defining the Tank class' constructor by creating an empty array with a number of elements equal to the number of bones in the model.

But what exactly are bones? When a 3D artist creates a model, they can define joints that determine how the various pieces of the model are connected. This process is referred to as "rigging" the model, and a model that has been set up this way is sometimes referred to as "rigged for animation".

The bones in the model are defined with relationships to each other, so that when a bone higher up in the hierarchy moves, all of the lower bones are moved in relation to it. Think for a moment of one of your fingers. It is composed of three distinct bones separated by joints. If you move the bone nearest to your palm, the other two bones move as well – they have to if your finger bones are going to stay connected!

The same is true of the components in our tank. When the tank rotates, all of its pieces rotate as well. Rotating the turret moves the cannon, but has no effect on the body or the wheels. Moving the cannon has no effect on any other parts of the model, but it is hinged at its base, so that rotating the cannon joint makes the cannon appear to elevate up and down around one end instead of spinning around its center.

We will come back to these bones in just a moment, but let's first look at the current `Draw()` method before we expand it to account for bone-based animation.

`Model.Root` refers to the highest level bone in the model's hierarchy. Transforming this bone will transform the entire model, so our basic scaling, rotation, and positioning happen here. Notice that we are drastically scaling down the model of the tank, to a scale of `0.005f`. The tank model is quite large in raw units, so we need to scale it to a size that is in line with the scale we used for our terrain.

Next, we use the `boneTransforms` array we created earlier by calling the model's `CopyAbsoluteBoneTransformsTo()` method. This method calculates the resultant transforms for each of the bones in the model, taking into account all of the parent bones above it, and copies these values into the specified array.

We then loop through each mesh in the model. A **mesh** is an independent piece of the model, representing a movable part. Each of these meshes can have multiple effects tied to it, so we loop through those as well, using an instance of `BasicEffect` created on the spot to render the meshes.

In order to render each mesh, we establish the mesh's world location by looking up the mesh's parent bone transformation and storing it in the `World` matrix. We apply our View and Projection matrices just like before, and enable default lighting on the effect. Finally, we draw the mesh, which sends the triangles making up this portion of the model out to the graphics card.

The tank model

The tank model we are using is from the **Simple Animation** sample for XNA 4.0, available on Microsoft's MSDN website at `http://xbox.create.msdn.com/en-US/education/catalog/sample/simple_animation`. The license document for the model is included in the graphics package archive for this chapter.

Bringing things down to earth

You might have noticed that our tank is not actually sitting on the ground. In fact, we have set our terrain scaling so that the highest point in the terrain is at 30 units, while the tank is positioned at 40 units above the X-Z plane.

Given a (X,Z) coordinate pair, we need to come up with a way to determine what height we should place our tank at, based on the terrain.

Time for action – terrain heights

To place our tank appropriately on the terrain, we first need to calculate, then place our tank there. This is done in the following steps:

1. Add a helper method to the `Terrain` class to calculate the height based on a given coordinate as follows:

```
#region Helper Methods
public float GetHeight(float x, float z)
{
    int xmin = (int)Math.Floor(x);
    int xmax = xmin + 1;
    int zmin = (int)Math.Floor(z);
    int zmax = zmin + 1;

    if (
        (xmin < 0) || (zmin < 0) ||
        (xmax > heights.GetUpperBound(0)) ||
        (zmax > heights.GetUpperBound(1)))
    {
        return 0;
    }
```

```
Vector3 p1 = new Vector3(xmin, heights[xmin, zmax], zmax);
Vector3 p2 = new Vector3(xmax, heights[xmax, zmin], zmin);
Vector3 p3;

if ((x - xmin) + (z - zmin) <= 1)
{
    p3 = new Vector3(xmin, heights[xmin, zmin], zmin);
}
else
{
    p3 = new Vector3(xmax, heights[xmax, zmax], zmax);
}

Plane plane = new Plane(p1, p2, p3);

Ray ray = new Ray(new Vector3(x, 0, z), Vector3.Up);

float? height = ray.Intersects(plane);

return height.HasValue ? height.Value : 0f;
}
#endregion
```

2. In the `LoadContent()` method of the `TankBattlesGame` class, modify the statement that adds a tank to the battlefield to utilize the `GetHeight()` method as follows:

```
tanks.Add(
    new Tank(
        GraphicsDevice,
        Content.Load<Model>(@"Models\tank"),
        new Vector3(61, terrain.GetHeight(61,61), 61)));
```

3. Execute the game and view the tank, now placed on the terrain as shown in the following screenshot:

What just happened?

You might be tempted to simply grab the nearest (X, Z) coordinate from the `heights[]` array in the `Terrain` class and use that as the height for the tank. In fact, in many cases that might work. You could also average the four surrounding points and use that height, which would account for very steep slopes.

The drawbacks with those approaches will not be entirely evident in **Tank Battles**, as our tanks are stationary. If the tanks were mobile, you would see the elevation of the tank jump between heights jarringly as the tank moved across the terrain because each virtual square of terrain that the tank entered would have only one height.

In the `GetHeight()` method that we just saw, we take a different approach. Recall that the way our terrain is laid out, it grows along the positive X and Z axes. If we imagine looking down from a positive Y height onto our terrain with an orientation where the X axis grows to the right and the Z axis grows downward, we would have something like the following:

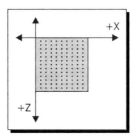

As we discussed when we created our index buffer, our terrain is divided up into squares whose corners are exactly 1 unit apart. Unfortunately, these squares do not help us in determining the exact height of any given point, because each of the four points of the square can theoretically have any height from 0 to 30 in the case of our terrain scale.

Remember though, that each square is divided into two triangles. The triangle is the basic unit of drawing for our 3D graphics. Each triangle is composed of three points, and we know that three points can be used to define a plane. We can use XNA's `Plane` class to represent the plane defined by an individual triangle on our terrain mesh.

To do so, we just need to know which triangle we want to use to create the plane. In order to determine this, we first get the (X, Z) coordinates (relative to the view in the preceding figure) of the upper-left corner of the square our point is located in. We determine this point by dropping any fractional part of the x and z coordinates and storing the values in `xmin` and `zmin` for later use.

We check to make sure that the values we will be looking up in the `heights[]` array are valid (greater than zero and less than or equal to the highest element in each direction in the array). This could happen if we ask for the height of a position that is outside the bounds of our map's height. Instead of crashing the game, we will simply return a zero. It should not happen in our code, but it is better to account for the possibility than be surprised later.

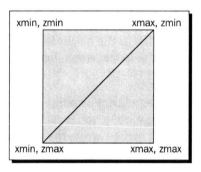

We define three points, represented as `Vector3` values `p1`, `p2`, and `p3`. We can see right away that no matter which of the two triangles we pick, the (`xmax`, `zmin`) and (`xmin`, `zmax`) points will be included in our plane, so their values are set right away.

To decide which of the final two points to use, we need to determine which side of the central dividing line the point we are looking for lies in. This actually turns out to be fairly simple to do for the squares we are using. In the case of our triangle, if we eliminate the integer portion of our X and Z coordinates (leaving only the fractional part that tells us how far into the square we are), the sum of both of these values will be less than or equal to the size of one grid square (1 in our case) if we are in the upper left triangle. Otherwise our point is in the right triangle.

The code `if ((x - xmin) + (z - zmin) <= 1)` performs this check, and sets the value of `p3` to either (`xmin`, `zmin`) or (`xmax`, `zmax`) depending on the result.

Once we have our three points, we ask XNA to construct a `Plane` using them, and then we construct another new type of object we have not yet used – an object of the `Ray` class. A `Ray` has a base point, represented by a `Vector3`, and a direction – also represented by a `Vector3`.

Think of a `Ray` as an infinitely long arrow that starts somewhere in our world and heads off in a given direction forever. In the case of the `Ray` we are using, the starting point is at the zero point on the Y axis, and the coordinates we passed into the method for X and Z. We specify `Vector3.Up` as the direction the `Ray` is pointing in. Remember from the FPS camera that `Vector3.Up` has an actual value of (0, 1, 0), or pointing up along the positive Y axis.

The `Ray` class has an `Intersects()` method that returns the distance from the origin point along the `Ray` where the `Ray` intersects a given `Plane`. We must assign the return value of this method to a `float?` instead of a normal float. You may not be familiar with this notation, but the question mark at the end of the type specifies that the value is nullable—that is, it might contain a value, but it could also just contain a null value. In the case of the `Ray.Intersects()` method, the method will return null if the object of `Ray` class does not intersect the object of the `Plane` class at any point. This should never happen with our terrain height code, but we need to account for the possibility.

When using a nullable float, we need to check to make sure that the variable actually has a value before trying to use it. In this case, we use the `HasValue` property of the variable. If it does have one, we return it. Otherwise we return a default value of zero.

Animating the tank

Now that we have a tank in our game, let's look at how we can animate the bones defined in the model in order to aim the turret and the cannon. We will be adding some temporary code to our `TankBattlesGame` class in order to see our animations in action.

Time for action – tank animation

In order to animate our tank, we perform the following steps:

1. In the constructor of the `Tank` class, add the following two lines to the end of the method:

   ```
   baseTurretTransform = model.Bones["turret_geo"].Transform;
   baseGunTransform = model.Bones["canon_geo"].Transform;
   ```

2. In the `Draw()` method of the `Tank` class, add the following before the call to `model.CopyAbsoluteBoneTransformsTo()`:

```
model.Bones["turret_geo"].Transform =
    Matrix.CreateRotationY(TurretRotation) * baseTurretTransform;

model.Bones["canon_geo"].Transform =
    Matrix.CreateRotationX(gunElevation) * baseGunTransform;
```

3. In the `Update()` method of the `TankBattlesGame` class, add some temporary code to allow us to animate the tank with the keyboard. Place this code after the existing camera movement code, inside the `if` block that checks for (`this.IsActive`) – directly after the current mouse position is stored in `previousMouse`:

```
// Begin temporary code
KeyboardState ks = Keyboard.GetState();
if (ks.IsKeyDown(Keys.A))
{
    tanks[0].TankRotation += 0.05f;
}

if (ks.IsKeyDown(Keys.Z))
{
    tanks[0].TankRotation -= 0.05f;
}

if (ks.IsKeyDown(Keys.S))
{
    tanks[0].TurretRotation += 0.05f;
}

if (ks.IsKeyDown(Keys.X))
{
    tanks[0].TurretRotation -= 0.05f;
}

if (ks.IsKeyDown(Keys.D))
{
    tanks[0].GunElevation += 0.05f;
}

if (ks.IsKeyDown(Keys.C))
{
    tanks[0].GunElevation -= 0.05f;
}
//End temporary code
```

4. Launch the game, use the mouse to zoom in on the tank, and then use the keyboard to rotate the tank with keys *A* and *Z*, the turret with keys *S* and *X*, and the cannon with keys *D* and *C*. Our tank would look like the one in the following screenshot:

What just happened?

Each of the bones within the tank model we are using has a name assigned to it. In this case, the turret bone is named `turret_geo`, while the bone for the gun is named `canon_geo`. In step 1, we store the base transformations for these bones so that we have their baseline positions, which we will use to apply our modifications to later.

When drawing the model, recall that we can produce a matrix that includes all of the transforms we wish to apply by multiplying the component matrices together. This is done in step 2.

Finally, we modify the `Update()` method of the `TankBattlesGame` class to allow us to use the keyboard to modify the various rotation values associated with the parts of our tank. We will pull this code back out of our project later, so it is marked with start and end comments to make it easy to recognize.

The combatants

Now that we can render and animate tanks, we will add a second tank to our game and position the two tanks randomly within the game world.

Time for action – positioning tanks

To position tanks within our game, perform the following steps:

1. Add the following fields to the declarations area of the TankBattlesGame class:

```
ContentManager p2Content;
Random rand = new Random();
```

2. In the Initialze() method of the TankBattlesGame class, add the following lines right before the call to base.Initialize():

```
p2Content = new ContentManager(this.Services);
p2Content.RootDirectory = "Content";
```

3. Add the StartNewRound() method to the TankBattlesGame class as follows:

```
public void StartNewRound()
{
    tanks.Clear();

    Vector3 p1Position =
        new Vector3(rand.Next(8, 56), 0, rand.Next(8, 56));
    Vector3 p2Position =
        new Vector3(rand.Next(8, 56), 0, rand.Next(8, 56));

    int p1Quadrant = rand.Next(0, 4);

    switch (p1Quadrant)
    {
        case 0:
            p2Position += new Vector3(64, 0, 64);
            break;

        case 1:
            p1Position += new Vector3(64, 0, 0);
            p2Position += new Vector3(0, 0, 64);
            break;

        case 2:
            p1Position += new Vector3(0, 0, 64);
            p2Position += new Vector3(64, 0, 0);
            break;

        case 3:
            p1Position += new Vector3(64, 0, 64);
            break;
    }

    p1Position.Y = terrain.GetHeight(p1Position.X, p1Position.Z);
```

```
        p2Position.Y = terrain.GetHeight(p2Position.X, p2Position.Z);

        tanks.Add(
            new Tank(
                GraphicsDevice,
                Content.Load<Model>(@"Models\tank"),
                p1Position));

        tanks.Add(
            new Tank(
                GraphicsDevice,
                p2Content.Load<Model>(@"Models\tank"),
                p2Position));
    }
```

4. In the `LoadContent()` method of the `TankBattlesGame` class, remove the current code that adds a tank to the `Tanks` list, and replace it with the following:

```
StartNewRound();
```

5. Execute the game. Verify that two tanks have been added to the battlefield in opposite quadrants of the map as shown in the following screenshot:

What just happened?

We logically divide our battlefield into four quadrants, numbered 0, 1, 2, and 3. As our battlefield is 128 units on a side, each quadrant is 64 by 64 units. Using this information we generate two positions within quadrant 0 (the upper left quadrant). We pad these positions a bit to keep the tanks from being too close to the outside edges of the map, or to the dividing lines between the quadrants.

Once we have two positions, we randomly select a quadrant for the first tank to occupy. In order to position it in the correct quadrant, we add 64 to the X, Z, both, or neither components of the position depending on the quadrant we selected. We similarly add offsets to the second tank based on the quadrant the first tank is located in, so that the two tanks are in diagonally opposite quadrants.

We calculate the height of each of the final points for the tanks and then generate and add both of them to the `tanks` list.

You might be wondering though, why we went through the trouble of creating a second instance of the `ContentManager` class to load the model for the second player's tank. This is because when we load a model (or any other resource) with `ContentManager`, it checks to see if it has already loaded that content. If it has, you simply get a pointer to the existing content object in memory. In most cases this is not a problem. If we are using the same texture in multiple classes in our game, there really is no need to have multiple copies of the same data in memory.

With our models, though, the transforms that make up the animations will be changing over time. This means that we have to have some way to separate the different instances of our tank models from each other. There are, of course, multiple ways to do this. You could write your own code to draw the model's meshes, taking each set of bone transforms into account and applying them separately.

The approach we have taken here is far simpler. By creating a second instance of `ContentManager`, it does not know that the first instance has already loaded, so it happily loads a new copy of it from the disk and supplies it for the second tank. Now both tanks can operate independently.

Summary

We have a pair of tanks on our battlefield now, and they are ready to fight! In this chapter, we covered the addition of 3D model content to our project along with the textures to support them, loading and displaying a 3D model, and animating a 3D model by applying bone transforms.

We have also seen how to precisely determine the elevation of a given point on our terrain using Ray/Plane intersection and how to lay the groundwork for our game flow by randomly positioning enemy tanks on the battlefield.

In *Chapter 7, Tank Battles – Shooting Things* we will add interface elements, mixing 2D with our 3D world, and allow our tanks to actually fire at each other!

7
Tank Battles – Shooting Things

We have two tanks facing off on the field of battle, but at the moment, the only way we have to control our tanks at all is a few temporary keyboard controls. In order to allow the players to interact with our game, we need to present some kind of user interface.

In this chapter, we will achieve the following:

- Implement pseudo event-driven user interface buttons
- Create and track shots fired by the player
- Determine where fired shots land
- Generate 3D particle-based explosions

Interface components

While we currently use an undocumented set of keyboard keys to rotate the various parts of our tank, such controls are not very user friendly. After all, if you did not know they were in the code, how would you ever know to press them without some kind of prompting?

Instead of using keys, we will implement a basic set of user interface controls right on the game screen itself. These will include buttons and text fields, both to provide the player with information about the game and to accept user input and commands.

Even in 3D games, most of the **user interface (UI)** elements will be composed of 2D items, so we will return to using `SpriteBatch` for the first time since our introduction to XNA in *Chapter 1, Introduction to XNA*.

In designing our user interface, we know we will need to accomplish two main goals:

- Allow each player to aim their cannon and fire at the opponent
- Display information about the current aiming values for the cannon, so the player can make the appropriate adjustments in subsequent turns to zero in on their target

In order to accomplish this, we will need user interface controls that perform roughly the same jobs as the Windows Forms `label` and `button` controls. We will create a hierarchy of classes to support our interface needs, starting with a simple base class that our other controls can build on.

The UIWidget class

We will begin the process of creating these controls by creating a base class for all of the controls our game will be able to handle, called the `UIWidget` class.

Time for action – creating the UIWidget class

In order to build a base class for all of the game controls, perform the following steps:

1. Download the `7089_07_GRAPHICSPACK.ZIP` file from the book's companion website and extract its contents to a temporary folder.

2. Select the two `.png` files (`button_50px.png` and `Explosion.png`) from the graphics package and copy them to the Windows clipboard.

3. In Visual Studio, right-click on the **Textures** folder in the **TankBattlesContent (Content)** project and select **Paste** to add the textures to your game.

4. Back in the temporary folder, select the `Sphere.x` file and the **Sphere** folder and copy them to the Windows clipboard.

5. Paste these items into the **Models** folder in **Solution Explorer**.

6. Right-click on the **Sphere** folder under **Models** in **Solution Explorer** and select **Exclude from Project**.

7. Add a new class file called `UIWidget.cs` to the `TankBattlesGame` project.

8. Add the following `using` declarations at the beginning of the `UIWidget.cs` file:

    ```
    using Microsoft.Xna.Framework;
    using Microsoft.Xna.Framework.Graphics;
    ```

9. Add properties to the `UIWidget` class as follows:

```
#region Properties
public string ID { get; private set; }
public bool Visible { get; set; }
public Vector2 Position { get; set; }
#endregion
```

10. Add a constructor to the `UIWidget` class as follows:

```
#region Constructor
public UIWidget(string id, Vector2 position)
{
    ID = id;
    Position = position;
    Visible = false;
}
#endregion
```

11. Add empty `Update()` and `Draw()` methods to the `UIWidget` class as follows:

```
#region Virtual methods
public virtual void Update(GameTime gameTime)
{

}

public virtual void Draw(SpriteBatch spriteBatch)
{

}
#endregion
```

What just happened?

In steps 1 through 6, we add the various content items we will use throughout this chapter to the game's content project. Just as with our tank model, we exclude the texture files for the sphere (contained in the **Sphere** folder) from the content project because they will be referenced by the model importer.

Beginning in step 7, we construct the `UIWidget`, which does not do a whole lot on its own. In fact, it only has two methods, and neither of them does anything at all! The real purpose of the `UIWidget` class is to provide the common properties that our different UI controls will have so that we do not need to duplicate them in each of our subsequent classes.

All of our UI components will have an ID that uniquely identifies the UI element. If you are familiar with Windows Forms programming, think of this as the object name of the textbox, button, label, or whatever other control you are creating.

Additionally, all UI elements will have a flag that marks them as visible and an onscreen position. These values are tracked in the `Visible` and `Position` properties, respectively. In the constructor, we set the `Visible` property to `false` by default, which will allow us to create all of our UI elements ahead of time and only show them when they should be displayed on the screen instead of creating them and setting each one invisible.

Using a base class also makes it possible to update and draw our UI elements as a group. As our text block and button classes will inherit from the `UIWidget` class, they can be treated as `UIWidget` objects from a code standpoint. We will look at this more closely after we have created our UI classes and added them to the game.

UITextblocks

The first type of `UIWidget` we create will hold text to be displayed on the screen. It will not have any type of associated graphics or interactivity, so it is not much complicated than the `UIWidget` itself.

Time for action – creating UITextblocks

To create the `UITextblock` class, perform the following steps:

1. Add a new class file called `UITextblock.cs` to the `TankBattlesGame` project.

2. Add the following `using` directives at the beginning of the `UITextblock` class file:

   ```
   using Microsoft.Xna.Framework;
   using Microsoft.Xna.Framework.Graphics;
   ```

3. Modify the declaration of the `UITextblock` class to derive it from `UIWidget` by adding `: UIWidget` at the end of the declaration. The class declaration should be as follows:

   ```
   class UITextblock : UIWidget
   ```

4. Add properties to the `UITextblock` class as follows:

   ```
   #region Properties
   public Vector2 TextOffset { get; set; }
   public SpriteFont Font { get; set; }
   public string Text { get; set; }
   public Color TextTint { get; set; }
   #endregion
   ```

5. Add a constructor to the `UITextblock` class as follows:

```
#region Constructor
public UITextblock(
    string id,
    Vector2 position,
    Vector2 textOffset,
    SpriteFont font,
    string text,
    Color textTint)
    : base(id, position)
{
    TextOffset = textOffset;
    Font = font;
    Text = text;
    TextTint = textTint;
}
#endregion
```

6. Add an override `Draw()` method to the `UITextblock` class as follows:

```
#region Draw
public override void Draw(SpriteBatch spriteBatch)
{

    if (Visible)
    {
        spriteBatch.DrawString(
            Font,
            Text,
            Position + TextOffset,
            TextTint);
    }

    base.Draw(spriteBatch);
}
#endregion
```

What just happened?

We have added a number of properties to our `UITextblock`, all dealing with the text that will be displayed. We store a text offset (which will be relative to the position of the widget itself), the font we will use to draw the text, the text to draw, and the color to use.

Remember that because a `UITextblock` is a `UIWidget`, it already has the `ID`, `Visible`, and `Position` properties available to it as well. We do not need to recreate them in the `UITextblock` class itself.

Our constructor passes the `id` and `position` parameters along to the base `UIWidget` constructor, and uses the text-related parameters to set the properties of this particular text block. As we are passing variables to the constructor of the `UIWidget` class, we only need to initialize properties here that are specific to the `UITextblock` class.

When drawing our text block, we make sure the control should be visible first, and then use `SpriteBatch.DrawString()` to render it if it should be displayed. Finally, the `Draw()` method calls its base class' `Draw()` method. In the case of the `UIWidget` base class, nothing further is drawn since the `Draw()` method is empty.

It may not be immediately obvious why we use `TextOffset` in the `UITextblock` class. After all, `UIWidget` itself has a `Position` property, so why not simply use that? While the text offset might have other uses, (for example, if you expanded the class to support right-aligned, or centered text) the primary reason we are implementing it here is because the buttons we create will actually be based on the `UITextblock` class.

UIButtons

Instead of deriving directly from `UIWidget`, the `UIButton` class will inherit from `UITextblock`. Specifying a text-specific offset allows us to treat the position of the text in any child control differently than the position of the control itself.

Time for action – creating buttons

The `UIButton` class for Tank Battles can be created as follows:

1. Add a new class file called `UIButtonArgs.cs` to the `TankBattlesGame` project.
2. Add the following `using` declaration at the beginning of the `UIButtonArgs` class file:

   ```
   using Microsoft.Xna.Framework;
   ```

3. Modify the declaration of the `UIButtonArgs` class to derive it from the `System.EventArgs` class by adding : `System.EventArgs` at the end of the declaration line. The declaration should read:

   ```
   class UIButtonArgs : System.EventArgs
   ```

4. Add properties to the `UIButtonArgs` class as follows:

```
#region Properties
public Vector2 Location { get; private set; }
public string ID { get; private set; }
#endregion
```

5. Add a constructor to the `UIButtonArgs` class as follows:

```
#region Constructor
public UIButtonArgs(string id, Vector2 location)
{
    ID = id;
    Location = location;
}
#endregion
```

6. Add another new class file, this time called `UIButton.cs` to the `TankBattlesGame` project.

7. Add the following `using` directives to the `UIButton` class:

```
using Microsoft.Xna.Framework;
using Microsoft.Xna.Framework.Graphics;
```

8. Change the declaration of the `UIButton` class to derive it from the `UITextblock` class by adding : `UITextblock` at the end of the line. The declaration should read:

```
class UIButton : UITextblock
```

9. Add properties to the `UIButton` class:

```
#region Properties
public Texture2D Texture { get; set; }
public bool Disabled { get; set; }
public bool Pressed { get; set; }
public Rectangle Bounds { get; private set; }
#endregion
```

10. Add a `delegate` and an `event` declaration to the `UIButton` class as follows:

```
#region Event-related Items
public delegate void ClickHandler(object sender, UIButtonArgs e);
public event ClickHandler Clicked;
#endregion
```

11. Add a constructor to the `UIButton` class as follows:

```
#region Constructor
public UIButton(
    string id,
```

```
            Vector2 position,
            Vector2 textOffset,
            SpriteFont font,
            string text,
            Color textTint,
            Texture2D texture)
            : base(id, position, textOffset, font, text, textTint)
    {
        Texture = texture;
        this.Bounds = new Rectangle(
            (int)position.X,
            (int)position.Y,
            Texture.Width,
            Texture.Height / 3);
    }
    #endregion
```

12. Add helper methods to the `UIButton` class as follows:

```
#region Helper Methods
public bool Contains(Point location)
{
    return Visible && Bounds.Contains(location);
}

public bool Contains(Vector2 location)
{
    return Contains(new Point((int)location.X, (int)location.Y));
}

public void HitTest(Point location)
{
    if (Visible && !Disabled)
    {
        if (Contains(location))
        {
            Pressed = true;
            Clicked(
                this,
                new UIButtonArgs(
                    this.ID,
                    new Vector2(location.X, location.Y)));
        }
        else
        {
```

```
                Pressed = false;
            }
        }
    }
    #endregion
```

13. Add a new `Draw()` method to the `UIButton` class as follows:

```
#region Draw
public override void Draw(SpriteBatch spriteBatch)
{
    if (Visible)
    {
        Point drawBase = Point.Zero;

        if (Disabled)
            drawBase = new Point(0, Bounds.Height);

        if (Pressed)
            drawBase = new Point(0, Bounds.Height * 2);

        spriteBatch.Draw(
            Texture,
            Position,
            new Rectangle(
                drawBase.X, drawBase.Y,
                Bounds.Width, Bounds.Height),
            Color.White);
    }

    base.Draw(spriteBatch);
}
#endregion
```

What just happened?

We actually create two classes to support our buttons here. The first is a small class derived from `System.EventArgs`, which we will use to pass information back to our game when the player clicks on a button object. When that happens, we will pass back the ID of the button that was clicked and the screen location of the mouse when the click happened. We will not actually make use of the screen location for our button code here, but if you were to create a spinner-type control, with two subbuttons on it (one for spinning up, one for spinning down) you could use this information to determine which of the subareas the user clicked on.

The UIButton class itself adds yet more properties in addition to those inherited from UIWidget and UITextblock. This time, we add a texture that will represent the button on the screen. We also declare two Boolean variables, Disabled and Pressed, which will alter the visual representation of the button on the screen. The Disabled flag will also be checked to determine if the user is allowed to interact with the button. Finally, we store a rectangle that holds the screen area the button occupies, so that we can easily check to see if any given point lies inside the button.

The next two declarations, labeled as the Event-related Items region, will allow us to hook up an event in our main game code that will be fired whenever the button is pressed. We will be implementing a quasi-event-driven system for the UI elements in our game.

In a Windows Forms application, we have Windows itself always watching what the user is doing and sending messages to controls that get clicked on, causing them to fire their events. We do not have the same type of built-in functionality in XNA, so we will implement a similar system inside the game's Update()/Draw() loop.

Events versus Polling

It would be completely valid to do away with all of the event-based code in our UI classes and instead poll each control during the Update() method. In fact, even though we are using an event-style system we will still have to implement a polling-style mechanism to tell each control to check if it should fire its event.

The biggest advantage to the event system we are implementing would be evident while adding new controls and new types of controls. Instead of modifying a large conditional statement to include functionality for the new controls, we would simply need to add instances of the control and create a new callback method to handle what happens when the user interacts with them.

In the constructor of UIButton, we cache the texture, and then calculate a rectangle to store the bounds of the image we want to draw to the screen. Notice that the height of the bounding rectangle is equal to the height of the image divided by three. We will be borrowing a trick from CSS-based web development to build buttons that contain multiple states (normal, disabled, and pressed) in the same image, stacked on top of each other.

The image files for our buttons have a normal button at the top, a grayed out disabled button in the middle, and a button with a beveled edge at the bottom to be displayed while the button is pressed.

We can see this in action if we skip briefly to the `Draw()` method in step 13. `Draw()` assumes a 0-pixel offset for the source rectangle when drawing the button. It then modifies this offset if the `Disabled` or `Pressed` properties are true.

Returning to step 12, we set up a pair of shortcut methods called `Contains()` to determine if a given point lies within the screen coordinates of the button. We then use these methods during the `HitTest()` method, which checks to see if the button is available for pressing—that is, it is both visible and not disabled. If the button can be clicked, we check to see if the passed location is within the button's area. If so, we set `Pressed` to `true` and call the `Clicked` delegate, which we will hook up when we create our buttons in the `TankBattlesGame` class shortly.

Working with our UI objects

Instead of embedding all of the code to create buttons and other UI elements into our game code, we will put together a static helper class, called `UIHelper`, to do some of this work for us.

Time for action – adding the UIHelper class

In order to add the static helper class, perform the following steps:

1. Add a new class file called `UIHelper.cs` to the Tank Battles project.

2. Add the following `using` directives at the beginning of the `UIHelper` class file:

   ```
   using Microsoft.Xna.Framework;
   using Microsoft.Xna.Framework.Graphics;
   using Microsoft.Xna.Framework.Input;
   ```

3. Modify the declaration of the class to add the modifier `static` before it. The new class declaration should read:

   ```
   static class UIHelper
   ```

4. Add fields to the `UIHelper` class as follows:

   ```
   #region Fields
   public static Texture2D ButtonTexture;
   public static SpriteFont ButtonFont;
   #endregion
   ```

5. Add methods to the `UIHelper` class as follows:

```
#region Helper Methods
public static UIButton CreateButton(
    string id,
    string text,
    int x,
    int y)
{
    UIButton b = new UIButton(
        id,
        new Vector2(x,y),
        new Vector2(25 - ButtonFont.MeasureString(text).X / 2,
10),
        ButtonFont,
        text,
        Color.White,
        ButtonTexture);

    b.Disabled = false;
    return b;
}

public static UITextblock CreateTextblock(
    string id,
    string text,
    int x,
    int y)
{
    UITextblock b = new UITextblock(
        id,
        new Vector2(x,y),
        Vector2.Zero,
        ButtonFont,
        text,
        Color.White);

    return b;
}

public static void SetButtonState(
    string prefix,
    Boolean disabled,
    Dictionary<string, UIWidget> uiElements)
{
```

```
        foreach (string widget in uiElements.Keys)
        {
            if (uiElements[widget].ID.StartsWith(prefix))
                if (uiElements[widget] is UIButton)
                    ((UIButton)uiElements[widget]).Disabled =
disabled;
        }
    }

    public static void SetElementVisibility(
        string prefix,
        Boolean visible,
        Dictionary<string, UIWidget> uiElements)
    {
        foreach (string widget in uiElements.Keys)
        {
            if (uiElements[widget].ID.StartsWith(prefix))
                ((UIWidget)uiElements[widget]).Visible = visible;
        }
    }

    public static void SetElementText(UIWidget uiElement, string text)
    {
        if (uiElement is UITextblock)
            ((UITextblock)uiElement).Text = text;
    }
    #endregion
```

6. In the **Solution Explorer** pane in Visual Studio, right-click on the **Fonts** folder in the **TankBattlesContent (Content)** project and select **Add | New Item**.

7. From the **Add New Item** window, select **Sprite Font** from the center pane.

8. Enter `Pericles14.spritefont` as the name of the font file and click on **Add**.

9. In the XML font definition document that opens automatically, change the font name (Between the **<FontName>** and **</FontName>** tags) from `Segoe UI Mono` to `Pericles`.

10. In the `LoadContent()` method of the `TankBattlesGame` class, initialize the `UIHelper` class with the texture we added at the beginning of this chapter, and the font we just created. Place this code before the call to `StartNewRound()` as follows:

```
UIHelper.ButtonTexture =
    Content.Load<Texture2D>(@"Textures\button_50px");
UIHelper.ButtonFont =
    Content.Load<SpriteFont>(@"Fonts\Pericles14");
```

What just happened?

The first thing to note about the `UIHelper` class is that the class itself is declared as `static`, meaning that we will never create an instance of `UIHelper`. Since the class is static, all of its members must also be static.

The `UIHelper` class has two basic jobs. First, it makes it easy for us to create instances of the `UIButton` and `UITextblock` classes via the `CreateButton()` and `CreateTextblock()` methods respectively. These methods accept the ID, text to display, and position of the element and use the preconfigured font and texture (for a button) settings to create the elements. In the case of a button, the text offset is calculated to center the text on the button's surface. In reality, these methods are just shortcuts to reduce the work we need to do in our main game code for each UI element we create.

The second job of the `UIHelper` class is to allow other parts of our code to easily interact with our UI elements. To accomplish this, we have the `SetButtonState()`, `SetElementVisibility()`, and `SetElementText()` methods. Two of these methods, `SetButtonState()` and `SetElementVisibility()`, accept an ID prefix and a dictionary of UI elements. They iterate through the list and apply the appropriate setting (enabled, disabled, visible, or hidden) to each matching element in the dictionary.

The `SetElementText()` method accepts a `UIWidget` and a text string. It ensures that the element can be cast as a `UITextBlock`. As long as this is true, the method goes ahead and sets the `Text` property of the passed `UIWidget` object to the text string provided to it.

What's with all the casting and type checking?

As we are using the `UIWidget` class as a base class from which the `UITextBlock` class is derived, all `UITextBlock` objects are `UIWidget` objects. Additionally, all `UIButton` objects are `UITextBlock` objects and therefore `UIWidget` objects. If we want to set the `Text` value of a button, which is a property of the `UITextBlock` class, we can ask C# to treat the button as a `UITextBlock` object so that we do not have to manage text blocks and buttons separately. In the case of `SetElementVisiblity()`, the `Visible` property is a property of the `UIWidget` class, so all three of our classes can be treated as `UIWidgets` for setting visibility.

In the remainder of the steps we just saw, we added a new `SpriteFont` object to our project and initialized the `UIHelper` class by setting both the `ButtonTexture` and `ButtonFont` values. These are then used by the `CreateButton()` method for all future buttons.

Creating the user interface

Now that we have the groundwork in place, we can actually start adding UI elements to our game screen. We will add a series of buttons for each player, and some informational text blocks to use when aiming shots.

Time for action – creating the UI

To create the user interface for our game, perform the following steps:

1. Add the following declaration to the declarations area of the `TankBattlesGame` class as follows:

```
Dictionary<string, UIWidget> uiElements =
    new Dictionary<string, UIWidget>();
```

2. Create a new region in the `TankBattlesGame` to hold UI-related code as follows:

```
#region User Interface
#endregion
```

3. In the new `User Interface` region, add a shell for a callback method for handling button-click events as follows:

```
void UIButton_Clicked(object sender, UIButtonArgs e)
{

}
```

4. Still inside the `User Interface` region, add the `CreateUIElements()` method as follows:

```
public void CreateUIElements()
{
    uiElements.Add("p1Up",
        UIHelper.CreateButton("p1Up", "U", 60, 10));
    uiElements.Add("p1Down",
        UIHelper.CreateButton("p1Down", "D", 60, 65));
    uiElements.Add("p1Left",
        UIHelper.CreateButton("p1Left", "L", 5, 35));
    uiElements.Add("p1Right",
        UIHelper.CreateButton("p1Right", "R", 115, 35));
    uiElements.Add("p1Fire",
        UIHelper.CreateButton("p1Fire", "Fire", 175, 35));
    uiElements.Add("p1Rotation",
        UIHelper.CreateTextblock("p1Rotation", "x", 5, 120));
    uiElements.Add("p1Elevation",
        UIHelper.CreateTextblock("p1Elevation", "x", 5, 135));

    uiElements.Add("p2Up",
        UIHelper.CreateButton("p2Up", "U", 685, 10));
    uiElements.Add("p2Down",
        UIHelper.CreateButton("p2Down", "D", 685, 65));
    uiElements.Add("p2Left",
        UIHelper.CreateButton("p2Left", "L", 630, 35));
    uiElements.Add("p2Right",
        UIHelper.CreateButton("p2Right", "R", 740, 35));
```

```
        uiElements.Add("p2Fire",
          UIHelper.CreateButton("p2Fire", "Fire", 570, 35));
        uiElements.Add("p2Rotation",
          UIHelper.CreateTextblock("p2Rotation", "x", 580, 120));
        uiElements.Add("p2Elevation",
          UIHelper.CreateTextblock("p2Elevation", "x", 580, 135));

        foreach (UIWidget widget in uiElements.Values)
        {
            if (widget is UIButton)
            {
                ((UIButton)widget).Clicked += new
                    UIButton.ClickHandler(UIButton_Clicked);
            }
        }
    }
```

5. In the `LoadContent()` method of the `TankBattlesGame` class, right after the
    initialization of the `ButtonTexture` and `ButtonFont` values of the `UIHelper`
    class, call the `CreateUIElements()` method as follows:

```
CreateUIElements();
UIHelper.SetElementVisibility("p", true, uiElements);
```

6. In the `Update()` method of the `TankBattlesGame` class, just before the line that
    reads `previousMouse = mouse;` add the following code:

```
if (mouse.RightButton == ButtonState.Released)
{
    if (mouse.LeftButton == ButtonState.Pressed)
    {
        foreach (UIWidget widget in uiElements.Values)
        {
            if (widget is UIButton)
            {
                ((UIButton)widget).HitTest(
                    new Point(mouse.X, mouse.Y));
            }
        }
    }
    else
    {
        foreach (UIWidget widget in uiElements.Values)
        {
            if (widget is UIButton)
            {
                ((UIButton)widget).Pressed = false;
            }
        }
    }
}
```

7. In the `Draw()` method of the `TankBattlesGame` class, just after the call to `GraphicsDevice.Clear()` add the following code:

```
GraphicsDevice.DepthStencilState = DepthStencilState.Default;
```

8. Still in the `Draw()` method of the `TankBattlesGame` class, just before the call to `base.Draw()`, add the following code:

```
spriteBatch.Begin();

foreach (UIWidget widget in uiElements.Values)
    widget.Draw(spriteBatch);

spriteBatch.End();
```

9. Execute the game to see the new interface buttons as shown in the following screenshot:

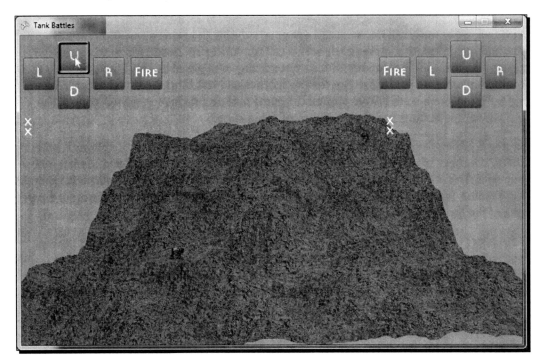

What just happened?

We keep all of our user interface elements in a `Dictionary` object, with the string-based ID that we assign to each element as the dictionary key.

In step 3, we define a shell for the `UIButton_Clicked()` method, which we will soon fill out to handle the user clicking on one of our user interface buttons. For now though, let's look at the largest of the code blocks that we just saw—the `CreateUIElements()` method.

In this method, we make repeated use of the `UIHelper` class' methods to create our interface elements and add them to the `UIElements` dictionary. Each element is assigned an ID, with the elements for the first player beginning with `p1` and the elements for the second player starting with `p2`.

After all of the elements have been created, we loop through each element in the dictionary and look for items of the `UIButton` type. For each button, we hook up the `UIButton_Clicked` event—the empty event handler we created in step 3.

In step 5, we actually call `CreateUIElements()` during the game's `LoadContent()` method. We follow this immediately with a call to `UIHelper.SetElementVisiblity()`, telling it to make all UI elements with names starting with `p` visible. This is actually only a temporary measure so that we can see the buttons and text blocks in this chapter. When we build the game-state system around the game in the next chapter, we will control the visibility of the buttons based on the current game state.

In step 6, we implement the code to check each of our buttons to see if the player is pressing them. We check to make sure that the right mouse button is not pressed and the left mouse button is. This is important because the mouse pointer is hidden when the player is using the right mouse button to move the camera. Potentially, the player could move the mouse over one of the buttons while it is invisible and cause the button to be pressed.

Assuming the buttons are in the correct configuration, we loop through each `UIElement` and call the `HitTest()` method on any button element, giving it the current location of the mouse. The `HitTest()` method will call the callback method we defined earlier (`UIButton_Clicked()`) if the mouse lies within the bounds of the button. `HitTest()` also sets the button's `Pressed` property to `true` if appropriate.

If the user is not pressing either mouse button, the update code runs through each button in the interface and sets `Pressed` to `false` to make sure they do not continue to be displayed as `Pressed` when they should not be.

We make two modifications to the `Draw()` method in steps 7 and 8. First, we set the `DepthStencilState` to `DepthStencilState.Default`. Whenever you mix 2D and 3D graphics in XNA, you need to remember to reset the value of the `DepthStencilState` setting, because drawing with `SpriteBatch` alters it internally. Go ahead and try commenting this line out and running the program, and you will notice that you can see through objects and terrain in strange ways, as if all of the pieces of them are piled up on top of each other.

We will go into more detail about the `DepthStencilState` when we discuss particle effects later in this chapter. For now, we simply need to set it back to its default value before we draw any of our 3D graphics.

Drawing the UI elements themselves is just a matter of looping through each item in the dictionary and calling its own `Draw()` method.

Responding to interface events

We have two sets of buttons (one set for each player), along with four informational text blocks on our display. We now need to hook these buttons up to the game controls so they actually do something. In order to accomplish this, we will flesh out the `UIButton_Clicked()` method that we added to the `TankBattlesGame` class.

Time for action – responding to events

To enable our buttons to do something, we need to add code to the `UIButton_Clicked()` method by performing the following steps:

1. Modify the `UIButton_Clicked()` method in the `TankBattlesGame` class to respond to button clicks as follows:

```
void UIButton_Clicked(object sender, UIButtonArgs e)
{
    int playerNumber = int.Parse(e.ID.Substring(1, 1)) - 1;
    string buttonName = e.ID.Substring(2);

    switch (buttonName)
    {
        case "Left":
            tanks[playerNumber].TurretRotation += 0.01f;
            break;

        case "Right":
            tanks[playerNumber].TurretRotation -= 0.01f;
```

```
                    break;

            case "Up":
                tanks[playerNumber].GunElevation -= 0.01f;
                break;

            case "Down":
                tanks[playerNumber].GunElevation += 0.01f;
                break;

            case "Fire":
                break;
        }
    }
}
```

2. In the `User Interface` region of the `TankBattlesGame` class, add a helper method for updating the contents of the four text blocks on the screen as follows:

```
private void UpdateTextBlocks()
{
    float p1Elevation =
        MathHelper.ToDegrees(tanks[0].GunElevation) * -1;
    float p1Rot = MathHelper.ToDegrees(tanks[0].TurretRotation);
    p1Rot = 180 - p1Rot;

    UIHelper.SetElementText(
        uiElements["p1Rotation"],
        "Angle: " + p1Rot.ToString("N2"));

    UIHelper.SetElementText(
        uiElements["p1Elevation"],
        "Elevation: " + p1Elevation.ToString("N2"));

    float p2Elevation =
        MathHelper.ToDegrees(tanks[1].GunElevation) * -1;
    float p2Rot = MathHelper.ToDegrees(tanks[1].TurretRotation);
    p2Rot = 180 - p2Rot;

    UIHelper.SetElementText(
        uiElements["p2Rotation"],
        "Angle: " + p2Rot.ToString("N2"));

    UIHelper.SetElementText(
        uiElements["p2Elevation"],
        "Elevation: " + p2Elevation.ToString("N2"));
}
```

3. In the `Update()` method of the `TankBattlesGame` class, call the `UpdateTextBlocks()` method right after the statement `previousMouse = mouse;`:

   ```
   UpdateTextBlocks();
   ```

4. Still in the `Update()` method of the `TankBattlesClass`, remove all of the temporary code that we added to allow for keyboard rotation of the tank elements. This code is marked with `//Begin Temporary Code` and `//End Temporary Code` comments.

5. Execute the game and use the buttons to rotate the tank turrets and elevate their cannons as shown in the following screenshot:

What just happened?

To determine which button event we are responding to, we dissect the ID value that is passed to the `UIButton_Clicked()` event handler. First, we extract the second character from the ID, which will have the player number that the button is intended for. Remember that the first tank in the `tanks` list is `tanks[0]`, so we subtract 1 from the player number to get the actual internal player number value.

The remainder of the string is stored in the `buttonName` variable, which is then checked for the various button types (`Left`, `Right`, `Up`, `Down`, and `Fire`). For most of these variables, all that is necessary is to increment or decrement one of the rotation values associated with the player's tank.

In `UpdateTextBlocks()`, we need to make a few adjustments to the raw values stored with the tanks for the sake of user friendliness. First, the elevation value for the tank's cannon ranges from `0` (horizontal) to `-90` (straight up). We multiply the elevation value by `-1` in order to make this value positive for display purposes.

Similarly, rotation is stored in radians, and when converted to degrees, will have a value between `-180` and `180`. In order to eliminate the negative value and align zero with what we have been considering the top of the map, we subtract the converted value of the rotation angle from 180. This gives us numbers in the range of 0 to 360 degrees as the player might expect.

The one button we have not yet accounted for is the **FIRE** button. In order to hook up this functionality, we will need to do a bit more groundwork. After all, we do not yet have any ammunition for the players to fire at each other!

Firing shots

We need some kind of visual representation of the cannonballs that will be fired between the players, and as it happens, we have already added a model file called `Sphere.x` to our content project.

This model is somewhat different than our `Tank` model. First of all, the model is really nothing more than a sphere created in a 3D graphics program with a very basic brick texture. The model was saved as a binary encoded `.x` file (Microsoft's DirectX model format), so we cannot open it up like we can open the tank's `.fbx` file and look at the contents with a simple text editor.

Time for action – ShotManager-part 1

To manage the shots fired at each other by the tanks, we will add a `ShotManager` class by performing the following steps:

1. Add a new class file called `ShotManager.cs` to the `Tank Battles` project.

2. Add the following declarations at the beginning of the `ShotManager` class file:

```
using Microsoft.Xna.Framework;
using Microsoft.Xna.Framework.Graphics;
```

3. Modify the declaration of the class to make it a static class. The class definition line should now read as follows:

```
static class ShotManager
```

4. Add fields to the `ShotManager` class as follows:

```
#region Fields
public static Model ShotModel;
public static Vector3 Position;
public static Vector3 Velocity;
public static Vector3 Gravity = new Vector3(0, -20, 0);
public static bool ShotActive = false;
public static bool HitProcessed = true;
public static Terrain Terrain;
private static float modelScale = 0.2f;
#endregion
```

5. Add a method to fire shots to the `ShotManager` class as follows:

```
#region Shot Handling
public static void FireShot(
    Vector3 startingPosition,
    Vector3 initialVelocity)
{
    if (!ShotActive)
    {
        Position = startingPosition;
        Velocity = initialVelocity;
        ShotActive = true;
        HitProcessed = false;
    }
}
#endregion
```

6. Add the `Update()` method to the `ShotManager` class as follows:

```
#region Update
public static void Update(GameTime gameTime)
{
    if (ShotActive)
    {
        float elapsed = (float)gameTime.ElapsedGameTime.
TotalSeconds;

        Position += (Velocity * elapsed);
        Velocity += (Gravity * elapsed);

        if (Position.Y < Terrain.GetHeight(Position.X,
Position.Z))
        {
```

```
                ShotActive = false;
            }
        }
    }
    #endregion
```

7. Add the `Draw()` method to the `ShotManager` class as follows:

```
#region Draw
public static void Draw(ArcBallCamera camera)
{
    if (ShotActive)
    {
        ShotModel.Root.Transform = Matrix.Identity *
            Matrix.CreateScale(modelScale) *
            Matrix.CreateTranslation(Position);

        foreach (ModelMesh mesh in ShotModel.Meshes)
        {
            foreach (BasicEffect basicEffect in mesh.Effects)
            {
                basicEffect.World = ShotModel.Root.Transform;
                basicEffect.View = camera.View;
                basicEffect.Projection = camera.Projection;

                basicEffect.EnableDefaultLighting();
            }

            mesh.Draw();
        }
    }
}
#endregion
```

8. In the declarations section of the `TankBattlesGame` class, add a float variable to control the power of fired shots:

```
float shotPower = 50f;
```

9. At the end of the `LoadContent()` method of the `TankBattlesGame` class, initialize the `ShotManager` class as follows:

```
ShotManager.ShotModel = Content.Load<Model>(@"Models\Sphere");
ShotManager.Terrain = terrain;
```

10. In the `Update()` method of the `TankBattlesGame` class, just before the call to `base.Update()` add the following line of code:

```
ShotManager.Update(gameTime);
```

11. In the `Draw()` method of the `TankBattlesGame` class, add the following to draw the `ShotManager` right before the `spriteBatch.Begin()` call that begins the drawing of the UI widgets:

```
ShotManager.Draw(camera);
```

12. In the `UIButton_Clicked()` method of the `TankBattlesGame` class, modify the `case` section for the **FIRE** buttons as follows:

```
case "Fire":
    Vector3 fireAngle = Vector3.Zero;
    float rotation = tanks[playerNumber].TankRotation;
    rotation += tanks[playerNumber].TurretRotation;
    float elevation = tanks[playerNumber].GunElevation;

    Matrix rotMatrix = Matrix.CreateFromYawPitchRoll(
        rotation,
        MathHelper.ToRadians(90) + elevation, 0);

    fireAngle = Vector3.Transform(Vector3.Up, rotMatrix);
    fireAngle.Normalize();

    ShotManager.FireShot(
        tanks[playerNumber].Position +
            new Vector3(0f, 1f, 0f) + fireAngle * 2,
        fireAngle * shotPower);
    break;
```

13. Execute the game and use the buttons to rotate the tank turrets, raise the gun elevations, and fire off a few shots as shown in the following screenshot:

What just happened?

We have quite a bit going on here, so we will break it down step-by-step to see how `ShotManager` works.

In steps 1 through 3 we create the `ShotManager` class, declaring the class to be `static`. Just like our `UIManager`, we will not be creating instances of the `ShotManager` class. It is available to the rest of our code as is.

We declare fields in step 4. We begin with the `ShotModel` field, which holds the sphere model we will use to represent the cannon ball. Next, the `Position` field tracks the current location of the shot in 3D space. The `Velocity` field represents how fast, and in what direction, the ball is currently moving.

Each time we apply the value of the shot's `Velocity` field to its `Position` field, we will also apply the value in the `Gravity` field to the `Velocity` field. In our case, the `Gravity` field is defined as a `Vector3` object pointing down with a length of `20` units.

When a shot is fired, `ShotActive` will be set to `true`, and `HitProcessed` will be set to `false`. We will eventually use these variables to determine when another shot can be fired and to check to see if the shot impacted close enough to the enemy tank to score a hit.

In order to determine where a shot has impacted, the `ShotManager` needs to know about the terrain being used in the game, so we store the current terrain in the `Terrain` field. Finally, as the raw sphere model is about as large as one of our scaled down tanks, we need to scale the cannon ball model down to a reasonable size. We define this size in the `modelScale` field, with a value of `0.2f`.

Actually firing a shot in step 5 is fairly straightforward from the point of view of the `ShotManager`. It accepts an initial position for the shot and a velocity. Assuming a shot is not already active, it sets these two values and sets the `ShotActive` and `HitProcessed` flags.

In step 6, we see how the fired shot actually travels. Each time through the update loop, the current value of the `Velocity` field is added to the shot's position. The value of the `Gravity` field is then added to the `Velocity` field, resulting in an ever-increasing downward pull on the shot's `Velocity` field. Both of these values are scaled according to the amount of game time that has passed since the last update, so even though the raw value of the `Gravity` field indicates downwards by `20` units, that much change in the `Velocity` would take a full second to be applied. One sixtieth of the `Gravity` field's value is added to the `Velocity` field during each `Update()` cycle if the game is running at the default frame rate.

Drawing our sphere in step 7 is a simplified version of the drawing code used for our tanks. In the case of the sphere, we do not need to worry about bone-based transformations, so we simply loop through the meshes in the model and draw them.

The `shotPower` field, defined in step 8, controls how much force is behind our cannon. This determines how quickly the cannon ball will be moving when it leaves the tank.

In steps 9 through 11, we integrate the `ShotManager` with the `TankBattlesGame` code, initializing the model and providing a link to the terrain we are using. The `Update()` and `Draw()` methods are integrated into the corresponding methods.

Finally, in step 12 we update the `UIButton_Clicked()` event handler to account for the **FIRE** buttons. When either of the **FIRE** buttons is clicked, we combine the rotation of both the tank itself and the turret into a single value. We also determine the elevation of the gun.

While we can use the resulting rotation value directly as the yaw parameter for the `Matrix.CreateFromYawPitchRoll()` method, the elevation needs to be modified to account for the fact that it runs from 0 to -90 degrees. We simply add 90 degrees to this value, and use the result as the pitch parameter. The roll value is zero since we are only rotating in two directions.

Using `Vector3.Transform()`, we apply the matrix we have just created to the standard `Vector3.Up` vector. Recall from our camera implementation that this vector is equal to (0, 1, 0), and points along the positive Y axis. By applying the rotation matrix generated prior to the `Vector.Up` vector, we obtain a vector pointing in the same direction as our cannon.

All that is left now is to call `ShotManager.FireShot()` to create our projectile. We supply the position of the tank firing the shot, but apply two modifications to it. First, we simply bump the position up by one unit along the Y axis. As the origin point of the tank is in the center of its base, this elevates the starting point of the projectile off the ground.

The second thing we add to the position is double the `fireAngle` vector to move the projectile out of the center of the tank and along its flight path slightly.

The velocity vector we supply to the `FireShot()` method is equal to the `fireAngle` multiplied by the `shotPower` value. This extends the length of the `fireAngle` vector and provides an initial thrust to propel the cannon ball into the air. After it has been fired, the rest of the projectile's movement is entirely up to gravity, as implemented in the `ShotManager` class.

Particles in 3D

What happens when the cannon ball hits the ground? Or the enemy tank? Right now, nothing, except that the `ShotManager` is freed up to fire another shot. We need some way to visually represent the impact of the cannon ball.

If you have worked with 2D game development, you may have used sprites to create a particle system. Particles are usually short-lived small images, many of which are added to the scene to create a flashy effect of some kind.

We can implement a similar system in 3D, but we are immediately faced with a problem. In a 2D game, we always see the sprites we draw head-on. The 2D pixel image is copied from the source and placed at the destination unchanged.

When working in 3D, however, all of our textures are mapped onto triangles (or surfaces composed of multiple triangles). If we use a standard **quad** (two triangles forming a square) to display our 3D particles, it will look just fine from one angle.

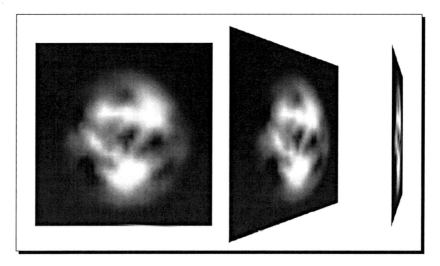

If our camera is not looking head-on at the image, however, it will shift perspective, until it disappears completely if we are looking at it either side-on or from the back (remember that all of our 3D drawings so far have been one-sided).

We can use a technique called billboarding to overcome this problem. In 3D terms, a **billboard** is a texture mapped onto a quad that is always rotated to face the camera. Billboards are commonly used in 3D games to represent trees (especially at a distance) without the need to display complex geometry for objects that will be so far away from the camera that the player will not be able to distinguish fine details anyway.

If you have ever been playing a 3D game and noticed that the trees suddenly change shape from flat images to full 3D objects as you get close to them, you have seen billboards working to simplify 3D rendering. Billboards also work well for particles, as they can ensure that the appropriate face of the texture is visible at all times.

Billboarded particles

We will begin building our 3D particle system by defining the `Particle` class to handle the particles themselves. We will be creating hundreds of instances of this class, each one responsible for its own drawing and updating.

Time for action – the Particle class-part 1

To add particles to our game using the `Particle` class, perform the following steps:

1. Add a new class file called `Particle.cs` to the Tank Battles project.

2. Add the following declarations at the beginning of the `Particle` class file:

    ```
    using Microsoft.Xna.Framework;
    using Microsoft.Xna.Framework.Graphics;
    ```

3. Add a region of static fields to the `Particle` class as follows:

    ```
    #region Static Fields
    public static GraphicsDevice GraphicsDevice;
    private static Vector3 Gravity = new Vector3(0, -5, 0);
    private static VertexBuffer vertexBuffer;
    private static IndexBuffer indexBuffer;
    #endregion
    ```

4. Add a region of non-static fields to the `Particle` class as follows:

    ```
    #region Instance Fields
    private Vector3 position;
    private Vector3 velocity;
    public float duration;
    private float initialDuration;
    private float scale;
    #endregion
    ```

5. Add the following property to the `Particle` class:

    ```
    #region Properties
    public bool IsActive { get { return (duration > 0); }}
    #endregion
    ```

6. Add a constructor to the `Particle` class as follows:

    ```
    #region Constructor
    public Particle()
    {
        if (vertexBuffer == null)
        {
            InitializeParticles();
        }
    }
    #endregion
    ```

7. Add the `InitializeParticles()` method to the `Particle` class as follows:

```
#region Static Methods
public static void InitializeParticles()
{
    VertexPositionTexture[] vertices = new
VertexPositionTexture[4];

    vertices[0] = new VertexPositionTexture(
        new Vector3(0, 1, 0), new Vector2(0, 0));
    vertices[1] = new VertexPositionTexture(
        new Vector3(1, 1, 0), new Vector2(1, 0));
    vertices[2] = new VertexPositionTexture(
        new Vector3(0, 0, 0), new Vector2(0, 1));
    vertices[3] = new VertexPositionTexture(
        new Vector3(1, 0, 0), new Vector2(1, 1));

    vertexBuffer = new VertexBuffer(
        GraphicsDevice,
        typeof(VertexPositionTexture),
        vertices.Length,
        BufferUsage.WriteOnly);

    vertexBuffer.SetData(vertices);

    int indexCount = 6;
    short[] indices = new short[indexCount];

    indices[0] = 0;
    indices[1] = 1;
    indices[2] = 2;
    indices[3] = 2;
    indices[4] = 1;
    indices[5] = 3;

    indexBuffer = new IndexBuffer(
        GraphicsDevice,
        IndexElementSize.SixteenBits,
        indices.Length,
        BufferUsage.WriteOnly);
    indexBuffer.SetData(indices);
}
#endregion
```

What just happened?

The `Particle` class is not yet complete, but let's stop here and take a look at what we have. The first thing you will notice is that the fields for the `Particle` class are split into two groups—static fields and instanced fields. Unlike many of our classes, we will make heavy use of static fields and methods in the `Particle` class, even though the class itself is not a fully static class.

The reason we have set the `Particle` class up this way is that there could be hundreds, or even thousands of instances of the `Particle` class in memory at the same time. Much of the data for each particle is shared across all of the particles, so pulling these items out as `static` reduces the resource requirements for our overall particle system.

For example, much like when building our terrain, we define a pair of triangles in the `InitializeParticles()` method and store them in a vertex/index buffer pair. There is really no need to store hundreds of these pairs in memory – they will all be identical.

The constructor for the `Particle` class just checks to see if the `InitializeParticles()` method has been run yet (by checking to see if `vertexBuffer` has been created). If not, it runs the `InitializeParticles()` method and exits. The first particle instance we create will cause the initialization routine to be run, after which creating a new particle involves no extra code.

The `InitializeParticle()` method itself should be very familiar. We have used the technique of building vertex and index buffers several times already. Here, we manually create four vertices and six indices to tie them together as a quad.

Time for action – finishing the Particle class

We will now finish the `Particle` class we just created by performing the following steps:

1. Add the `Activate()` method to the `Particle` class as follows:

```
#region Particle Activation
public void Activate(
    Vector3 position,
    Vector3 velocity,
    float duration,
    float scale)
{
    this.duration = duration;
    initialDuration = duration;
    this.position = position;
    this.velocity = velocity;
    this.scale = scale;
}
#endregion
```

2. Add the `Update()` method to the `Particle` class as follows:

```
#region Update
public void Update(GameTime gameTime)
{
    float elapsed = (float)gameTime.ElapsedGameTime.TotalSeconds;
    duration -= elapsed;
    velocity += (Gravity * elapsed);
    position += (velocity * elapsed);
}
#endregion
```

3. Add the `Draw()` method to the `Particle` class as follows:

```
#region Draw
public void Draw(ArcBallCamera camera, Effect effect)
{
    Matrix billboard = Matrix.CreateBillboard(
        position,
        camera.Position,
        Vector3.Up,
        null);

    effect.Parameters["World"].SetValue(
        Matrix.CreateScale(scale) * billboard );

    effect.Parameters["alphaValue"].SetValue(
        duration/initialDuration);

    foreach (EffectPass pass in effect.CurrentTechnique.Passes)
    {
        pass.Apply();
        GraphicsDevice.SetVertexBuffer(vertexBuffer);
        GraphicsDevice.Indices = indexBuffer;
        GraphicsDevice.DrawIndexedPrimitives(
            PrimitiveType.TriangleList,
            0,
            0,
            6,
            0,
            2);
    }
}
#endregion
```

What just happened?

Activating a particle sets the instanced values to the passed parameters. As long as the duration is greater than zero, the particle is considered active. We will actually check for active particles outside the `Particle` class itself, when we create a manager class to deal with our particles as a group.

Just like our cannon ball, a particle's `Update()` method applies its current velocity to its position and then modifies the velocity by adding the value of the `Gravity` field to it. In the case of the particle system, we have lowered the gravity value compared to the cannon ball to allow our particles to float in the air a bit as they drift downwards.

There are a few odd things you may have noticed about the `Draw()` method for particles. First, we seem to be missing all of the preliminaries about setting the current technique for the effect we are using. We also never set a texture, or even the view and projection matrices.

As all of our particles will be drawn at the same time, most of this code has been moved out of the actual `Particle` class. When we build the `ParticleManager` class, we will set all of these parameters once before we start drawing. We can save quite a bit of processing time simply by not setting the same values several hundred times for each frame.

You will also notice that we use the `Matrix.CreateBillboard()` method to create the matrix that we use when specifying the `World` matrix for our particle. The `Matrix.CreateBillboard()` method does the work of figuring out for us how the quad that represents our particle should be rotated to face the camera. Given an object's position, a camera position, and the direction that we consider to be up, (our standard `Vector3.Up` in this case) the matrix we get back will position the quad appropriately for viewing the full texture, regardless of where our camera is located.

Lastly, we set a parameter on the effect we are using called `alphaValue`. As this is not one of the standard effect parameters, we can tell right away that there is a bit of **High Level Shader Language (HLSL)** work in our future. As a particle gets older, we want it to fade out slowly. By setting the `alphaValue` parameter to `duration/initialDuration`, we get a value ranging between `0.0f` and `1.0f` that represents how long the particle has left to live. The lower the number, the closer the particle is to expiration, and hence lower will be the alpha value we wish to use for this particle.

Managing particles

Our `Particle` class on its own is missing quite a bit of the required drawing code for efficiency reasons. To easily deal with a large number of particles, we will create a `ParticleManager` class that will not only maintain a list of particles in our game, but also be responsible for completing the steps necessary to successfully draw them on the screen.

Time for action – the ParticleManager class

To manage the particles in our game, we will create the `PraticleManager` class by performing the following steps:

1. Add a new class called `ParticleManager.cs` to the Tank Battles project.

2. Add the following declarations at the beginning of the `ParticleManager` class file:

   ```
   using Microsoft.Xna.Framework;
   using Microsoft.Xna.Framework.Graphics;
   ```

3. Modify the declaration of the `ParticleManager` class to make it a static class. The declaration should now read as follows:

   ```
   static class ParticleManager
   ```

4. Add fields to the `ParticleManager` class as follows:

   ```
   #region Fields
   private static GraphicsDevice graphicsDevice;
   private static List<Particle> particles = new List<Particle>();
   private static Effect particleEffect;
   private static Texture2D particleTexture;
   private static Random rand = new Random();
   #endregion
   ```

5. Add the `Initialize()` method to the `ParticleManager` class as follows:

   ```
   #region Initialization
   public static void Initialize(
       GraphicsDevice device,
       Effect effect,
       Texture2D texture)
   {
       graphicsDevice = device;
       particleEffect = effect;
       particleTexture = texture;
       Particle.GraphicsDevice = device;
       for (int x = 0; x < 300; x++)
       {
           particles.Add(new Particle());
       }
   }
   #endregion
   ```

6. Add the `AddParticle()` method to the `ParticleManager` class as follows:

```
#region Particle Creation
public static void AddParticle(
    Vector3 position,
    Vector3 velocity,
    float duration,
    float scale)
{
  for (int x = 0; x < particles.Count; x++)
  {
    if (!particles[x].IsActive)
    {
        particles[x].Activate(position, velocity, duration,
scale);
        return;
    }
  }
}
#endregion
```

7. Add the `Update()` method to the `ParticleManager` class as follows:

```
#region Update
public static void Update(GameTime gameTime)
{
    foreach (Particle particle in particles)
    {
        if (particle.IsActive)
            particle.Update(gameTime);
    }
}
#endregion
```

8. Add the `Draw()` method to the `ParticleManager` class as follows:

```
#region Draw
public static void Draw(ArcBallCamera camera)
{
    graphicsDevice.BlendState = BlendState.Additive;

    particleEffect.CurrentTechnique =
        particleEffect.Techniques["ParticleTechnique"];

    particleEffect.Parameters["particleTexture"].SetValue(
        particleTexture);
```

```
    particleEffect.Parameters["View"].SetValue(camera.View);

    particleEffect.Parameters["Projection"].SetValue(
        camera.Projection);

    graphicsDevice.RasterizerState = RasterizerState.CullNone;
    graphicsDevice.BlendState = BlendState.Additive;
    graphicsDevice.DepthStencilState = DepthStencilState.
DepthRead;

    foreach (Particle particle in particles)
    {
        if (particle.IsActive)
            particle.Draw(camera, particleEffect);
    }
    graphicsDevice.RasterizerState =
        RasterizerState.CullCounterClockwise;
    graphicsDevice.BlendState = BlendState.Opaque;
    graphicsDevice.DepthStencilState = DepthStencilState.Default;
}
#endregion
```

9. Add a helper method to the `ParticleManager` class as follows:

```
#region Helper Methods
public static void MakeExplosion(Vector3 position, int
particleCount)
{
    for (int i = 0; i < particleCount; i++)
    {
        float duration = (float)(rand.Next(0, 20)) / 10f + 2;
        float x = ((float)rand.NextDouble() - 0.5f) * 1.5f;
        float y = ((float)rand.Next(1, 100)) / 10f;
        float z = ((float)rand.NextDouble() - 0.5f) * 1.5f;
        float s = (float)rand.NextDouble() + 1.0f;
        Vector3 direction = Vector3.Normalize(
            new Vector3(x, y, z) *
            (((float)rand.NextDouble() * 3f) + 6f);

        AddParticle(
            position + new Vector3(0, -2, 0),
            direction,
            duration, s);
    }
}
#endregion
```

What just happened?

The `ParticleManager` class maintains a list of particles, as well as references to the graphics device, the texture used for particles, and the effect used to draw them.

During initialization, the `ParticleManager` class creates 300 particles and adds them to the `particles` list. These 300 particles will not be displayed anywhere (there is no duration set for them, so they are inactive). By precreating the particles, we can save .NET from the work of creating and disposing off hundreds of objects as particles come and go. We will simply re-use particles that have expired as new particles.

We implement this logic in the `AddParticle()` method. This method loops through the `particles` list looking for an inactive particle. When it finds one, it calls the particle's `Activate()` method, passing it the new parameters for the active particle. When a particle has been activated, the method exits. If all of the particles in the list are currently active, the method will end without doing anything. In this way, we have set a limit of 300 particles active at a time in our game. That will be plenty for the effects we will be creating, but you could raise or lower this value depending on the resource requirements of your game. This would also be a good value over which the player have some influence, if you were to expand Tank Battles and add the ability for the player alter the configuration of the game. Dropping the number of active particles can improve performance on low-end hardware, and it is one of the most frequently modified settings in commercial games.

When `Draw()` is called, we do the work of setting up the effect we will be using to draw all of our particles. We set the current technique, the texture, view, and projection matrices.

In addition, we make several changes to the way the graphics device displays the objects we give it to render. The first thing we do is set the `RasterizerState` property to `CullNone`. Recall that when we define vertices, we need to define them in a clockwise order. This is because the normal setting for `RasterizerState` is `CullCounterClockwise`. One of the quirks of the `Matrix.CreateBillboard()` method is that the matrix we get back actually has the particles facing away from us, meaning that we will not see them with the default culling enabled. We could handle this in several different ways, including modifying the matrix or changing the order we specify the vertices for the quad that makes up the particle. Instead, however, we simply tell the graphics device to show us the triangles no matter what the winding order of the vertices is.

The second thing is to set the particle's `BlendState` to `Additive`. In `Additive` mode, the current value of the pixels being drawn is blended with the value of the particle. As more particles are drawn on the same spot, a more intense effect will be created. We might be tempted to use `BlendState.AlphaBlending` here, and that will certainly work (try it out once we have the full particle system in place) but it does not look as convincing as additive blending for the explosions we are creating. With additive blending, the central areas of the explosion will look brighter while the edges fade away.

Finally, we set the `DepthStencilState` property to `DepthRead`. You might remember that we saw the `DepthStencilState` briefly when drawing our 2D buttons to the screen with existing 3D graphics. The `DepthStencilState` property controls how objects that overlap get drawn. When in default mode, each time an object is drawn, the pixels of that object are compared with the depths of the objects that have already been drawn. If the new object is closer to the camera, its pixel value will be selected and it will be drawn to the display.

Because our explosion is a square texture with a circular flame image, if we allow the depth stencil to function in this manner, we will have strange looking box outlines around each of the particle sprites instead of a smooth blending of the particle images.

After looping through all of the active particles and drawing them, we reset each of these values to their defaults.

In the final step, we add a helper method called `MakeExplosion()`, which accepts a location and a desired particle count. The method generates a random duration, direction, and scale for the particle. These values are skewed so that the y component is generally larger than the x and z components, giving the particle a boost upwards. The resulting direction is then scaled six to nine times its length so that the particles will naturally spread themselves randomly across the area of the explosion.

HLSL for our particles

We already know that we need to create a new effect for our particles, so let's go ahead and build the effect file.

Time for action – building Particles.fx

In order to create effects for our particles, perform the following steps:

1. Right-click on the **Effects** folder in the game's content project and select **Add | New Item**.

2. From the **Add New Item** dialog box, select the **Effect File** type from the central pane.

3. Name the effect file `Particles.fx` and click on **Add**.

4. In the declarations area at the beginning of the file, add the following new declarations:

```
float alphaValue;

texture particleTexture;

sampler2D textureSampler = sampler_state {
  Texture = (particleTexture);
  AddressU = Wrap;
  AddressV = Wrap;
};
```

5. Replace the current `VertexShaderInput` and `VertexShaderOutput` structs with new ones that include texture coordinates as follows:

```
struct VertexShaderInput
{
    float4 Position : POSITION0;
    float2 TextureCoordinate : TEXCOORD0;
};

struct VertexShaderOutput
{
    float4 Position : POSITION0;
    float2 TextureCoordinate : TEXCOORD0;
};
```

6. Replace the current `VertexShaderFunction()` method with a new version that supports the texture coordinates we added to the structs as follows:

```
VertexShaderOutput VertexShaderFunction(VertexShaderInput input)
{
    VertexShaderOutput output;

    float4 worldPosition = mul(input.Position, World);
    float4 viewPosition = mul(worldPosition, View);
    output.Position = mul(viewPosition, Projection);

    output.TextureCoordinate = input.TextureCoordinate;

    return output;
}
```

7. Replace the `PixelShaderFunction()` method with a new version that supports both texture coordinates and the `alphaValue` parameter as follows:

```
float4 PixelShaderFunction(VertexShaderOutput input) : COLOR0
{
    return tex2D(
        textureSampler, input.TextureCoordinate) * alphaValue;
}
```

8. Replace `Technique1` technique with `ParticleTechnique` as follows:

```
technique ParticleTechnique
{
    pass Pass1
    {
        VertexShader = compile vs_2_0 VertexShaderFunction();
        PixelShader = compile ps_2_0 PixelShaderFunction();
    }
}
```

What just happened?

Our `Particle.fx` effect file is very similar to the effect we are currently using to render our terrain with a texture. In fact, the only real difference is the inclusion of the `alphaValue` parameter. Recall that we set this value in relation to the time the particle has left to live during each frame. As the particle is about to disappear, this value will approach `0.0f`.

In the `PixelShaderFunction()` method of the `Particle.fx` effect, we use a texture sampler to read from the texture for the particle, just like we do for our terrain, but we multiply the result by the `alphaValue` parameter for the particle. Multiplying a color by the `alphaValue` parameter's value will scale all of the components of that color (red, green, blue, and alpha) by the desired alpha level, resulting in a darker, partially transparent pixel.

Adding particles

Now that we have a system in place to add 3D particles to Tank Battles, it is time to actually get them into the game! Let's go ahead and make the necessary modifications to bring our explosions to life inside the game world.

Time for action – implementing particles

To implement the particles for our game, perform the following steps:

1. In the `LoadContent()` method of the `TankBattlesGame` class, initialize the `ParticleManager` as follows:

```
ParticleManager.Initialize(
    GraphicsDevice,
    Content.Load<Effect>(@"Effects\Particles"),
    Content.Load<Texture2D>(@"Textures\Explosion"));
```

2. Add the `CheckForShotImpacts()` helper method to the `TankBattlesGame` class as follows:

```
private void CheckForShotImpacts()
{
    if (!ShotManager.ShotActive && !ShotManager.HitProcessed)
    {
        Vector3 impactPoint = new Vector3(
            ShotManager.Position.X, 0, ShotManager.Position.Z);
        impactPoint.Y = terrain.GetHeight(
            impactPoint.X, impactPoint.Z);
        ParticleManager.MakeExplosion(impactPoint, 200);
        ShotManager.HitProcessed = true;
    }
}
```

3. In the `Update()` method of the `TankBattlesGame` class, add the following lines of code right after the `ShotManager` is updated:

```
CheckForShotImpacts();
ParticleManager.Update(gameTime);
```

4. In the `Draw()` method of the `TankBattlesGame` class, draw the `ParticleManager` right after the `ShotManager` is drawn as follows:

```
ParticleManager.Draw(camera);
```

5. Execute the game, position the camera, align the guns, and fire. When the cannon ball lands, you should see an explosion at the point of impact as shown in the following screenshot:

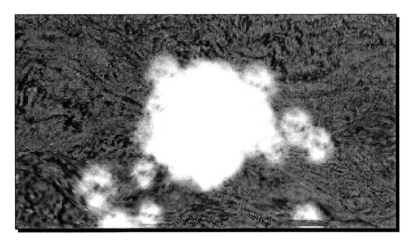

What just happened?

When a projectile has been fired, we need some way to identify that it has landed and should produce an explosion. We track two Boolean variables in the `ShotManager` class. One of these, `ShotActive`, indicates whether a shot is currently in flight. The second, `HitProcessed`, is set to `false` when a shot is fired.

In the `CheckForShotImpacts()` method, we are interested in the point where a shot has finished flying, but we have not yet done anything as a result. When this is the case, both `ShotActive` and `HitProcessed` will be `false`. In that case, we retrieve the position of the shot and calculate that point's elevation (the shot could have travelled significantly below the terrain if it is falling particularly fast, so we do not use the y coordinate of the shot itself).

We ask the `ParticleManager` class to create an explosion consisting of `200` particles at that location, and set the `HitProcessed` flag to `true`.

Summary

We have covered a lot of ground in this chapter, bringing Tank Battles to the point where it is almost a playable game. You have now implemented the user interface widgets to display text values and button images, event-driven responses to UI button clicks, creation and tracking of projectiles as they fly across the game world, and particle explosions based on billboards.

In *Chapter 8, Tank Battles – Ending the War*, we will finish up the Tank Battles game by wrapping a game structure around our code and looking at ways we can polish some of our existing systems to improve the visual quality of the game.

8
Tank Battles – Ending the War

We almost have a playable game on our hands now!

In this chapter, we will finish up the Tank Battles game by covering the following tasks:

- Creating a basic game flow structure to surround the game play
- Cycling between game states based on player input and the results of the gameplay
- Allowing two players to take turns adjusting their aim and firing shots
- Determining when a player has scored a hit on the opposing tank – or their own
- Enhancing the visual appeal of our terrain by adding lighting and multitexturing effects

Managing game states

While we could certainly get very elaborate with our game state management system, we are going to take a simple approach. Our game will have three basic states as follows:

- **TitleScreen**
- **Playing**
- **GameOver**

Our simple state system will progress through a loop of these three states, as illustrated in the following diagram:

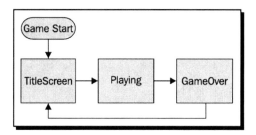

The state cycle will be a simple loop between our three states, so from the title screen, we play the game. When someone wins, we display a game over message and then return to the **TitleScreen**.

In addition, while in the **Playing** state, we will track turns for each player, enabling and disabling interface components as appropriate depending on the currently active player.

Time for action – implementing a title screen

1. Download the `7089_08_GRAPHICSPACK.ZIP` file from the book's website and extract the files it contains to a temporary location.

2. In Windows Explorer, select all of the `.png` files in the temporary folder and copy them to the clipboard.

3. Switch back to Visual Studio, right-click on the **Textures** folder in the content project, and select **Paste**.

4. To the `TankBattlesGame` class' declarations area, add the following declarations:

```
Texture2D titleScreen;
int currentPlayer = 0;
enum GameState { TitleScreen, Playing, GameOver }
GameState gameState = GameState.TitleScreen;
```

5. In the `LoadContent()` method of the `TankBattlesGame` class, remove the line that reads `StartNewRound();`.

6. At the bottom of the `LoadContent()` method of the `TankBattlesGame` class, initialize the `titleScreen` texture field as follows:

```
titleScreen = Content.Load<Texture2D>(@"Textures\TitleScreen");
```

7. In the `Update()` method of the `TankBattlesGame` class, use the mouse to highlight everything within the `if (this.IsActive)` block, excluding the `if` statement itself.

8. Right-click on the highlighted code and select **Refactor | Extract Method**.

9. In the **Extract Method** dialog box, enter `ProcessPlayingInput` as the name of the new method. For clarity, the `ProcessPlayingInput()` method should now be as follows:

```
private void ProcessPlayingInput()
{
    if (this.IsActive)
    {

        MouseState mouse = Mouse.GetState();

        if (moveMode)
        {
            camera.Rotation += MathHelper.ToRadians(
                (mouse.X - screenCenter.X) / 2f);
            camera.Elevation += MathHelper.ToRadians(
                (mouse.Y - screenCenter.Y) / 2f);

            Mouse.SetPosition(screenCenter.X, screenCenter.Y);
        }

        if (mouse.RightButton == ButtonState.Pressed)
        {
            if (!moveMode &&
                previousMouse.RightButton == ButtonState.Released)
            {
                if (graphics.GraphicsDevice.Viewport.Bounds.
Contains(
                    new Point(mouse.X, mouse.Y)))
                {
                    moveMode = true;
                    saveMousePoint.X = mouse.X;
                    saveMousePoint.Y = mouse.Y;
                    Mouse.SetPosition(
                        screenCenter.X,
                        screenCenter.Y);
                    this.IsMouseVisible = false;
                }
            }
        }
        else
        {
            if (moveMode)
```

```
            {
                moveMode = false;
                Mouse.SetPosition(
                    saveMousePoint.X,
                    saveMousePoint.Y);
                this.IsMouseVisible = true;
            }
        }

        if (mouse.ScrollWheelValue -
            previousMouse.ScrollWheelValue != 0)
        {
            float wheelChange = mouse.ScrollWheelValue -
                previousMouse.ScrollWheelValue;

            camera.ViewDistance -= (wheelChange / 120) *
scrollRate;
        }

        if (mouse.RightButton == ButtonState.Released)
        {
            if (mouse.LeftButton == ButtonState.Pressed)
            {
                foreach (UIWidget widget in uiElements.Values)
                {
                    if (widget is UIButton)
                    {
                        ((UIButton)widget).HitTest(
                            new Point(mouse.X, mouse.Y));
                    }
                }
            }
            else
            {
                foreach (UIWidget widget in uiElements.Values)
                {
                    if (widget is UIButton)
                    {
                        ((UIButton)widget).Pressed = false;
                    }
                }
            }
        }
```

```
        previousMouse = mouse;

        UpdateTextBlocks();

    }
}
```

10. Replace the current `Update()` method with the following:

```
protected override void Update(GameTime gameTime)
{
    if (this.IsActive)
    {
        switch (gameState)
        {
            case GameState.TitleScreen:
                KeyboardState ks = Keyboard.GetState();
                if (ks.IsKeyDown(Keys.Space))
                {
                    gameState = GameState.Playing;
                    UIHelper.SetElementVisibility(
                        "p", true, uiElements);
                    StartNewRound();
                }
                break;

            case GameState.Playing:
                ProcessPlayingInput();
                break;

            case GameState.GameOver:
                break;
        }
    }

    ShotManager.Update(gameTime);
    CheckForShotImpacts();
    ParticleManager.Update(gameTime);

    base.Update(gameTime);
}
```

11. Modify the current `Draw()` method to encapsulate the existing code within a conditional statement that either draws the title screen or executes the existing code. The entire new draw method should look like the following code:

```
protected override void Draw(GameTime gameTime)
{
    GraphicsDevice.Clear(Color.CornflowerBlue);

    GraphicsDevice.DepthStencilState = DepthStencilState.Default;

    if (gameState == GameState.TitleScreen)
    {
        spriteBatch.Begin();
        spriteBatch.Draw(titleScreen, Vector2.Zero, Color.White);
        spriteBatch.End();
    }
    else
    {
        terrain.Draw(camera, effect);

        foreach (Tank tank in tanks)
        {
            tank.Draw(camera);
        }

        ShotManager.Draw(camera);
        ParticleManager.Draw(camera);

        spriteBatch.Begin();

        foreach (UIWidget widget in uiElements.Values)
            widget.Draw(spriteBatch);

        spriteBatch.End();
    }

    base.Draw(gameTime);
}
```

12. Execute the game. Press the Space bar at the title screen to begin a new game. The title screen of the game should look like the following screenshot:

What just happened?

We define an enumeration (GameState) which can have three possible values, each corresponding to one of the game states we are dealing with—TitleScreen, Playing, or GameOver. The gameState variable holds the current state, and defaults to the TitleScreen state, meaning that when we first execute the game, we want the title screen to appear, as a player might expect.

Because we are no longer jumping directly into the game, we have removed the code to start a new round from the LoadContent() method, and replaced it with the code necessary to load the title screen into memory.

Beginning with step 7, we need to restructure our existing code in order to accommodate the game state system. We do this by using one of Visual Studio's refactoring features. By highlighting a section of code and selecting **Refactor | Extract Method** from the right-click popup menu, we are telling Visual Studio that the code we have selected can stand on its own as a method and to extract the highlighted code from its current location and create a new method.

In steps 7 and 8, we perform this refactoring on the Update() method of the TankBattlesGame class, generating the ProcessPlayingInput() method. Notice that Visual Studio performs enough analysis on the code to realize that the code we have selected needs to make use of the gameTime variable, so it automatically includes it as a parameter for the new method.

Refactoring

In general, **refactoring** refers to techniques for altering the internal workings of a piece of code while leaving its functionality unchanged. Visual Studio provides several tools (available under the **Refactor** menu option, which appears in a popup menu on right-clicking the highlighted code) to assist with code refactoring. Besides extracting methods, you can also rename a field, property, method, or class and Visual Studio will rename it everywhere where it is referenced in your code. Other tools can generate properties to encapsulate fields in your classes, and change the order of parameters in a method, including updating all calls to that method.

All of the code that we extract from the `Update()` method is replaced with a single line that calls the extracted method. In step 10, we perform some additional tasks by replacing the `Update()` method entirely while keeping the call to the `ProcessPlayingInput()` method in the proper location.

This new `Update()` method, which we will be expanding on shortly, decides what actions to take based on the current value of the `gameState` variable. While displaying the title screen, the only processing necessary during `Update()` is to watch for the player starting a new game by pressing the Space bar.

When in the `Playing` state, all of the previous code is executed by calling `ProcessPlayingInput()`. Finally, when in the `GameOver` state, we currently do not perform any additional state-specific processing.

Outside the game state conditional logic, we continue to update the `ShotManager` and `ParticleManager` classes, and check for shot impacts. We still want particle effects to process in the event that one player scores a hit and the game moves to the `GameOver` state. If we did not continue this processing when the state changes, the explosions would freeze in place at that point instead of continuing to settle downward and fade away.

Similarly, we update the `Draw()` method in step 11 to account for varying game states. This time, however, we only need to consider two possibilities. Either we are in the `TitleScreen` state, in which case we only want to display the title screen, or we are in one of the two other states, and wish to draw all of our normal game components.

Again, this is because we do not want to stop drawing the terrain, tanks, and particles during the `GameOver` state. They will continue to show while the winning player is displayed and we pause before returning to the title screen.

From Playing to GameOver

Tank Battles currently begins in the `TitleScreen` state, and we have code in place in the `Update()` method to allow us to start a new game, transitioning to the `Playing` state. At the moment, however, we do not have any way of getting out of the `Playing` state. Since we are not detecting hits against players, the game never comes to an end.

For our purposes, the game will end when a shot comes close enough to a tank to destroy it. In Tank Battles, we will use simple distance measurement to make this determination. We will implement a more detailed collision detection system in *Chapter 10, Mars Runner – Reaching the Finish Line*. The winning player will be the player whose tank survives – note that potentially, the player could fire a shot that hits their own tank, so the player firing the final shot is not necessarily the winner of the game.

We already know where a shot lands (we are creating an explosion there, after all) and we know the positions of each of the tanks, so determining if a tank is hit by a shot is a relatively straightforward matter of determining the distance between these two locations.

Time for action – detecting hits

To detect hits, perform the following steps:

1. To the `TankBattlesGame` class' declarations area, add the following fields:

    ```
    float gameOverTimer = 0.0f;
    float gameOverDelay = 8.0f;
    float impactDistance = 2.5f;
    ```

2. In the `CreateUIElements()` method of the `TankBattlesGame` class, create a new text block to hold the **Game Over** message when it should be displayed by adding the following to the end of the method:

    ```
    uiElements.Add("gameOverText",
        UIHelper.CreateTextblock("gameOverText", "", 220, 100));
    ```

3. Replace the current `case GameState.GameOver` section of the `Update()` method with:

    ```
    case GameState.GameOver:
        gameOverTimer += (float)gameTime.ElapsedGameTime.TotalSeconds;
        if (gameOverTimer > gameOverDelay)
        {
            UIHelper.SetElementVisibility(
                "gameOverText",
                false,
    ```

```
            uiElements);
        gameState = GameState.TitleScreen;
    }
    break;
```

4. To the `CheckForShotImpacts()` method inside the `if` statement and just before setting `ShotManager.HitProcessed` to true, add the following lines of code:

```
int hitPlayer = -1;
if (Vector3.Distance(
    impactPoint, tanks[0].Position) < impactDistance)
{
    hitPlayer = 0;
}

if (Vector3.Distance(
    impactPoint, tanks[1].Position) < impactDistance)
{
    hitPlayer = 1;
}

if (hitPlayer >= 0)
{
    string gameOverText;
    int winner = currentPlayer;
    if (hitPlayer == currentPlayer)
    {
        winner = (currentPlayer == 0 ? 1 : 0);
    }
    if (currentPlayer == hitPlayer)
    {
        gameOverText = "Player " + currentPlayer.ToString() +
            " blew themselves up! Player " +
            winner.ToString() + " wins!";
    }
    else
    {
        gameOverText = "Player " + currentPlayer.ToString() +
            " scores a hit! Player " +
            winner.ToString() + " wins!";
    }
    gameOverTimer = 0;
    UIHelper.SetElementText(
        uiElements["gameOverText"],
```

```
        gameOverText);
    UIHelper.SetElementVisibility("p", false, uiElements);
    UIHelper.SetElementVisibility("gameOverText", true,
uiElements);
    gameState = GameState.GameOver;
}
```

5. Execute the game and fire shots until you hit one of the two tanks. (Hint: If you fire straight up, the shot will land on the tank that fired it.)

What just happened?

We add a `UITextblock` object as one of our `UIElements` to hold the text that will be displayed when the game ends. By implementing it this way, we do not have to do anything else to draw the message – it will be drawn if it is `Visible` when the `UIElements` list is drawn in the `Draw()` method.

When in the `GameOver` state, we run a timer, waiting for the amount of time dictated by `gameOverDelay` to pass. During this time, we are not accepting any player input. After the delay expires, we hide the game over text block and switch back to the `TitleScreen` state.

In order to determine when one of the tanks has been hit, we measure the distance between each tank and the location where the shot landed. If either of these distances is small enough, we store which one of the tanks has been hit in the `hitPlayer` variable.

If a player has been hit, we know that we are going to switch to the `GameOver` state. If we did not want to give an indication of who won the game, we could simply do that immediately. Instead, we check to see if the player that was hit is the same player that fired the shot. If it was, we know that the player has hit themselves. If not, the player has hit their opponent. In either case, we set the text of the `gameOverText` UI element to indicate the results of the game.

After hiding all other UI elements (elements that start with `p`), we show the `gameOverText` and switch to the `GameOver` state.

Managing turns

Either tank can fire bullets at this point, but since there is only one mouse, the player who physically has it, has a distinct advantage in the game! In order to rectify this rather significant game balance issue, we need to implement a controlled sequence of turns.

Time for action – managing turns

1. Add the `Turn Management` region and its two methods to the `TankBattlesGame` class as follows:

```
#region Turn Management
private void ActivatePlayer(int playerNumber)
{
    UIHelper.SetElementVisibility("p", true, uiElements);
    UIHelper.SetButtonState(
        "p" + (playerNumber+1).ToString(), false, uiElements);
    currentPlayer = playerNumber;
}


private void DeactivatePlayer(int playerNumber)
{
    UIHelper.SetButtonState(
        "p" + (playerNumber+1).ToString(), true, uiElements);
}
#endregion
```

2. In the `checkForShotImpacts()` method of the `TankBattlesGame` class, just after the line that reads `ShotManager.HitProcessed = true`, add the following lines of code:

```
if (gameState != GameState.GameOver)
{
    ActivatePlayer((currentPlayer + 1) % 2);
}
```

3. At the end of the `StartNewRound()` method in the `TankBattlesGame` class, set the initial state of the players when a new game is started, as follows:

```
DeactivatePlayer(1);
ActivatePlayer(0);
```

4. In the `UIButton_Clicked()` method of the `TankBattlesGame` class (inside the `User Interface` region) just before the final `break` in the method, add the following line of code:

```
DeactivatePlayer(playerNumber);
```

5. Launch the game and fire shots back and forth between the players. We can see that the distant tank just missed the nearer combatant in the following screenshot:

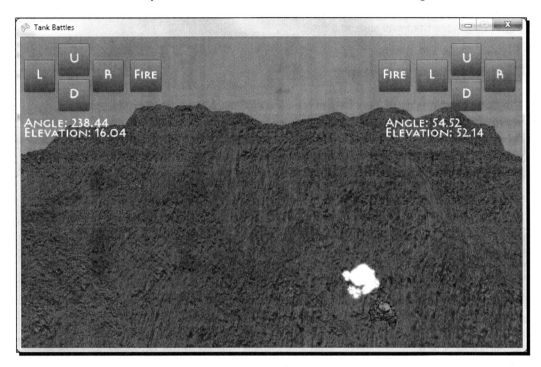

What just happened?

We introduced two new methods in the Turn Management region that allow us to activate and deactivate the controls for each player. Remember that while our players are internally referred to as players 0 and 1, our buttons have IDs beginning with p1 and p2, so we need to add one to the player number in order to modify the correct set of controls.

Deactivating a player simply sets the Disabled property of all of the player's controls to true. On the other hand, activating a player takes the additional steps of making sure all of the controls are visible and setting the currentPlayer variable to the player number that was passed to the method.

When the game has finished processing a shot, it activates the controls for the player that is up next by calling activatePlayer((currentPlayer + 1) % 2). This is a shorthand way of making sure that the value passed to activatePlayer will always be either 0 or 1. This works because the following mathematical expressions are true: $0 + 1 \% 2 = 1$, and $1 + 1 \% 2 = 0$. By using the modulo operator (%) we can wrap the player number around back to 0 when it reaches 2, preventing us from having to construct an if...else... structure.

When beginning a new round, we deactivate the controls for player 1 and activate the controls for player 0, setting up player 0 as the first player to take a turn in the new game. Each time a shot is fired, the firing player's controls are all disabled. This prevents the player from firing more than one shot at a time.

Visual improvements

The game functionality of Tank Battles is now complete, but aside from gameplay improvements (see the end of this chapter for suggestions on things you could implement) there are a number of graphical improvements we can make to Tank Battles to make it more visually appealing. We will add lighting to our terrain, and implement multitexturing to vary the appearance of areas of the terrain based on their elevation.

While we will still only scratch the surface of what we could potentially do with XNA and HLSL, let's look at a few topics that will give us a taste of the graphical power at our disposal.

Lighting

Right now, our terrain is fairly drab. Everything is uniformly lit, which gives the terrain a bland appearance. By adjusting and expanding the way we create the vertex buffer for our terrain, along with a little HLSL modification, we can give our landscape a realistic lighting.

Our first step is to generate normals for each of the vertices in the vertex buffer. A **normal** is a vector that is perpendicular to a triangle or vertex in our 3D environment. In the case of a triangle, this is fairly easy to visualize, as shown in the following figure:

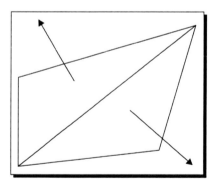

For the two triangles in the previous image, imagine they are bent along the center line, facing away from each other. The vectors pointing away from the surfaces of the triangles represent the normals of each triangle.

We are interested in the normals of our vertices. While not as straightforward to visualize, these are, fortunately, easy to calculate. The normal of a given vertex is equal to the sums of the normal of the triangles it is a part of. The following diagram illustrates the various possibilities for triangles contributing to vertex normals:

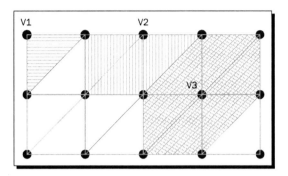

We have several different scenarios for the number of triangle normals that will be added together to give a vertex normal. In the preceding diagram, only one triangle contributes to the normal of vertex **V1**. This will be the case for the upper-left and lower-right corners of our terrain. The other two corners will each have two triangles contributing to their normal.

Vertices along the sides of our terrain will have three triangles contributing to their normal, as does vertex **V2**. Finally, the internal vertices of the terrain will have six different triangles contributing the values of their normals to the vertex normal as is the case with vertex **V3**.

Why do we need these normals anyway? When we compute the light falling on a surface, we use the dot product of the light direction vector and the normal of each vertex. The result of this calculation gives the intensity of the light at that vertex. Once we get to the HLSL, we simply need to apply this intensity when computing the color of a pixel.

Time for action – computing normals

To complete the normals, perform the following steps:

1. Near the end of the `BuildVertexBuffer()` method of the `Terrain` class, modify the code that defines the `vertexBuffer` variable by changing `BufferUsage.WriteOnly` to `BufferUsage.None`. The new statement should read as follows:

```
vertexBuffer = new VertexBuffer(
    device,
    typeof(VertexPositionNormalTexture),
    vertices.Length,
    BufferUsage.None);
```

2. Similarly, near the end of the `BuildIndexBuffer()` method, when the `indexBuffer` is defined, change `BufferUsage.WriteOnly` to `BufferUsage.None`. The statement should be as follows:

```
indexBuffer = new IndexBuffer(
    device,
    IndexElementSize.SixteenBits,
    indices.Length,
    BufferUsage.None);
```

3. In the `Helper Methods` region of the `Terrain` class, add the `CalculateNormals()` method as follows:

```
private void CalculateNormals()
{
    VertexPositionNormalTexture[] vertices =
        new VertexPositionNormalTexture[vertexBuffer.VertexCount];
    short[] indices = new short[indexBuffer.IndexCount];

    vertexBuffer.GetData(vertices);
    indexBuffer.GetData(indices);

    for (int x = 0; x < vertices.Length; x++)
        vertices[x].Normal = Vector3.Zero;

    int triangleCount = indices.Length / 3;

    for (int x = 0; x < triangleCount; x++)
    {
        int v1 = indices[x * 3];
        int v2 = indices[(x*3) + 1];
        int v3 = indices[(x*3) + 2];

        Vector3 firstSide =
            vertices[v2].Position - vertices[v1].Position;
        Vector3 secondSide =
            vertices[v1].Position - vertices[v3].Position;
        Vector3 triangleNormal =
            Vector3.Cross(firstSide, secondSide);
        triangleNormal.Normalize();

        vertices[v1].Normal += triangleNormal;
        vertices[v2].Normal += triangleNormal;
        vertices[v3].Normal += triangleNormal;
    }
```

```
        for (int x = 0; x < vertices.Length; x++)
            vertices[x].Normal.Normalize();

        vertexBuffer.SetData(vertices);
    }
```

4. In the constructor of the `Terrain` class, after both the vertex and index buffers have been built, add a call to `CalculateNormals()` as the last line of the method, as follows:

```
CalculateNormals();
```

What just happened?

In the past, we have been fine with `BufferUsage.WriteOnly` because our C# code never needed to look at the vertex or index buffers after they had been set. We simply passed them to the shader code as whole units.

Now, however, we not only need to view their contents inside our C# code, but we will also be updating each of the vertices to set the normal vector. For these reasons, we need to change the initialization of both buffers to remove the `WriteOnly` declaration, otherwise XNA will give us an error when we try to execute the `GetData()` method.

To compute the normals themselves, we begin by copying both buffers to arrays to make them easier to work with. Even without the `WriteOnly` buffer mode, we cannot access elements of the buffers individually.

We will be adding up one normal per triangle connected to a vertex, and we need to begin with a known value, so we loop through all of the vertices and set the normal vector to `Vector3.Zero`.

We calculate the number of triangles we are going to process by dividing the number of indices in the index buffer by three. Remember that the index buffer stores a list of points that make up triangles, so dividing the number of points by three gives us the total number of triangles in the terrain.

We then loop through the triangles, extracting the three vertex positions that make up each triangle. We derive two vectors that describe sides of the triangle by subtracting their positions from each other. Thanks to the magic of vector math, computing the cross product of these two vectors returns the vector that is perpendicular to a plane that would contain those two vectors. As the triangle would also be contained in this plane, the vector is normal to the triangle.

We normalize the normal vector (setting its length to 1 unit, while keeping the same direction) and add this normal vector to the current normal vectors for the three vertices that make up the triangle.

When we have done this for all of the triangles in the terrain, we run through each vertex once again and normalize the normal vectors. Finally, we place our modified vertex data back into our vertex buffer.

We saw earlier, that any given vertex may have one, two, three, or six triangles contributing to its normal. Instead of trying to determine this number for each of our vertices, we simply calculate normals for each triangle and have them update their three connected vertices. That way, we never need to know if a vertex is in a corner, on the side, or in the middle of our terrain.

Diffuse lighting

We have attached normals to all of our vertices, but if we were to run the code right now we would not see any difference in our terrain. As it exists, our HLSL code does not take these normals into account when determining the color of each pixel. We now need to expand our shader code to work with this new data.

Time for action – HLSL for lighting

To implement HLSL lighting, perform the following steps:

1. In the declarations area of the `Terrain.fx` effect file, after `textureSampler` is declared, add the following variable declarations:

    ```
    float3 lightDirection;
    float4 lightColor;
    float lightBrightness;
    ```

2. In the `VertexShaderInput` struct definition, add a new struct component to pass in the normal associated with the vertex as follows:

    ```
    float3 Normal : NORMAL0;
    ```

3. In the `VertexShaderOutput` struct definition, add a new struct component to hold the calculated lighting value for the vertex as follows:

    ```
    float4 LightingColor : COLOR0;
    ```

4. In the `VertexShaderFunction()` function, add the following lines of code before the line that reads `return output;`:

    ```
    float4 normal = normalize(mul(input.Normal, World));
    float lightLevel = dot(normal, lightDirection);
    output.LightingColor = saturate(
        lightColor * lightBrightness * lightLevel);
    ```

5. Replace the current `PixelShaderFunction()` method with the following:

```
float4 PixelShaderFunction(VertexShaderOutput input) : COLOR0
{
    float4 pixelColor = tex2D(
        textureSampler, input.TextureCoordinate);
    pixelColor *= input.LightingColor;
    pixelColor.a = 1.0;
    return pixelColor;
}
```

6. In the `Draw()` method of the `Terrain` class, add the following code to set the additional parameters defined in the effect file, before the `foreach` loop that draws the terrain:

```
Vector3 lightDirection = new Vector3(-1f, 1f, -1f);
lightDirection.Normalize();
effect.Parameters["lightDirection"].SetValue(lightDirection);
effect.Parameters["lightColor"].SetValue(new Vector4(1,1,1,1));
effect.Parameters["lightBrightness"].SetValue(0.8f);
```

7. Execute the game and observe the lighting applied to the terrain. A comparison of the game's visuals with and without lighting is shown in the following screenshot:

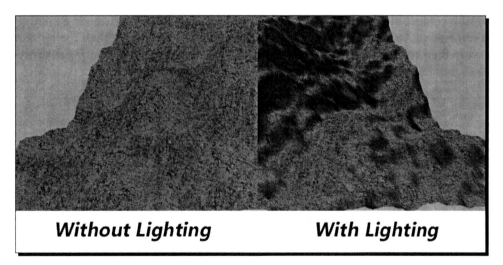

Without Lighting   **With Lighting**

What just happened?

The lighting effect we have created here is known as diffuse lighting. Specifically, we are implementing directional diffuse lighting, meaning that the unseen light source is so far away that it appears to light everything in our game world uniformly. This type of lighting works well for simulating daylight – the sun is so far away that all objects in any specific area on the ground cast shadows in essentially the same direction.

In order to implement our light, we specify the direction the light is coming from, the light color, and its brightness level. We add these three factors to our HLSL code so that we can pass them in as parameters from our `Draw()` method.

Because we are now utilizing the normal portion of the `VertexPositionNormalTexture` vertex format that our terrain uses, we need some way to let our HLSL code know what it is. We do this by assigning the `NORMAL0` semantic to the `Normal` variable in the `VertexShaderInput` structure.

We also need a way to pass the color information we calculate in the vertex shader on to the pixel shader, so we define a new component of the `VertexShaderOutput` structure called `LightingColor`. We assign the `COLOR0` semantic to it.

In order to calculate the light level at a particular vertex, we first transform the normal vector for the vertex into world space, and normalize it—giving it a length of 1 unit. When the dot product is computed between this vector and the light direction vector, we get a number that corresponds to how closely the two vectors are aligned with each other. The resulting value can then be thought of as how directly the light source is shining on any given vertex, or the light's intensity at this point.

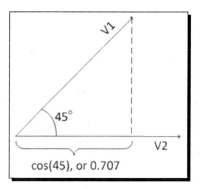

In order to keep things simple, let's look at a 2D example. If we create a vector pointing from the origin to point (1, 1) in 2D space, it will be at a 45 degree angle to a vector from the origin to point (1, 0). In the preceding figure, these vectors are represented as **V1** and **V2**, after **V1** has been normalized to a 1 unit length, making it (**0.707**, **0.707**). Vector **V2** already has a length of 1.

For 2D vectors, the dot product is calculated as:

$$X_1 * X_2 + Y_1 * Y_2$$

In our case, that would be: **0.707** * 1 + **0.707** * 0 or **0.707** + 0.

When both of the vectors have a length of 1, the result of the dot product is equal to the cosine of the angle between the vectors. As shown in the preceding figure and calculations, it represents the projection of the first vector onto the second, or in other words how far in the direction of **V2** does **V1** extends.

Three dimensional vectors work the same way, except that the formula is expanded to include the z component of the vectors:

$$X_1 * X_2 + Y_1 * Y_2 + Z_1 * Z_2$$

We use this value, called the scalar projection because it projects **V1** in terms of **V2**, to indicate how well aligned our vertices and the directional light are. The higher the scalar projection, the closer the alignment of the two vectors, and the more intense the light from the light source is at that location.

Given that both of our vectors are normalized, the lighting value will be between `-1` and `1`. We then use the HLSL function `saturate()` to calculate the overall effect of the light at this vertex given the color, brightness, and localized intensity of the light. The `saturate()` function actually just clamps the value passed into it between zero and one. If we pass in a negative number (because the dot product returns a negative number) we will end up with a zero for the return value of the `saturate()` function. This information is stored in the `LightingColor` component so that we can utilize it in the pixel shader.

In order to do so, we retrieve the pixel color from the texture just as we did before, but this time we multiply it by the lighting color we calculated in the vertex shader. Note that we also set the alpha value of the pixel to `1.0` explicitly. Because we are multiplying the colors from the texture by a calculated color, we will end up with partial transparency in the resulting color value. Setting the alpha level manually eliminates this.

Ambient lighting

Our terrain now looks a bit better, but it sure is dark! Our first thought might be to increase the brightness of the directional light we are already using. That would certainly work up to a point, but it would begin to wash out the lit areas while making the dark areas seem even darker.

Instead, we will add an ambient light to our terrain. Ambient light refers to the directionless, reflected light that generally fills an area. The sun is a very bright directional light source, but if you are standing in the shadow of a telephone pole, you are not enveloped in absolute darkness. The ground around you, walls of buildings, even the sky, all reflect less intense light that makes even shadowed areas not quite so dark.

Time for action – using ambient light

To implement ambient light, perform the following steps:

1. Add two more declarations to the declarations area of the `Terrain.fx` effect file:

```
float4 ambientLightColor;
float ambientLightLevel;
```

2. In the `PixelShaderFunction()` of the `Terrain.fx` file, just before setting the alpha value of the pixel to `1.0` add the following line of code:

```
pixelColor += (ambientLightColor * ambientLightLevel);
```

3. In the `Draw()` method of the `Terrain` class, add two additional parameter settings before the terrain is drawn:

```
effect.Parameters["ambientLightLevel"].SetValue(0.15f);
effect.Parameters["ambientLightColor"].SetValue(
    new Vector4(1,1,1,1));
```

4. Execute the game and view the newly lit terrain. The game should look like the following screenshot:

What just happened?

That certainly looks better! The dark areas are still dark, but they haven't completely lost their detail now. Ambient lighting is quite a bit simpler to implement than diffuse lighting. All we need to know is the color of the light and the overall ambient light level. We then simply add the ambient light to each pixel.

Ambient light and effects

Ambient lights can be used to produce quick effects across the whole terrain. Try changing the ambient light color to red (1, 0, 0, 1) and see how the whole landscape is now tinted a nice shade of Mars. If such an ambient light varied in intensity up and down over time, you would have a quick "red alert" type effect.

Multitexturing

One way we can introduce a bit more variety into the look of our terrain is by using different textures for different elevations. For the sake of Tank Battles, we will use three different terrain textures as shown in the following figure:

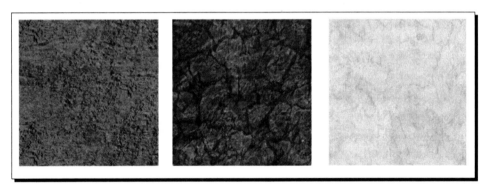

The first will be the grass texture we are familiar with. To this, we will add a rocky brown texture for the mid-range elevations and a snowy white texture for the highest areas of the map.

Open Game Art

The brown rock and snow textures (the latter is actually a white stone texture) were downloaded from the texture area of OpenGameArt.org. These particular textures are licensed as CC0 (Public Domain). If you are looking for artwork for your independent or open source game project, give http://www.opengameart.org a look. A lot of talented artists contribute a wide range of artwork available under creative commons, GPL, and public domain licenses to the archive there.

In order to give our multitexturing approach a smooth appearance, we will not simply change textures at a certain elevation, but will instead blend the textures at the transition points, smoothly ramping up the ratio of the two textures over the course of a small distance in our terrain. This will prevent us from having a sharp dividing line between grass, rocks, and snow.

Time for action – multitexturing

1. In the declarations area of the `Terrain.fx` effect file, add two new texture variables to hold the additional textures we will be using, as follows:

```
texture terrainTexture2;
texture terrainTexture3;
```

2. Still in the declarations area, add samplers for the new textures as follows:

```
sampler2D textureSamplerMid = sampler_state {
  Texture = (terrainTexture2);
  AddressU = Wrap;
  AddressV = Wrap;
};

sampler2D textureSamplerHigh = sampler_state {
  Texture = (terrainTexture3);
  AddressU = Wrap;
  AddressV = Wrap;
};
```

3. Also in the declarations area, add the following items to control how the textures are split between elevations:

```
float maxElevation;
float trans1 = 0.50;
float trans2 = 0.75;
```

4. In the `VertexShaderOutput` structure, add a new structure member to allow us to pass the elevation of the current vertex to the pixel shader as follows:

```
float Elevation : TEXCOORD1;
```

5. In the `VertexShaderFunction()` method, right after declaring the output variable, store the raw elevation of this vertex as follows:

```
output.Elevation = input.Position.y;
```

6. Replace the existing `PixelShaderFunction()` in the `Terrain.fx` file with the following lines of code:

```
float4 PixelShaderFunction(VertexShaderOutput input) : COLOR0
{
    float elevation = input.Elevation / maxElevation;

    float4 lowColor = tex2D(
      textureSampler, input.TextureCoordinate);
    float4 midColor = tex2D(
      textureSamplerMid, input.TextureCoordinate);
    float4 highColor = tex2D(
      textureSamplerHigh, input.TextureCoordinate);

    float4 pixelColor = lowColor;

    if ((elevation >= trans1 - 0.05 ) && (elevation <= trans1 +
0.05))
        {
        float transWeight = ((trans1 + 0.05) - elevation) / 0.10;
        pixelColor = lowColor * transWeight;
        pixelColor += midColor * (1 - transWeight);

        }

    if ((elevation > trans1 + 0.05) && (elevation <= trans2 -
0.05))
        {
        pixelColor = midColor;
        }

    if ((elevation > trans2 - 0.05) && (elevation <= trans2 +
0.05))
        {
        float transWeight = ((trans2 + 0.05) - elevation) / 0.10;
        pixelColor = midColor * transWeight;
        pixelColor += highColor * (1 - transWeight);
        }

    if (elevation > trans2 + 0.05)
        pixelColor = highColor;

    pixelColor *= input.LightingColor;
    pixelColor += (ambientLightColor * ambientLightLevel);
    pixelColor.a = 1.0;
    return pixelColor;
}
```

7. In the `Terrain` class, add the following new fields to the class declarations area:

```
private Texture2D terrainTexture2;
private Texture2D terrainTexture3;
private float maxHeight;
```

8. Modify the declaration of the constructor for the `Terrain` class to include the two additional textures. The new declaration should read as follows:

```
public Terrain(
    GraphicsDevice graphicsDevice,
    Texture2D heightMap,
    Texture2D terrainTexture,
    Texture2D terrainTexture2,
    Texture2D terrainTexture3,
    float textureScale,
    int terrainWidth,
    int terrainHeight,
    float heightScale)
```

9. Inside the constructor for the `Terrain` class, cache the newly created fields just after setting the value of `this.TerrainTexture`, as follows:

```
this.terrainTexture2 = terrainTexture2;
this.terrainTexture3 = terrainTexture3;
maxHeight = heightScale;
```

10. In the `Draw()` method of the `Terrain` class, set the new parameters for our effect in the block of parameter sets as follows:

```
effect.Parameters["terrainTexture2"].SetValue(terrainTexture2);
effect.Parameters["terrainTexture3"].SetValue(terrainTexture3);
effect.Parameters["maxElevation"].SetValue(maxHeight);
```

11. In the `LoadContent()` method of the `TankBattlesGame` class, modify the code that creates the terrain object to include the two new textures. The new statement should read as follows:

```
terrain = new Terrain(
    GraphicsDevice,
    Content.Load<Texture2D>(@"Textures\HeightMap_02"),
    Content.Load<Texture2D>(@"Textures\Grass"),
    Content.Load<Texture2D>(@"Textures\Rocky"),
    Content.Load<Texture2D>(@"Textures\Snowy"),
    32f,
    128,
    128,
    30f);
```

12. Execute the game and view the smooth texture transitions between height ranges as shown in the following screenshot:

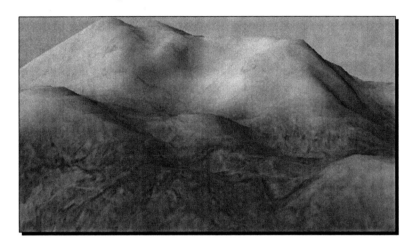

What just happened?

In order to use more than one texture, we need to define both texture variables and samplers inside our HLSL to manage them. We also need to know the highest elevation in our map so that we can determine where shifts in the terrain are going to occur.

In step 3, we set these shifts in the terrain to occur at 50% and 75% of the maximum height, so any terrain below 50% of the maximum height will use the grass texture. Terrain between 50% and 75% will use the rock texture, and anything above 75% will be snow covered.

When we modify the `VertexShaderOutput` structure in step 4 to add the `Elevation` value, it might seem odd that we assign it the `TEXCOORD1` semantic. After all, it is not a texture coordinate. Everything in our structure needs to be assigned to some semantic, and `TEXCOORD1` is not used by anything else in our shader so it is available to us. We are just going to treat it as a simple float value and ignore the fact that it is mapped to a semantic.

To set the elevation value of a given vertex, we extract the Y component of the vertex's position based on the input position of the vertex and not the output position (after it has been transformed by the world, view, and projection matrices). This gives us the relative elevation of the terrain compared to the other vertices. If we had used `output.Position.y` as the base instead, the terrain texture would be based on the position of the vertex on the screen instead of relative to the other terrain areas. It is an interesting effect (go ahead and try it out), but that's not what we want here.

The real work of our multitexturing code comes into play in the `PixelShaderFunction()` method. We begin by extracting the pixel for this texture's position from each of our three textures and storing it in the `lowColor`, `midColor`, and `highColor` variables. We assume that the pixel will be a grass pixel to begin with, so we set `pixelColor` to the retrieved `lowColor` value.

We then begin a series of checks to determine if the pixel really is a grass pixel or not. We start by checking to see if the pixel lies within `0.05` units of the first transition zone (at the 0.5 or 50% elevation mark).

If the elevation does lie within this zone, we calculate how far the pixel rests along the 0.1 unit span, and use this value to come up with a weight for the two colors that will be mixed to create the final color for this pixel. If the value is right at the transition zone, for example (`0.50`), we will use 50% of the grass texture and 50% of the rock texture colors for this pixel.

If the pixel is higher than the first transition zone and lower than the second, we know that the pixel should be entirely from the rock texture. The same pair of checks apply to the rock-to-snow transition zone and the snowy area above it.

Once we have a blended color value for our pixel, we apply the lighting values just as we did earlier to come up with the final color for the pixel.

In steps 7 through 11, we modify our existing code to supply the required textures and parameters to our newly modified shader, and we are ready to use our multitexturing HLSL code!

Have a go hero!

There are almost limitless ways you could expand the `Tank Battles` game. Here are a few suggestions to try out:

- Use billboarding to create a pointer that can be placed above the current player's tank to highlight their location.
- Implement movement controls, allowing each player to move their tank a limited distance on each turn.
- Add health bars for each player's tank. Compute the distance between a shell impact and the tank to determine how badly the shot damages the tank. Players can then play until their tank is destroyed by multiple hits.
- Implement gamepad controls for each player, detecting when gamepads are present and removing the onscreen buttons and allowing both players to move and fire at the same time.

Summary

In addition to wrapping our game in a basic state-based game structure, we have expanded the graphical appeal of Tank Battles by including both lighting and smoothly transitioning textured terrain.

The basic techniques used in Tank Battles—`heightMap` terrain generation, 3D model rendering and animation, billboard particle effects, and 2D/3D interaction for interface objects, form a solid foundation for a wide variety of 3D games. As we can see, the possibilities of interesting graphical effects utilizing advanced HLSL are almost limitless.

Now that Tank Battles is complete, we are going to shift gears in the next chapter and begin a new game – driving a rover on the surface of Mars while under attack by alien saucers!

9
Mars Runner

For our final game, we will revisit some of the topics we have already covered, like heightmaps and vertex-based terrain, with a few new twists to their implementation. We will also take a look at a couple of new techniques we can use to implement 3D worlds in XNA.

In this chapter, we will cover:

- ◆ Working with the Game State Management sample project provided by Microsoft
- ◆ Building 3D skyboxes to provide background images for a 3D world
- ◆ Using heightmap terrain pieces as tiles to form a larger playing area

Design of Mars Runner

In Mars Runner, the player drives a vehicle on the surface of Mars, jumping over craters strewn about the Martian terrain while also attempting to shoot down the UFOs flying overhead and dropping bombs down onto both the player and the player's pathway. The gameplay is reminiscent of the classic arcade game Moon Patrol.

We will utilize a randomly generated pathway for each level, including rules about the placement of obstacles to keep the levels playable. The player's score will be based on the distance they travel along the track and the number of aliens they are able to shoot down along the way.

In order to implement these goals, we will need to come up with a way to create a continuous pathway the player can drive their vehicle on. Though we could certainly lay out the entire world (as we did for Cube Chaser), we have an opportunity to use a different approach given the constraints of our gameplay.

Instead of moving the player's vehicle along a predesigned landscape and having the camera follow it, we will instead utilize a camera at a fixed location and move the entire world in front of the camera as required, to produce the movement effect we are looking for.

In addition, we will utilize the **Game State Management (GSM)** code sample provided by Microsoft on the MSDN website to build our game structure in order to see how to use the GSM sample in your own projects.

Getting started with the GSM sample

Available as a code sample from the **education** section of the MSDN website, the GSM sample code provides a framework for building your games that includes precoded menu screens, input processing, and screen stacking flow.

We will use the GSM to act as the foundation of our Mars Runner game project, customizing and adding screens to implement our gameplay.

Time for action – creating the Mars Runner solution

To create the Mars Runner solution, perform the following steps:

1. Visit the GSM sample page of the App Hub website at `http://xbox.create. msdn.com/en-US/education/catalog/sample/game_state_management` and download `GSMSample_4_0_WIN_XBOX.zip`, and extract the contents of the file to a temporary location.

2. Select all of the files and folders from the archive and copy them to the Windows clipboard.

3. In your Visual Studio 2010 **Projects** folder (by default, the `Visual Studio 2010\ Projects` folder inside your `Documents` folder) create a new folder for the `Mars Runner` project, called `Mars Runner`.

4. Paste the files from the clipboard into this new location.

5. Still in Windows Explorer, select the `GameStateManagementSample (Windows). sln` file and rename it to `Mars Runner.sln`.

6. Double-click on the `Mars Runner.sln` file to open the solution in Visual Studio.

7. In the **Solution Explorer** pane, right-click on the **GameStateManagementSample (Windows)** project entry and select **Rename**. Rename the project to `Mars Runner`.

8. Double-click on the `Game.cs` file in the newly renamed project and right-click on `GameStateManagmenetGame` on the line that reads `namespace GameStateManagement`. Select **Refactor | Rename** and change the name to `Mars_Runner`. Click on **Ok**, click on **Apply**, and then click on **Yes** on the subsequent alerts that appear about the rename function.

9. Execute the game to verify that the base GSM code is functioning properly as shown in the following screenshot:

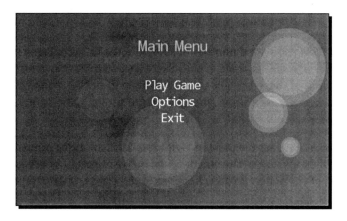

What just happened?

We have now downloaded the GSM sample code and renamed the components of the project to match our Mars Runner game's name. With the base GSM code, you can navigate the onscreen menu with either the keyboard or game pad. Selecting the **Play Game** option will start a simple text-based sample screen.

The **Options** menu item brings up a second menu screen that has various made-up settings that can be altered via the interface.

Finally, the **Exit** menu item uses a pop-up window to verify that you really wish to exit, and ends the game and returns to Visual Studio if you decide to do so.

Before we dive too deeply into customizing the GSM code for Mars Runner, let's look at the structure of the GSM system and how each screen operates within the system. At its heart, the GSM system is composed of three components as follows:

- **The ScreenManager class**: This is a class derived from the `DrawableGameComponent` class that is responsible for keeping track of all the defined screens and letting each screen know what it should be doing at any given time.

- ♦ **The InputState class**: This is a helper class for dealing with keyboard, gamepad, and touchpad input and supplying it in a format that game screens can consume. The `InputState` class handles input for up to four players, though this implies that each player is using a separate physical game pad since there is usually only one keyboard connected to a PC.

- ♦ **The GameScreen class**: This is an abstract class that acts as the base for all screens in the game. The `GameScreen` class provides code to handle transitioning a screen on and off, base `Update()` and `Draw()` methods, and a method for removing the screen from the `ScreenManager` class.

Included with the GSM code are a number of sample screens, including a background screen, loading overlay screen, menu screens, a pause screen, and a sample gameplay screen. We will make use of some of these screens that will remain basically unchanged (the loading screen, for example), customize some (the main menu screen), and completely replace others (the gameplay screen).

If you open the `Game.cs` class file included with the GSM solution, you will see that it is a somewhat simplified version of the standard default game class. There is no `Update()` method, and most of the action actually happens in the class constructor, named `GameStateManagementGame()`.

Inside the constructor, an instance of the `ScreenManager` class is created and added to the `Components` collection. Two screens, `BackgroundScreen` and `MainMenuScreen`, are then added to the instance of the `ScreenManager` class.

While running, whenever a new screen is added to the instance of the `ScreenManager` class, it will become the topmost screen of the game. When this happens, other screens will receive a flag in their respective `Update()` methods indicating that they are covered by something else. The `Update()` method will still run for each screen, but we can use this flag to determine if we should actually do any game-related processing.

In addition to the `Update()` method, each screen can implement a `HandleInput()` method. This method will only be called on the currently active screen, so a screen covered by another screen will not receive any player input.

The GameScreen abstract class

As a base for other screens, most of the methods in the `GameScreen` class are empty virtual methods meant to be overridden and implemented by custom code in our individual screens.

One important exception here is how transitions are handled. Each screen has a defined state of `TransitionOn`, `Active`, `TransitionOff`, or `Hidden`. Screens begin in the `TransitionOn` state and the `Update()` method of the base `GameScreen` class is responsible for managing the progress of each transition and the switch between states when a transition has completed.

By default, the duration of each transition is zero, so transitions will be immediate and invisible to the player. If we do choose to implement a transition, we need to build support for it into the game screens we create. The `GameScreen` class handles the sequencing of transitions automatically, but what effect the transition has on the display of the screen is completely up to us.

The GSM sample code includes a couple of transition samples, which you can see when running our current game project. When the menu screen appears as the game starts, the menu options slide in from the edges of the screen. Selecting **Play Game** from the menu causes the menu to slide out, the loading screen to fade in and then back out, and then the gameplay screen to fade in.

Customizing the default ScreenManager screens

Let's take a closer look at the two screens that get created automatically in the constructor of the `GameStateManagementGame` class. The first is an instance of the `BackgroundScreen` class. As its name implies, the `BackgroundScreen` class loads a background image and displays it behind other screens that, presumably, have at least some transparency to their content.

The `BackgroundScreen` class defines both `TransitionOnTime` and `TransitionOffTime` properties as `0.5f`, meaning that instead of the default instant transitions, `BackgroundScreen` instances will take half a second to become fully visible after being created and half a second to fade out when being hidden. Looking at the `Draw()` method for `BackgroundScreen`, we can see the implementation of the fading transition effect as follows:

```
spriteBatch.Draw(backgroundTexture, fullscreen,
    new Color(TransitionAlpha, TransitionAlpha, TransitionAlpha));
```

Just by adjusting the draw color for the background image based on the `TransitionAlpha` (a property of the `GameScreen` class that computes the progress through the current transition), we can create the fading effect simply by switching out the color used to tint the texture.

Time for action – customizing the BackgroundScreen class

To customize the background image for Mars Runner, perform the following steps:

1. Download the `7089_09_GRAPICSPACK.zip` file from the book's website and extract the contents to a temporary location.

2. Select the `Textures`, `Models`, and `HeightMaps` folders from the temporary location and copy them to the Windows clipboard.

3. In Visual Studio, right-click on **Content** (the name of the content project for a GSM project) and select **Paste** to add the folders and their contents to the project.

4. Expand the `Models` folder in the content project and exclude all of the PNG files, along with the `Sphere` folder from the project.

5. In the `LoadContent()` method of the `BackgroundScreen` class (located inside the `Screens` folder in the project), change the name of the texture that is loaded from `"background"` to `@"textures\marsrunner"`. The new line should read:

```
backgroundTexture = content.Load<Texture2D>@("textures\
marsrunner");
```

6. Launch the game and view the new background image as shown in the following screeenshot:

What just happened?

There is, of course, nothing very complicated about replacing the image used for the background. It does point out an issue though—we are utilizing our background image as a title screen of sorts, but the menu title (Main Menu) in this case, overlaps with the game title built into the title screen. In the preceding image, you can see **Main Menu** in gray text inside the **Mars Runner** title.

The second screen that is automatically created in the `GameStateManagementGame` class is an instance of `MainMenuScreen`. This class inherits from the `MenuScreen` class, which is in turn derived from `GameScreen`.

The code of the `MainMenuScreen` defines the menu entries that will be displayed and implements the callbacks associated with selecting a menu entry. The base code of the `MenuScreen` class implements updating and drawing the menu, and handles input from the player to move between menu items and select menu items.

The locations of the menu items are hard coded by default in the GSM, so we will modify the `MenuScreen` class to allow us to specify the locations of these items. In addition, we will remove the **Options** menu item for now, as we will not be implementing options in Mars Runner.

Time for action – updating the menu

To update the menu for Mars Runner, perform the following steps:

1. In the `MenuScreen` class file, add two new fields to the `Fields` region as follows:

```
int menuTitleYPos = 80;
int menuEntryYStart = 175;
```

2. Add a new constructor to the `MenuScreen` class, in addition to the existing constructor (located in the `Initialization` region) as follows:

```
public MenuScreen(string menuTitle, int titleYPos, int menuYPos)
{
    this.menuTitle = menuTitle;

    TransitionOnTime = TimeSpan.FromSeconds(0.5);
    TransitionOffTime = TimeSpan.FromSeconds(0.5);
    menuTitleYPos = titleYPos;
    menuEntryYStart = menuYPos;
}
```

3. In the `Update and Draw` region of the `MenuScreen` class, modify the line of code in the `UpdateMenuEntryLocations()` method that specifies the base `position` vector, replacing `175f` with our new `menuEntryYStart` variable, as follows:

```
Vector2 position = new Vector2(0f, menuEntryYStart);
```

4. In the `Draw()` method, modify the line that sets the `titlePosition` vector by replacing the `80` value with the `menuTitleYPos` field as follows:

```
Vector2 titlePosition =
    new Vector2(graphics.Viewport.Width / 2, menuTitleYPos);
```

5. In the `MainMenuScreen` class file, modify the declaration of the constructor to include new positions in the call to the base class' constructor as follows:

```
public MainMenuScreen()
    : base("Main Menu", 175, 225)
```

6. In the constructor, comment out the line that adds the `optionsMenuEntry` to the `MenuEntries` list as follows:

```
//MenuEntries.Add(optionsMenuEntry);
```

7. Execute the game and view the relocated menu as shown in the following screenshot:

What just happened?

By adding a second constructor to the MenuScreen class and setting the default values of the menu positions equal to the existing hardcoded values, we can ensure that we will not break the MenuScreen code for other screens that may be derived from it.

After modifying the menu positions, we simply eliminate the addition of the **Options** menu item from the MenuItems list. The **Options** menu still gets created, but is never displayed. This way, if you choose to implement your own screen to display options later, you just need to uncomment the line to return the menu entry to its place.

Adding a new screen

The game in the GameplayScreen class is not too terribly exciting. It simply bounces a bit of text around the screen, admonishing the player to "Insert Gameplay Here". In order to implement our design for Mars Runner, we will create a new gameplay screen to house our code.

Time for action – creating the MarsRunnerPlayScreen class

To create a new gameplay screen for Mars Runner, perform the following steps:

1. Add a new class file to the Screens folder of the Mars Runner project. Name the class file MarsRunnerPlayScreen.cs.

2. Modify the namespace line in the newly created class by removing .Screens from the end of the namespace. The new line should read as follows:

```
namespace Mars_Runner
```

3. Add the following `using` directives at the beginning of the class file:

```
using Microsoft.Xna.Framework;
using Microsoft.Xna.Framework.Content;
using Microsoft.Xna.Framework.Graphics;
using Microsoft.Xna.Framework.Input;
```

4. Modify the declaration of the class to derive it from the `GameScreen` class as follows:

```
class MarsRunnerPlayScreen : GameScreen
```

5. Add fields to the `MarsRunnerPlayScreen` class as follows:

```
#region Fields
ContentManager content;
Random random = new Random();
#endregion
```

6. In the `MainMenuScreen` class, inside the `Handle Input` region, modify the `PlayGameMenuEntrySelected()` event handler by replacing the reference to `GameplayScreen` with a reference to our new `MarsRunnerPlayScreen`. The new line should read as follows:

```
LoadingScreen.Load(ScreenManager, true, e.PlayerIndex,
    new MarsRunnerPlayScreen());
```

7. Execute the game and select **Play Game** from the main menu.

What just happened?

At the moment, our `MarsRunnerPlayScreen` class is even less exciting than the default GSM game! All we get now after selecting **Play Game** is a black screen. We have created the shell for our gameplay class, but we need to do quite a bit of background work before we are ready to actually implement the gameplay. Note that we needed to modify the namespace associated with the `MarsRunnerPlayScreen` class because Visual Studio automatically appends the folder name any time you create a class file inside a folder in your project. We are using folders strictly for organization, so we are fine keeping our code in a single namespace.

A new camera

As we saw at the beginning of this chapter, the camera in Mars Runner will remain in a single location, facing a fixed point throughout the game. This simplifies the `Camera` class somewhat from the cameras we have previously implemented, but we also want to add a couple of new capabilities to allow us to play a few tricks with the skybox that will form the background of our gameplay.

Time for action – the stationary camera

To implement a stationary camera in Mars Runner, perform the following steps:

1. Create a new class file in the `Mars Runner` project called `Camera.cs`.

2. Add the following `using` declaration to the `Camera` class file:

```
using Microsoft.Xna.Framework;
```

3. Add the following fields to the `Camera` class:

```
#region Fields
private Vector3 position = Vector3.Zero;
private float rotation;

private Vector3 lookAt;
private Vector3 baseCameraReference = new Vector3(0, 0, 1);
private bool needViewResync = true;

private Matrix cachedViewMatrix;
#endregion
```

4. Add the following properties to the `Camera` class:

```
#region Properties
public Matrix Projection { get; private set; }
public Matrix WideProjection { get; private set; }

public Vector3 Position
{
    get
    {
        return position;
    }
    set
    {
        position = value;
        updateLookAt();
    }
}

public float Rotation
{
    get
    {
        return rotation;
```

```
        }
        set
        {
            rotation = value;
            updateLookAt();
        }
    }

    public Matrix View
    {
        get
        {
            if (needViewResync)
                cachedViewMatrix = Matrix.CreateLookAt(
                    Position,
                    lookAt,
                    Vector3.Up);

            return cachedViewMatrix;
        }
    }
    #endregion
```

5. Add a constructor to the `Camera` class as follows:

```
#region Constructor
public Camera(
    Vector3 position,
    float rotation,
    float aspectRatio,
    float nearClip,
    float farClip)
{
    Projection = Matrix.CreatePerspectiveFieldOfView(
        MathHelper.PiOver4,
        aspectRatio,
        nearClip,
        farClip);
    WideProjection = Matrix.CreatePerspectiveFieldOfView(
        MathHelper.PiOver4,
        aspectRatio/2,
        nearClip,
        farClip);
    MoveTo(position, rotation);
}
#endregion
```

6. Add helper methods to the `Camera` class as follows:

```
#region Helper Methods
private void updateLookAt()
{
    Matrix rotationMatrix = Matrix.CreateRotationY(rotation);
    Vector3 lookAtOffset = Vector3.Transform(
        baseCameraReference,
        rotationMatrix);
    lookAt = position + lookAtOffset;
    needViewResync = true;
}


public void MoveTo(Vector3 position, float rotation)
{
    this.position = position;
    this.rotation = rotation;
    updateLookAt();
}
#endregion
```

7. In the `MarsRunnerPlayScreen` class, add a new field to the `Fields` region as follows:

```
Camera camera;
```

8. Also in the `MarsRunnerPlayScreen` class, add the `LoadContent()` method as follows:

```
#region Initialization
public override void LoadContent()
{
    camera = new Camera(
        new Vector3(0, 2, 115),
        MathHelper.ToRadians(180),
        ScreenManager.GraphicsDevice.Viewport.AspectRatio,
        0.1f,
        1000f);

    base.LoadContent();
}
#endregion
```

What just happened?

The `Camera` class should look very familiar. In fact, it is nearly identical to the camera from Cube Chaser, with the `PreviewMove()` and `MoveForward()` methods removed, and a new property added.

This property, `WideProjection`, is initialized in the constructor with mostly the same parameters as the normal `Projection` matrix, but with half of the aspect ratio. As we saw when experimenting with the projection matrix in Cube Chaser, this will cause anything drawn using the `WideProjection` matrix to appear stretched out horizontally. This will help us mask the fact that the background we will be using is essentially plastered onto the inside of a cube and rotating around the player's viewpoint continuously.

When we create the instance of the `Camera` class, we will specify a position slightly above the XZ plane, and `115` pixels towards the player along the Z axis. By specifying a view angle of `180` degrees, we are looking back straight along the Z axis.

At the moment we have nothing for our camera to show us. Let's rectify that.

Creating the background

If the player is good at playing Mars Runner, they could drive along the surface of the planet for quite a while. This creates a challenge when displaying the planetary background—how do we display a continuous background image no matter how far the player travels?

We have a couple of options here. We could create a background panel with a seamless texture on it and place multiple copies of it in the right position so they march past the camera at the appropriate rate. We are going to do exactly that to implement the track that our player will drive on.

We could also revert to using 2D images for the background. We would simply need to draw enough copies of the image, offsetting it as the player travels, to fill the display.

Both of these approaches would work for Mars Runner as we are implementing it in this book, but what would happen if we allowed the camera to move or rotate? Our flat background panels would quickly be revealed for what they are, and if we were using a repeated 2D image the background might not change at all.

Instead, we will implement a very common and handy technique for 3D games: the skybox. By creating a cube and mapping a texture to its inside walls, we can draw it large enough that it encompasses our entire viewing area. The texture on the inner surfaces of the cube will appear to be a seamless background image.

As with most coding tasks, there are multiple ways we could go about creating a skybox. It is quite common to load a model with the skybox mapped to it. On the other hand, we only need a cube with six faces, and we happen to have most of the code we need to create—in the Cube Chaser game.

Time for action – creating a skybox

To create a skybox for Mars Runner, perform the following steps:

1. Add a new class file called `Skybox.cs` to the `Mars Runner` project.

2. Add the following `using` declaration at the beginning of the `Skybox` class file:

```
using Microsoft.Xna.Framework;
using Microsoft.Xna.Framework.Graphics;
```

3. Add fields to the `Skybox` class as follows:

```
#region Fields
private GraphicsDevice device;
private Texture2D texture;
private VertexBuffer cubeVertexBuffer;
private List<VertexPositionTexture> vertices = new
    List<VertexPositionTexture>();
private float rotation = 0f;
#endregion
```

4. Create a constructor for the `Skybox` class as follows:

```
#region Constructor
public Skybox(
    GraphicsDevice graphicsDevice,
    Texture2D texture)
{
    device = graphicsDevice;
    this.texture = texture;

    // Create the cube's vertical faces
    BuildFace(
        new Vector3(0, 0, 0),
        new Vector3(0, 1, 1),
        new Vector2(0, 0.25f)); // west face
    BuildFace(
        new Vector3(0, 0, 1),
        new Vector3(1, 1, 1),
        new Vector2(0.75f, 0.25f)); // south face
    BuildFace(
```

```
        new Vector3(1, 0, 1),
        new Vector3(1, 1, 0),
        new Vector2(0.5f, 0.25f)); // east face
    BuildFace(
        new Vector3(1, 0, 0),
        new Vector3(0, 1, 0),
        new Vector2(0.25f, 0.25f)); // North face

    // Create the cube's horizontal faces
    BuildFaceHorizontal(
        new Vector3(1, 1, 0),
        new Vector3(0, 1, 1),
        new Vector2(0.25f, 0)); // Top face
    BuildFaceHorizontal(
        new Vector3(1, 0, 1),
        new Vector3(0, 0, 0),
        new Vector2(0.25f, 0.5f)); // Bottom face

    cubeVertexBuffer = new VertexBuffer(
        device,
        VertexPositionTexture.VertexDeclaration,
        vertices.Count,
        BufferUsage.WriteOnly);

    cubeVertexBuffer.SetData<VertexPositionTexture>(
        vertices.ToArray());
}
#endregion
```

5. Add helper methods to implement the `BuildFace()`, `BuildFaceHorizontal()`, and `BuildVertex()` methods in the `Skybox` class as follows:

```
#region Helper Methods
private void BuildFace(Vector3 p1, Vector3 p2, Vector2 txCoord)
{
    vertices.Add(BuildVertex(
        p1.X, p1.Y, p1.Z, txCoord.X + 0.25f, txCoord.Y + 0.25f));
    vertices.Add(BuildVertex(
        p2.X, p2.Y, p2.Z, txCoord.X, txCoord.Y));
    vertices.Add(BuildVertex(
        p1.X, p2.Y, p1.Z, txCoord.X + 0.25f, txCoord.Y));

    vertices.Add(BuildVertex(
        p1.X, p1.Y, p1.Z, txCoord.X + 0.25f, txCoord.Y + 0.25f));
    vertices.Add(BuildVertex(
```

```
        p2.X, p1.Y, p2.Z, txCoord.X, txCoord.Y + 0.25f));
    vertices.Add(BuildVertex(
        p2.X, p2.Y, p2.Z, txCoord.X, txCoord.Y));
}

private void BuildFaceHorizontal(
    Vector3 p1, Vector3 p2, Vector2 txCoord)
{

    vertices.Add(BuildVertex(
        p1.X, p1.Y, p1.Z, txCoord.X, txCoord.Y + 0.25f));
    vertices.Add(BuildVertex(
        p2.X, p2.Y, p2.Z, txCoord.X + 0.25f, txCoord.Y));
    vertices.Add(BuildVertex(
        p2.X, p1.Y, p1.Z, txCoord.X + 0.25f, txCoord.Y + 0.25f));

    vertices.Add(BuildVertex(
        p1.X, p1.Y, p1.Z, txCoord.X, txCoord.Y + 0.25f));
    vertices.Add(BuildVertex(
        p1.X, p1.Y, p2.Z, txCoord.X, txCoord.Y));
    vertices.Add(BuildVertex(
        p2.X, p2.Y, p2.Z, txCoord.X + 0.25f, txCoord.Y));
}

private VertexPositionTexture BuildVertex(
    float x,
    float y,
    float z,
    float u,
    float v)
{
    return new VertexPositionTexture(
    new Vector3(x, y, z),
    new Vector2(u, v));
}
#endregion
```

6. Add the Draw() method to display the skybox as follows:

```
#region Draw
public void Draw(Camera camera, BasicEffect effect)
{
    effect.VertexColorEnabled = false;
    effect.TextureEnabled = true;
    effect.Texture = texture;
```

```
effect.LightingEnabled = false;

Matrix center = Matrix.CreateTranslation(
    new Vector3(-0.5f, -0.5f, -0.5f));
Matrix scale = Matrix.CreateScale(200f);

Matrix translate = Matrix.CreateTranslation(camera.Position);

Matrix rot = Matrix.CreateRotationY(rotation);

effect.World = center * rot * scale * translate;
effect.View = camera.View;
effect.Projection = camera.WideProjection;

foreach (EffectPass pass in effect.CurrentTechnique.Passes)
{
    pass.Apply();
    device.SetVertexBuffer(cubeVertexBuffer);
    device.DrawPrimitives(
        PrimitiveType.TriangleList,
        0,
        cubeVertexBuffer.VertexCount / 3);
}
}
#endregion
```

7. In the `MarsRunnerPlayScreen` class, add a field for the skybox and an effect that we will use to draw it to the `Fields` region as follows:

```
Skybox skybox;
BasicEffect effect;
```

8. In the `LoadContent()` method of the `MarsRunnerPlayScreen` class, initialize the skybox and the effect that we will use just before the call to `base.LoadContent()` as follows:

```
if (content == null) content = new
    ContentManager(ScreenManager.Game.Services, "Content");

skybox = new Skybox(
    ScreenManager.GraphicsDevice,
    content.Load<Texture2D>(@"textures\mars_skybox"));

effect = new BasicEffect(ScreenManager.GraphicsDevice);
```

9. Finally, add an override for the `Draw()` method to the `MarsRunnerPlayScreen` class as follows:

```
#region Draw
public override void Draw(GameTime gameTime)
{

    ScreenManager.GraphicsDevice.DepthStencilState =
        DepthStencilState.Default;

    skybox.Draw(camera, effect);

    base.Draw(gameTime);
}
#endregion
```

10. Execute the game and view the skybox from the camera's position as shown in the following screenshot:

What just happened?

We have quite a bit of code here, but most of it is straight from the Cube Chaser `Cube` class, with a few small modifications.

You will recall that the cube in Cube Chaser rotated in two directions, around the Y axis and around the Z axis and could be placed anywhere in the game level. Our skybox only needs to rotate around the Y axis, so we have removed all references to the `zrotation` field from the original Cube Chaser code. The `location` field has also been eliminated, because the skybox will never need to have a position within the game world.

The second important difference between this cube and the cube we made for Cube Chaser is the way we want to map textures to it. Our skybox will be viewed from the inside, while Cube Chaser's cube was displayed from the outside. When the skybox is drawn, it will be positioned so that the camera is at the center of the box. If we used the same vertex creation order for the skybox as for the cube, we would not see any of our textures – remember that the triangles we draw are one-sided. By reversing the order, we are flipping each face of the cube around so that the textured surfaces face inward.

For this reason, we flip the second and third coordinate of each triangle's vertex in `BuildFace()` and `BuildFaceHorizonal()`. This gives us the vertices in the reverse order, allowing the triangles to be seen from the inside. Additionally, instead of specifying absolute (u, v) coordinates for texture mapping, we have instead passed in a `Vector2` instance, which represents the base location inside a larger texture for each triangle to use.

We can see the reason for this by looking at the following actual texture image used for the skybox:

Recall that, while not strictly necessary for many of today's modern video cards, our texture sizes work out best when they are powers of two (64, 128, 256, and so on). In the case of our skybox texture, we are using a texture that is 2048 x 2048 pixels. The visuals are placed on the texture to form an unwrapped cube shape. If you were to print out the texture image, cut away the black areas, and fold the remaining shape into a box, you would have a physical representation of the skybox we are building, though from the outside all you would see is plain white paper.

As our texture is sized to a power of two, we can divide it up nicely for texture coordinates in increments of $0.25f$ units. Remember that in (u, v) coordinates, the upper-left corner of the texture is ($0f$, $0f$), while the lower-right corner is ($1f$, $1f$). As the vertical faces of our cube are laid out in four sections horizontally along the texture and one quarter of the way down, they have (u,v) coordinates as ($0f$, $0.25f$) for the leftmost face, ($0.25f$, $0.25f$) for the second face, and so on across the texture. The portion of the texture used for each face is $0.25f$ units wide and $0.25f$ units tall.

The final major difference between this code and the code in Cube Chaser comes in the `Draw()` method. We still center the cube at the origin, but we now scale the cube by a factor of 200. The actual scale is not too important (by itself, it would look exactly the same without any scaling or scaled dramatically higher). The important thing is that it is scaled large enough to appear behind anything else that we will be drawing in the scene. Otherwise 3D objects such as our rover and alien craft could be hidden behind the sky.

Further, instead of calculating the translation matrix based on a world position for the skybox, we use the camera's current location to determine the translation matrix. This means the skybox will always be drawn with the camera at its center. This is not too critical for Mars Runner since the camera will never move anyway, but in a game using an FPS camera, this keeps the sky in the right position as the player moves around in the level.

Also changed in the `Draw()` method is the projection matrix we use for drawing the skybox. This particular change is specific to the way we will be using the skybox in Mars Runner. You would normally want to use the standard projection matrix for an FPS-style game. The reason we are using a wider projection is that we are going to slowly rotate the skybox to simulate the player travelling in a straight line along the Martian terrain. With a standard projection, the fact that the background is rotating is easily visible as features of the background enter from the sides and dip downward as they approach the center of the screen. The wider projection helps to mask that effect somewhat, even though it does not eliminate it entirely.

What happens to the corners of the skybox? Since the camera is always in the center of the box, the texture that is mapped onto the cube's faces is seamless, and as there is no lighting applied to the skybox, the seams visually disappear. Here is a view of the skybox rendered from outside:

From the preceding screenshot, it is a little easier to see that the image is actually being mapped to the inside of the box. As the faces of the box closest to the viewpoint in the preceding screenshot are turned inward, we do not see them from outside, allowing us to see into the box.

Creating your own skyboxes

The skybox image used in Mars Runner was created with Terragen Classic, available for no cost at `http://www.planetside.co.uk/`. If you search the web for "terragen skybox tutorial" you will find any number of tutorials on creating skybox images.

One last important point: In the updated `Draw()` method for the `MarsRunnerPlayScreen` class, before we draw our skybox, we set the `GraphicsDevice.DepthStencilState` property to its default. This might seem odd at first as we are not setting it to anything else, and we have not been mixing 2D and 3D graphics. Or have we? The GSM system uses `SpriteBatch` extensively for backgrounds and menu text, and as we saw when adding our UI to Tank Battles, the `SpriteBatch.End()` method does not reset all of the rendering parameters that the `SpriteBatch.Begin()` method changes. Remember that our background screen is still being drawn, even though we have covered it up with other graphics. As we never know what kind of state we might have been left in, it is safest just to reset this value before we draw any of our 3D meshes.

We will come back and add rotation to our skybox to give it the appearance of motion after we have a surface for our player to drive their rover on. In order to do that, we will revisit heightmaps.

Building the Martian surface

Just as we have been able to make use of the concepts and code we have learned previously to allow us to build a skybox, we can also call upon our knowledge of heightmap-based terrain in order to create the track that the player will drive along. As earlier, we will customize and streamline the code a bit to implement the features we need for Mars Runner.

Simplified heightmaps

In Tank Battles, we used large, detailed heightmaps to create a nicely varied terrain. Our goal in Mars Runner is somewhat different, so our heightmap implementation will change to accommodate that difference. The heightmaps we will be using in Mars Runner are shown in the following image:

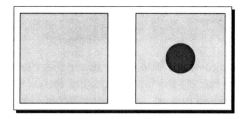

As you can see, our heightmaps are very simple. Each of our two heightmaps is a 16 x 16 pixel image. The image on the left-hand side is a solid shade of gray, meaning that the entire map will have the same elevation if we made no changes to the code that creates the mesh.

The image on the right-hand side represents a crater in the Martian surface. It has the same shade of gray for the border as the first heightmap, but with a darker spot at the center which will produce a deeply plunging pit at the center of the mesh.

In order to form the track the player will drive on, we will create an array of integers representing either a clear, flat track section, or a cratered section. When we draw the track, we will only draw the pieces that happen to be in front of the camera at the time.

Time for action – beginning the MarsTrack class

To create a track for the player to drive on, perform the following steps:

1. Add a new class file called `MarsTrack.cs` to the `Mars Runner` project.

2. Add the following `using` directives to the top of the `MarsTrack` class file:

```
using Microsoft.Xna.Framework.Graphics;
using Microsoft.Xna.Framework.Content;
using Microsoft.Xna.Framework;
```

3. Add fields to the `MarsTrack` class as follows:

```
#region Fields
private GraphicsDevice device;
private Texture2D marsTexture;

private List<VertexBuffer> vertexBuffers = new
List<VertexBuffer>();
private List<IndexBuffer> indexBuffers = new List<IndexBuffer>();

private float terrainScale = 30f;

private int[] track;
#endregion
```

4. Add a constructor to the `MarsTrack` class as follows:

```
#region Constructor
public MarsTrack(GraphicsDevice device, ContentManager content)
{
    this.device = device;
    track = GenerateTrack(100);
    marsTexture = content.Load<Texture2D>(@"Textures\mars_
surface");
    BuildHeightMap(
        content.Load<Texture2D>(@"HeightMaps\NormalPath"),
        new Vector3(0, -35, 49));
    BuildHeightMap(
        content.Load<Texture2D>(@"HeightMaps\CraterPath"),
        new Vector3(0, -35, 49));

}
#endregion
```

5. Add the `Height Maps` region and the `BuildHeightMap()` method to the `MarsTrack` class as follows:

```
#region Height Maps
private void BuildHeightMap(Texture2D texture, Vector3
vertexOffset)
{
    int width = texture.Width;
    int height = texture.Height;
    int elements = width * height;
    VertexPositionNormalTexture[] vertices =
        new VertexPositionNormalTexture[elements];
```

```
Random rand = new Random();

Color[] colorData = new Color[elements];
texture.GetData(colorData);

for (int x = 0; x < width; x++)
    for (int z = 0; z < height; z++)
    {
        int randFactor = rand.Next(8) - 4;
        if (x == 0 || x == width - 1)
            randFactor = 0;

        float y = (float)(colorData[x + z * width].R +
            randFactor) / 255f * terrainScale;

        vertices[x + z * width].Position =
            new Vector3(x * 2, y, z * 2) + vertexOffset;

        vertices[x + z * width].TextureCoordinate =
            new Vector2(
                (float)x / (float)width,
                (float)z / (float)height);

        vertices[x + z * width].Normal = Vector3.Zero;
    }

int indexCount = (width - 1) * (height - 1) * 6;
short[] indices = new short[indexCount];
int counter = 0;

for (short z = 0; z < height - 1; z++)
    for (short x = 0; x < width - 1; x++)
    {
        short upperLeft = (short)(x + (z * width));
        short upperRight = (short)(upperLeft + 1);
        short lowerLeft = (short)(upperLeft + width);
        short lowerRight = (short)(upperLeft + width + 1);

        indices[counter++] = upperLeft;
        indices[counter++] = lowerRight;
        indices[counter++] = lowerLeft;
        indices[counter++] = upperLeft;
        indices[counter++] = upperRight;
        indices[counter++] = lowerRight;
```

```
    }

int triangleCount = indices.Length / 3;

for (int x = 0; x < triangleCount; x++)
{
    int v1 = indices[x * 3];
    int v2 = indices[(x * 3) + 1];
    int v3 = indices[(x * 3) + 2];

    Vector3 firstSide =
        vertices[v2].Position - vertices[v1].Position;

    Vector3 secondSide =
        vertices[v1].Position - vertices[v3].Position;

    Vector3 triangleNormal =
        Vector3.Cross(firstSide, secondSide);

    triangleNormal.Normalize();

    vertices[v1].Normal += triangleNormal;
    vertices[v2].Normal += triangleNormal;
    vertices[v3].Normal += triangleNormal;

    if (x % width == 0)
    {
        if (v1 + width < width * height)
            vertices[v1 + width].Normal += triangleNormal;

        if (v3 + width < width * height)
            vertices[v3 + width].Normal += triangleNormal;
    }

    if (x % width == width - 1)
    {
        if (v2 - width >= 0)
            vertices[v2 + width].Normal += triangleNormal;
    }
}

for (int x = 0; x < vertices.Length; x++)
```

```
        vertices[x].Normal.Normalize();


    VertexBuffer vertexBuffer = new VertexBuffer(
        device,
        typeof(VertexPositionNormalTexture),
        vertices.Length,
        BufferUsage.None);

    vertexBuffer.SetData(vertices);

    IndexBuffer indexBuffer = new IndexBuffer(
        device,
        IndexElementSize.SixteenBits,
        indices.Length,
        BufferUsage.None);

    indexBuffer.SetData(indices);

    vertexBuffers.Add(vertexBuffer);
    indexBuffers.Add(indexBuffer);
}
#endregion
```

What just happened?

The `BuildHeightMap()` method contains quite a bit of code, so let's pause here and see what we have so far. As with the code to construct the skybox, much of this code comes directly from our existing work. This time, we pull it from the `Terrain` class in Tank Battles.

There are three new fields of interest in the `MarsTrack` class. The most obvious is the `track` array. `track` is an array of integers, each one representing a segment along the course of the track. For each entry in the array, a zero represents a flat portion of the track, while a one represents a crater.

We also have two new `List` objects declared, `vertexBuffers` and `indexBuffers`. Because we are going to have what is essentially a tile-based system of track pieces, we will build our mesh buffers and store them in these lists. The index into each list will determine which buffer will be drawn when we go to draw a track segment.

The constructor caches the `GraphicsDevice` and loads the texture we will be using for the Mars surface. This is actually just a recolored version of the rock/dirt texture we used for the central region of the landscape in Tank Battles.

Next, the constructor calls `BuildHeightMap()` to create meshes based on the two heightmaps in the previous image. In addition to the heightmap image to use, a new parameter allowing us to specify an offset for each of the vertices generated for the heightmap has been added to the method call. The value here `(0, -35, 49)` positions the resulting mesh so that, given the position of our camera, it will align with the bottom of our display window by lowering it along the Y axis by 35 units. It is also pushed forward toward the player's viewpoint by 49 units along the Z axis.

Finally, the constructor calls the `generateTrack()` method, which we have not yet implemented. We will get to that shortly, but first let's look at the new `BuildHeightMap()` method.

The `BuildHeightMap()` method is actually a combination of the `ReadHeightMap()`, `BuildVertexBuffer()`, `BuildIndexBuffer()`, and `CalculateNormals()` methods from the `Terrain` class in Tank Battles, all rolled into one. Because we are doing everything at the same time, we can tweak the code a bit.

Instead of creating an array of heights like we did in Tank Battles, we loop through the color data for the heightmap and create the vertex positions directly from the image. Inside the nested `for` loops where we do this, we introduce something new, a randomization factor, giving each point in the height map a range of plus or minus eight from its actual color value everywhere except the left and right-hand sides of the heightmap (where `x==0` or `x==width-1`). The randomization of the vertices will create a nice bumpy effect to keep our landscape from looking like a simple flat plane, but we also want the edges of the segments to match up seamlessly, so we ensure there is no randomization along the edges where the two track segments meet.

The X and Z coordinates of the vertex are multiplied by two, so given our 16 x 16 pixel heightmap (which would normally produce a 15 x 15 unit terrain) we will end up with a piece of terrain that is 30 x 30 units in size.

The indices and normals are calculated just as they are in Tank Battles. The only difference here is that they are calculated at the time the vertex buffer is generated instead of splitting them into their own methods. Since we still have the vertex and index arrays at this point, (they have not been placed into their respective buffers yet) we do not need to extract their data from the buffers. We simply use the arrays as they are.

Once all of the normals have been calculated, we build both `VertexBuffer` and `IndexBuffer` and store the data from our arrays into them. Finally, we add these buffers to the `vertexBuffers` and `indexBuffers` list so we can retrieve them for display later. Before we can draw our track, though, we need to generate it.

Time for action – generating the track

To generate the track for our Mars Runner, perform the following steps:

1. Add the `Helper Methods` region, along with the `GenerateTrack()` method to the `MarsTrack` class as follows:

```
#region Helper Methods
private int[] GenerateTrack(int length)
{
    Random rand = new Random();

    int[] track = new int[length];
    for (int x = 0; x < length; x++)
    {
        track[x] = 0;

        if (x < 5)
            continue;

        if (x > length - 6)
            continue;

        if (track[x - 1] != 1)
        {
            if (rand.Next(0, 4) == 0)
            {
                track[x] = 1;
            }
        }
    }

    return track;
}
#endregion
```

What just happened?

We loop through each segment of the track, beginning with the assumption that each segment will represent solid ground (a value of zero). If we are within the first or last five segments of the track, we continue the loop, we do not want to have crater segments show up too soon or the player will not have an opportunity to jump the first crater. We also want a clear ending area where the player can come to a stop at the end of the level.

If we are not within five segments of either end of the track, we need to randomly determine if we should change this segment of track into a crater. First, though, we check to see if the previous segment is a crater. We do not want to place two craters in a row, or the player will not have a place to land between jumps.

Assuming we actually can place a crater at a given segment, we then determine if we should do so. There is a one in four chance of a track space that passes the criteria ending up as a crater – a probability you could increase to raise the difficulty as the player progressed through multiple levels if you expand on the Mars Runner game. If a segment is going to become a crater, we set its value to one.

Drawing the track

Just like our terrain from Tank Battles, we will use the `DrawIndexedPrimitives()` method to display our Martian surface. On the other hand, we want to display one or both of our two possible terrain meshes multiple times. Each one will need to be drawn with an offset along the X axis so it appears in the appropriate position.

Time for action – drawing the track

To draw the track for Mars Runner, perform the following steps:

1. Add the `Draw` region and its two methods to the `MarsTrack` class as follows:

```
#region Draw
public void Draw(Camera camera, BasicEffect effect, float offset)
{
    effect.View = camera.View;
    effect.Projection = camera.Projection;
    effect.TextureEnabled = true;
    effect.Texture = marsTexture;
    effect.EnableDefaultLighting();

    float drawBase = 60f;
    drawBase += offset % 30f;
    int firstSector = (int)(offset / 30f);

    for (int x = 0; x < 5; x++)
    {
        if (firstSector + x >= 0 && firstSector + x < track.
Length)
        {
            DrawTerrainMeshInstance(
                track[firstSector + x],
```

```
                                    effect,
                                    drawBase - (x * 30f));
                    }
            }
    }

    private void DrawTerrainMeshInstance(
        int meshIndex,
        BasicEffect effect,
        float horizontalOffset)
    {
        effect.World = Matrix.Identity *
            Matrix.CreateTranslation(
                new Vector3(-horizontalOffset, 0, 0));

        foreach (EffectPass pass in effect.CurrentTechnique.Passes)
        {
            pass.Apply();
            device.SetVertexBuffer(vertexBuffers[meshIndex]);
            device.Indices = indexBuffers[meshIndex];
            device.DrawIndexedPrimitives(
                PrimitiveType.TriangleList,
                0,
                0,
                vertexBuffers[meshIndex].VertexCount,
                0,
                indexBuffers[meshIndex].IndexCount / 3);
        }
    }
    #endregion
```

2. In the `MarsRunnerPlayScreen` class, add a new field for the track itself and the position of the player as follows:

```
MarsTrack track;
float playerPosition = 0f;
```

3. In the `LoadContent()` method of the `MarsRunnerPlayScreen` class, initialize the track just before the call to `base.LoadConent()` method as follows:

```
track = new MarsTrack(ScreenManager.GraphicsDevice, content);
```

4. In the `Draw()` method of the `MarsRunnerPlayScreen` class, draw the track after the skybox has been drawn:

```
track.Draw(camera, effect, playerPosition);
```

5. Execute the game and view the track drawn in front of the skybox as shown in the following screenshot:

What just happened?

The Draw() method sets up the parameters for the BasicEffect class which we will use to draw our heightmaps. We also call the effect.EnableDefaultLighting() method, which tells the BasicEffect class to use a built-in default lighting setup designed to simulate a standard three-light rig. Details on the default lighting setup for the BasicEffect class can be found in Shawn Hargreaves' blog entry on the subject here: http://blogs.msdn.com/b/shawnhar/archive/2007/04/09/the-standard-lighting-rig.aspx

Why BasicEffect?

You may have noticed that we are not implementing any custom HLSL for Tank Battles. There are a couple of reasons for this. First, we are not implementing any visual effects that the BasicEffect class cannot already handle, so adding our own effect file would just be extra work. Second, if you intend to target the Windows Phone platform with your XNA games, custom effect files are not supported. You will need to find ways to produce the effects you want with the built-in effects.

Next, we need to determine where we are going to draw the ground segments that make up the track. Remember that our camera is positioned along the positive Z axis, slightly above the XZ plane. It is looking back along the Z axis towards the origin. As the vertices in our terrain are designed with the upper-left corner at the origin, if we were to simply draw our terrain as is, each piece would be stacked on top of each other to the right-hand side of the center from our camera's view.

Each segment of terrain is 30 units wide. If we were to offset the draw position of the first terrain segment 30 units along the negative X axis, it would appear to the right-hand side of the center of the viewpoint, but it would not extend all the way off the screen. For this reason, we want to start drawing terrain segments two positions to the left-hand side of the center. This is the reason for the `drawBase` variable and its initial value of `60f`.

Although we have not yet implemented the player's rover, and therefore not allowed the player to move along the track, we allow for the player's current position (how far they have travelled from their initial position of zero) to be passed to the `Draw()` method. Since our terrain tiles are 30 units wide, as the player's position slowly increments towards a multiple of 30, we need to shift our drawing offset further to the left-hand side of the screen. To do this, we divide the offset by 30 and add the remainder of the division to the `drawBase` variable.

In order to determine which style segment to draw for each position, we need to determine the index into the track array that corresponds to a given offset. We can do this simply by dividing the offset by 30 and truncating the result.

After we have this `drawBase` and the index of the first segment to draw, we loop and draw five segments, subtracting 30 from the `drawBase` location each time. The actual drawing of the terrain is handled by the `DrawTerrainMeshInstance()` method.

In order to draw a terrain segment, the `DrawTerrainMeshInstance()` method calculates a world matrix based on the offset passed to it. With the translation matrix corresponding to this offset calculated, we draw the terrain just as we have before, passing the `TriangleList` enumeration to the `DrawIndexedPrimitives()` method.

Summary

We have laid the groundwork for the Mars Runner game, integrating our own code into the Game State Management sample system and creating both a skybox and a track for our player to drive along.

We have seen how the code concepts we have implemented in earlier games can be tweaked and updated for our new endeavors. We will continue this trend in *Chapter 10, Mars Runner – Reaching the Finish Line*, as we complete the Mars Runner game by adding the player's rover, the alien ship, and all of the gameplay elements we need, to tie the various pieces of the game together.

10
Mars Runner – Reaching the Finish Line

The Mars Runner game is in pretty good shape so far. We have implemented the GSM system from the GSM sample code provided by Microsoft, and we have created a skybox to represent the Martian landscape. We have built heightmaps in such a way that they sequence as segments of a track along the surface of Mars for our player to drive their rover on.

Of course, to drive the rover, we actually need to implement it! Because the resource is available to us, we will use the same 3D model for the rover that we used for the tanks in Tank Battles.

In this chapter, we will cover the following:

- Generalizing our code for using and displaying 3D models
- Adding the player's Mars rover to the game, including movement controls
- Animating the background, track, and rover
- Adding an enemy UFO and allowing the player to fire shots at it
- Detecting collisions between the player, enemy, craters, and fired shots

Abstracting support for 3D models

We know we will need to support at least three different models in Mars Runner. The player will need a vehicle to drive, the alien enemy will be flying a saucer, and we will need projectiles for both the player and the enemy to fire.

Instead of building all of the code to support 3D model rendering into separate classes for each of the entities, we will create a base class that will handle the common functionality for our different objects' need.

Time for action – the GameEntity class

To add a class for implementing the common functionality in Mars Runner, perform the following steps:

1. Add a new class file called `GameEntity.cs` to the `Mars Runner` project.

2. Add the following `using` directives at the beginning of the `GameEntity` class file:

```
using Microsoft.Xna.Framework;
using Microsoft.Xna.Framework.Graphics;
```

3. Add fields to the `GameEntity` class as follows:

```
#region Fields
protected Model model;
protected GraphicsDevice device;
protected Vector3 position = Vector3.Zero;
protected float scale = 1.0f;
protected float yaw = 0f;
protected float pitch = 0f;
protected float roll = 0f;
protected Dictionary<string, Matrix> baseTransforms =
    new Dictionary<string, Matrix>();
protected Dictionary<string, Matrix> currentTransforms =
    new Dictionary<string, Matrix>();
protected Matrix[] boneTransforms;
protected Vector3 minVector;
protected Vector3 maxVector;
protected Vector3 drawOffset = Vector3.Zero;
#endregion
```

4. Add properties to the `GameEntity` class as follows:

```
#region Properties
public virtual Vector3 Position
{
    get { return position; }
    set { position = value; }
}

public float Scale
{
```

```
            get { return scale; }
            set { scale = value; }
        }

    public BoundingBox Bounds
    {
        get
        {
            Matrix scaleMatrix = Matrix.CreateScale(scale);
            Matrix rotate = Matrix.CreateFromYawPitchRoll(
                yaw, pitch, roll);
            Matrix translate = Matrix.CreateTranslation(position);

            Matrix transform = scaleMatrix * rotate * translate;

            Vector3 v1 = Vector3.Transform(minVector, transform);
            Vector3 v2 = Vector3.Transform(maxVector, transform);
            Vector3 boxMin = Vector3.Min(v1, v2);
            Vector3 boxMax = Vector3.Max(v1, v2);

            return new BoundingBox(
                boxMin,
                boxMax);
        }
    }
    #endregion
```

5. Add a constructor for the GameEntity class as follows:

```
#region Constructor
public GameEntity(
    GraphicsDevice device,
    Model model,
    Vector3 position)
{
    this.device = device;
    this.model = model;
    Position = position;
    BasicEffect effect = null;

    boneTransforms = new Matrix[model.Bones.Count];

    for (int i = 1; i < model.Bones.Count; i++)
    {
        baseTransforms[model.Bones[i].Name] =
```

```
                model.Bones[i].Transform;

        currentTransforms[model.Bones[i].Name] =
            model.Bones[i].Transform;
    }

    minVector = new Vector3(
        float.MaxValue, float.MaxValue, float.MaxValue);
    maxVector = new Vector3(
        float.MinValue, float.MinValue, float.MinValue);

    foreach (ModelMesh mesh in model.Meshes)
    {
        foreach (ModelMeshPart part in mesh.MeshParts)
        {
            if (effect == null)
                effect = (BasicEffect)part.Effect.Clone();

            part.Effect = effect.Clone();

            VertexPositionNormalTexture[] vertexData = new
            VertexPositionNormalTexture[part.VertexBuffer.
VertexCount];
  part.VertexBuffer.GetData<VertexPositionNormalTexture>(vertexDa
ta);

            for (int i = 0; i < part.VertexBuffer.VertexCount; i++
)
            {
                minVector = Vector3.Min(
                    minVector,
                    vertexData[i].Position);
                maxVector = Vector3.Max(
                    maxVector,
                    vertexData[i].Position);
            }
        }
    }
}
#endregion
```

6. Add an empty `Update()` method to the `GameEntity` class as follows:

```
#region Update
public virtual void Update(GameTime gameTime)
{

}
#endregion
```

7. Add the `Draw()` method to the `GameEntity` class as follows:

```
#region Draw
public virtual void Draw(Camera camera)
{
    model.Root.Transform = Matrix.Identity *
        Matrix.CreateScale(scale) *
        Matrix.CreateFromYawPitchRoll(yaw, pitch, roll) *
        Matrix.CreateTranslation(position + drawOffset);

    foreach (string s in currentTransforms.Keys)
    {
        model.Bones[s].Transform = currentTransforms[s];
    }

    model.CopyAbsoluteBoneTransformsTo(boneTransforms);

    foreach (ModelMesh mesh in model.Meshes)
    {
        foreach (BasicEffect basicEffect in mesh.Effects)
        {
          basicEffect.World = boneTransforms[mesh.ParentBone.
Index];
            basicEffect.View = camera.View;
            basicEffect.Projection = camera.Projection;

            basicEffect.EnableDefaultLighting();
        }

        mesh.Draw();
    }
}
#endregion
```

What just happened?

Much of the `GameEntity` class is based on the code we used to set up and draw the tank model in Tank Battles. We have expanded the functionality a bit, so let's go over the whole thing, as it will be the basis for the other classes that we will implement later.

We store fields for familiar things like the `Model`, `GraphicsDevice`, location and rotation information, and the bone transformations we will apply to animate the model. We have also added two dictionary objects (`baseTransforms` and `currentTransforms`), and three `Vector3` values (`minVector`, `maxVector`, and `drawOffset`).

The `baseTransforms` dictionary is populated in the constructor to store the transforms for each bone in the model when the model is initialized. Recall that in Tank Battles, we stored the base transforms for the pieces of the tank we were going to be animating. Here, we are really doing the same thing in a more generic way. Each bone's base transform can be accessed by the bone's name in the dictionary.

Along the same lines, in Tank Battles we stored rotation information for the turret and the cannon. These values were stored as floats and translated to matrices when the model was drawn back then. By moving this functionality to a dictionary that stores the final transforms, we create a generic interface for setting the bone transforms on our models.

The `minVector` and `maxVector` values are calculated in the constructor as well. In the constructor's nested `foreach` loop, we examine each vertex to create a pair of coordinates that describe the outermost limits of the model. Note that the `Vector3.Min()` and `Vector3.Max()` methods do not simply compare the two vectors passed to them and return the smaller or larger vector. They match up each of the individual vector components (X, Y, and Z) and return a new vector with the most extreme of each component for each vector passed to it. For example, the `Max()` method's result for the vectors (10, 10, 10) and (8, 500, 1) will return (10, 500, 10). The `Min()` method's result for the same two vectors would return (8, 10, 1).

The `Bounds` property makes use of the `minVector` and `maxVector` values, along with the scale, rotation, and positional information for the model, to build a bounding box around the model that we can use for collision detection later.

The other important job performed by the constructor is the extraction of the effects from the model. Beginning with `effect` set to `null`, we clone the first effect we find in the model, and replace all of the effects with clones of the effect. Why in the world would we do this? If you remember, back in Tank Battles we resorted to using a separate `ContentManager` object to load a second copy of the tank model into memory in order to draw our second tank. It is actually the effects on the models that cause problems if we simply attempt to draw a model in two different positions.

By cloning the effects for each instance of the model we wish to draw, we can draw multiple copies of a model without the need for a second `ContentManager`.

Our `GameEntity` class does not need to do anything during the `Update()` method's execution, but we include an empty method so that our subclasses can override it. That just leaves `Draw()` to be implemented.

Again, to support drawing more than one instance of the model, we have a few minor changes from our tank drawing code. We now simply set the model's root transform to `Matrix.Identity` and handle scaling, rotating, and translating our model in a separate matrix. This matrix (called `world` in our code) is applied to each effect instead of being set on the root transform.

The only other change is in how we copy the current transforms. In Tank Battles, we were setting the transforms manually at this point. For the `GameEntity` class, we loop through the `currentTransforms` dictionary and read the desired values from there.

Building the rover

Now that we have a base class to handle 3D models, it is time to add our first game entity— the player's rover. We will do this over a couple of small steps, as it is important to see that with only a few lines of code, we can get a model up and into our game. The rest of the coding that we will need to do is for customizing the behaviors of each particular entity.

Time for action –building the rover

To build the player's rover, perform the following steps:

1. Add a new class file called `Rover.cs` to the `Mars Runner` project.

2. Add the following `using` directives to the top of the `Rover` class file:

   ```
   using Microsoft.Xna.Framework;
   using Microsoft.Xna.Framework.Graphics;
   ```

3. Modify the declaration of the `Rover` class to inherit from `GameEntity`. The new class declaration should read as follows:

   ```
   class Rover : GameEntity
   ```

4. Add a constructor for the `Rover` class as follows:

   ```
   #region Constructor
   public Rover(GraphicsDevice device, Model model, Vector3 position)
        : base(device, model, position)
   {
       scale = 0.015f;
   ```

```
yaw = MathHelper.ToRadians(90);
currentTransforms["canon_geo"] =
    Matrix.CreateRotationX(MathHelper.ToRadians(-90)) *
    baseTransforms["canon_geo"];
}
#endregion
```

5. In the `MarsRunnerPlayScreen` class, add a new field to hold an instance of the `Rover` class as follows:

```
Rover rover;
```

6. In the `LoadContent()` method of the `MarsRunnerPlayScreen` class, initialize the rover as follows:

```
rover = new Rover(ScreenManager.GraphicsDevice,
    content.Load<Model>(@"Models\tank"),
    new Vector3(0, -14, 64));
```

7. In the `Draw()` method of the `MarsRunnerPlayScreen` class, draw the rover after the track has been drawn as follows:

```
rover.Draw(camera);
```

8. Execute the game and view the rover as shown in the following screenshot:

What just happened?

Getting the rover into the game is pretty straightforward. All we need to do is set the scale (remember that the raw tank model is very large), set the yaw value to 90 degrees (causing the tank to face right from the camera's point of view) and point the cannon up at the sky. When we create the rover instance, we specify its position so that it is sitting on the track we created earlier. In the case of the rover, we specify -14 for the Y coordinate, which is different from the -35 value that we used for the track. Why the difference? Remember that the track is a heightmap. By giving it a Y position of -35, we set the zero-height of the terrain to -35. The gray color used in the heightmap image places the visible terrain somewhat above that zero point.

Now that we have the rover visible, it is time to add a little movement. Remember, though, that the way Mars Runner is designed, the movement range of the rover is very restricted. We will have the environment moving around the rover much more than the other way around.

In order to allow the player to move the rover, we need to add support for handling user input to the MarsRunnerPlayScreen class.

Time for action – accepting user input

To add support for handling user input to the MarsRunnerPlayScreen class, perform the following steps:

1. In the Fields region of the MarsRunnerPlayScreen class, add two new fields to track the player's desired movement direction and the base movement speed as follows:

```
int moveState = 0;
int moveSpeed = 8;
```

2. Add the HandleInput() override method to the MarsRunnerPlayScreen class as follows:

```
#region Handle Input
public override void HandleInput(InputState input)
{
    moveState = 0;
    if (
        (input.CurrentKeyboardStates[0].IsKeyDown(Keys.Left)) ||
        (input.CurrentGamePadStates[0].ThumbSticks.Left.X < -0.3f)
        )
    {
        moveState = 1;
```

```
        }

        if (
            (input.CurrentKeyboardStates[0].IsKeyDown(Keys.Right)) ||
            (input.CurrentGamePadStates[0].ThumbSticks.Left.X > 0.3f)
            )
        {
            moveState = 2;
        }

        if (
            (input.CurrentKeyboardStates[0].IsKeyDown(Keys.Up)) ||
            (input.CurrentGamePadStates[0].Buttons.A ==
                ButtonState.Pressed)
            )
        {
            rover.Jump();
        }

        base.HandleInput(input);
    }
    #endregion
```

3. Add the `Update()` method to the `MarsRunnerPlayScreen` class as follows:

```
#region Update
public override void Update(
    GameTime gameTime,
    bool otherScreenHasFocus,
    bool coveredByOtherScreen)
{
    if (IsActive)
    {
        float elapsed = (float)gameTime.ElapsedGameTime.
TotalSeconds;
        if (moveState == 1)
        {
            rover.Position = new Vector3(
                rover.Position.X - (moveSpeed * elapsed),
                rover.Position.Y,
                rover.Position.Z);
        }
        if (moveState == 2)
        {
```

```
        rover.Position = new Vector3(
            rover.Position.X + (moveSpeed * elapsed),
            rover.Position.Y,
            rover.Position.Z);
    }

    rover.Update(gameTime);


}

base.Update(gameTime, otherScreenHasFocus,
coveredByOtherScreen);
}
#endregion
```

4. In the `Rover` class, add five new fields that we will use to control how the rover moves, as follows:

```
#region Fields
public float groundElevation = -14;
private float minX = -25f;
private float maxX = 25f;
public Vector3 velocity = new Vector3(0, 0, 0);
public Vector3 gravity = new Vector3(0, -30, 0);
#endregion
```

5. Still in the `Rover` class, override the `Position` property as follows:

```
#region Properties
public override Vector3 Position
{
    get { return position; }
    set
    {
        position = new Vector3(
            MathHelper.Clamp(value.X, minX, maxX),
            value.Y,
            value.Z);
    }
}
#endregion
```

6. Add an additional property to the `Properties` region of the `Rover` class to determine if the rover is currently on the ground or not, as follows:

```
public bool IsOnGround
{
    get
    {
        return (position.Y <= groundElevation);
    }
}
```

Add an `Update()` method to the `Rover` class:

```
#region Update
public override void Update(GameTime gameTime)
{
    float elapsed = (float)gameTime.ElapsedGameTime.TotalSeconds;

    velocity += gravity * elapsed;
    position += velocity * elapsed;

    if (position.Y < groundElevation)
        position.Y = groundElevation;

    base.Update(gameTime);
}
#endregion
```

7. Add the `Jump()` method to the `Rover` class as follows:

```
#region Helper Methods
public void Jump()
{
    if (IsOnGround)
    {
        velocity = new Vector3(0, 30, 0);
    }
}
#endregion
```

8. Launch the game and move the rover around with the arrow keys on the keyboard or a gamepad. The rover in motion is shown in the following screenshot:

What just happened?

One oddity of the way the GSM sample code is set up is that the `HandleInput()` method does not get a `GameTime` value passed to it, so if we want to scale our movement based on the elapsed time (and we do, to avoid choppy movement), we need to store our intended movement for use in the next `Update()` cycle. Our `HandleInput()` method does this by setting a variable called `moveState` when the player wishes to move to the left-hand side or to the right-hand side.

The other interesting thing to note about the way the GSM handles input is that the `Update()` method for all screens gets called first, and then `HandleInput()` is called on the topmost screen. The results of our input will not actually happen until the following `Update()`/`Draw()` cycle.

When the GSM processes input, it gathers all of the possible input sources and consolidates their current states into an `InputState` instance. When we check for input, we check the first keyboard state and the first gamepad state. As the GSM is set up to handle multiple players, the second state value in each array would correspond to the second player, the third to the third, and so on.

Touch and mouse input

By default, the `InputState` class of GSM handles touch points and gesture support on platforms that support them (Windows Phone) but does not offer built-in support for mouse input. This can easily be added to the `InputState` class without breaking existing code that uses the class if you should wish to do so.

In the `Update()` method, we check for input we should respond to and make the appropriate alterations to the position of the rover. In order to constrain that position, we override the `GameEntity` class' default `Position` property in order to apply a clamping value to the X component of the position vector. This clamping range will keep the rover positioned within the view of the camera while allowing the tank to move to the left and right-hand side of the screen.

In order to implement the ability to jump (which will be critical if the player is to survive), we also need to implement a simple gravity simulation. In our case, we define `gravity` as a vector pointing down along the Y axis. In each `Update()` cycle, the `gravity` vector is added to the `velocity` vector for the rover, and the `velocity` vector is added to the rover's position. If the result of these modifications would take the rover below ground level, the Y position of the rover is reset to ground level.

All we need to do to begin a jump is set the Y component of `velocity` to a positive value. In our case, we have chosen 30 units/second as the initial jump velocity. Gravity will rapidly overcome this velocity, slowing the rover's upward movement until it starts to fall back toward the ground.

Animating the planet

We can now slide our rover back and forth along a small strip of ground, but otherwise Mars Runner is still relatively static. To simulate the rover actually crossing the terrain, we need to move both the track and the skybox in relation to the camera.

Time for action – moving the world

To move both the track and the skybox in relation to the camera, perform the following steps:

1. In the `Skybox` class, add a new property to allow us to set the rotation while maintaining a valid angle as follows:

```
#region Properties
public float Rotation
{
```

```
        get { return rotation; }
        set { rotation = MathHelper.WrapAngle(value); }
    }
    #endregion
```

2. Inside the `if` statement in the `Update()` method of the `MarsRunnerPlayScreen` class, just before the rover is updated, update the variable that controls the track position and rotate the skybox as follows:

```
if (playerPosition < 2880)
{
    playerPosition += 15 * elapsed;
    skybox.Rotation += 0.1f * elapsed;
}
```

3. Execute the game.

What just happened?

The way the track is drawn is based on the `playerPosition` variable. Hence, updating this value causes the track to scroll slowly past the camera. Similarly, slowly rotating the skybox to match the speed that the track is moving gives the illusion that the player is now rolling along the surface of Mars.

Animating the rover

Currently, the rover seems to glide along the surface of the planet. We know that we have wheels, and we already know the basics of animating parts of the tank model, so at the very least we should make the wheels roll while the tank is moving.

With a little added effort, we can actually do better than that, and bounce the wheels vertically to simulate driving over the rough Martian terrain.

Time for action – animating the rover

To animate the rover, perform the following steps:

1. Add several new fields to the `Fields` region of the `Rover` class to support wheel animation, as follows:

```
Random rand = new Random();
private float wheelRotation = 0f;
private float wheelBounceDelta = 0.01f;
private int wheelBounceRange = 20;
private float[] wheelBounceTargets = new float[4] {0f, 0f, 0f, 0f}
;
```

```
private float[] wheelBounceCurrent = new float[4] { 0f, 0f, 0f, 0f
};
private string[] wheelNames = new string[4]
{
    "r_back_wheel_geo",
    "l_back_wheel_geo",
    "r_front_wheel_geo",
    "l_front_wheel_geo"
};
```

2. Add the `Wheel Animation` region and the `GenerateWheelTarget()` method to the `Rover` class as follows:

```
#region Wheel Animation
private void GenerateWheelTarget(int wheel)
{
    float newBounceTarget = (float)rand.Next(0,
wheelBounceRange+1);
    newBounceTarget -= wheelBounceRange / 2;

    wheelBounceTargets[wheel] = newBounceTarget / 100f;
}
#endregion
```

3. Add the `HasWheelReachedTarget()` method to the `Wheel Animation` region of the `Rover` class as follows:

```
private bool HasWheelReachedTarget(int wheel)
{
    return (Math.Abs(wheelBounceTargets[wheel] -
        wheelBounceCurrent[wheel]) <= wheelBounceDelta);
}
```

4. Add the `UpdateWheels()` method to the `Wheel Animation` region of the `Rover` class as follows:

```
private void UpdateWheels()
{
    wheelRotation = MathHelper.WrapAngle(wheelRotation + 0.02f);

    for (int w = 0; w < 4; w++)
    {
        if (IsOnGround)
        {
            if (HasWheelReachedTarget(w))
            {
                GenerateWheelTarget(w);
```

```
                }

                if (wheelBounceTargets[w] > wheelBounceCurrent[w])
                {
                    wheelBounceCurrent[w] += wheelBounceDelta;
                }
                else
                {
                    wheelBounceCurrent[w] -= wheelBounceDelta;
                }
            }

            currentTransforms[wheelNames[w]] =
                Matrix.CreateRotationX(wheelRotation) *
                Matrix.CreateRotationZ(wheelBounceCurrent[w]) *
                baseTransforms[wheelNames[w]];
        }
    }
```

5. In the `Update()` method of the `Rover` class, call `UpdateWheels()`. Place the following call just before the call to the `base.Update()` method:

```
UpdateWheels();
```

6. Execute the game and watch the wheels rotate and bounce along the surface.

What just happened?

Of the two animations we are applying to the rover's wheels, the basic rotation is by far the simplest. We track a rotation amount and simply increase it by `0.02f` every `update()` cycle in order to spin the wheel. If we had not rotated the rover 90 degrees, the X axis would be parallel to the axel through the wheels, so the rotation we want to apply to the rover's wheels is around the X axis.

Letting the wheels bounce is slightly more involved, but not overly complicated. We begin by creating two arrays to hold information about the wheels. The first, `wheelBounceTargets`, holds the amount of skew the wheels should work their way towards, while the second, `wheelBonceCurrent`, tracks how much progress toward their goals each wheel has made.

When we generate a new target for a wheel to work towards, we get a random number between 0 and 20, and then subtract 10 from it, giving a total range of -10 to +10 for the new wheel target. As all of our angles are expressed in radians, this would be a very large (several full rotations) range of wheel movement. We divide the target by `100` in order to get a more reasonable bounce range for the wheel.

During each `Update()` cycle while on the ground (the wheels would not bounce up and down while the rover is jumping), the `wheelBounceDelta` value is added to or subtracted from the current wheel value until the desired target position has been reached. When it has, a new target is generated and the process starts all over again.

By setting the values of each wheel's component of the `currentTransforms` dictionary, we can combine the rotation matrices for both the wheel rotation and the wheel bounce, which is a rotation around the Z axis, in order to animate the model.

Crashing into craters

There are two ways the player can die in Mars Runner. The first is to fall into one of the craters on the track while driving. We will add support for this type of ending in a temporary fashion now, simply returning to the main menu when the player crashes into a crater. The second way to die is to be hit by a shot from the enemy saucer. That will have to wait until we actually create the saucer.

Time for action – detecting craters

To detect the craters on the track, perform the following steps:

1. Add the `GetTrackSegment()` method to `Helper Methods` region of the `MarsTrack` class as follows:

```
public int GetTrackSegment(float position)
{
    return track[(int)(position / 30f)];
}
```

2. Add a new field to the `Fields` region of the `MarsRunnerPlayScreen` class to flag the game as having ended as follows:

```
bool gameEnded = false;
```

3. At the very beginning of the `Update()` method in the `MarsRunnerPlayScreen` class, add the following lines of code to return to the main menu if the game has ended:

```
if (gameEnded && !otherScreenHasFocus)
{
    ScreenManager.AddScreen(new BackgroundScreen(), null);
    ScreenManager.AddScreen(new MainMenuScreen(), null);
    ExitScreen();
}
```

4. Still in the `Update()` method, inside the `if (IsActive)` block, add the following lines of code just after the call to the `rover.Update()` method:

```
if (CheckFallInPit())
{
    EndGame();
}
```

5. Add the `checkFallInPit()` method to the `MarsRunnerPlayScreen` class as follows:

```
#region Helper Methods
private bool CheckFallInPit()
{
    float trackPosition = 60f + playerPosition + rover.Position.X;
    int trackType = track. GetTrackSegment(trackPosition);
    float trackSubPosition = trackPosition % 30f;

    bool isPit = false;

    if ((trackType == 1) &&
        (rover.IsOnGround) &&
        (trackSubPosition > 5) &&
        (trackSubPosition < 25))
    {
        isPit = true;
    }

    return isPit;
}
#endregion
```

6. Add the `endGame()` method to the `Helper Methods` region of the `MarsRunnerPlayScreen` class as follows:

```
private void EndGame()
{
    gameEnded = true;
}
```

7. Execute the game and fall into a crater.

What just happened?

When we detect that the game has ended, we need to restore the screens that were in `ScreenManager` before `MarsRunnerPlayScreen` was loaded. Because the menu screen uses an instance of the `LoadScreen` class to load `MarsRunnerPlayScreen`, all of the other screens we have created and stored in `ScreenManager` are exited while `MarsRunnerPlayScreen` is loading.

Recall that `BackgroundScreen` and `MainMenuScreen` are the two screens added to `ScreenManager` during the initialization of the `Game` class. To return to that state, we simply add these same screens to the `ScreenManager` and exit our play screen.

Actually, detecting the player falling into a crater involves determining which segment on the track the player's rover is currently on. This involves several different variables. The `playerPosition` variable tracks how far along the track the screen has scrolled, while the rover's `Position` property determines the rover's position relative to the edge of the screen. By adding these two values, along with the same offset value (`60f`) that we used to offset the drawing of the track, we can determine which track segment the player is currently on by calling the track's `GetTrackSegmentAtPosition()` method.

Because the untransformed tank model would be centered at the origin, the model's `Position` property actually represents the position of the center of the model. Therefore, the position we just calculated is the position of the center of the rover along the track.

Additionally, the crater in our terrain mesh does not completely fill a track segment. For both of these reasons, we want to give the rover a bit of a cushion when it comes to detecting craters. We calculate `trackSubPosition` as the remainder obtained when dividing `trackPosition` by `30`. This will give us how far into the current segment the center of the rover is.

If the rover is between units `6` and `24` of a segment with a crater, and the rover is not jumping, we consider the player to have driven into a crater. We therefore set the `gameEnded` flag to `true`, which will be picked up and acted upon by the next `Update()` cycle.

Why not simply call `ExitScreen()` and reload the menu right here? Two reasons: first, we do not want to write the same code for the second way the player can be killed (being hit by the alien saucer's attacks), and second, we will expand on what happens when the game ends later, displaying a `GameOver` screen instead of just dropping back to the menu.

Adding an enemy

If all the player had to do to survive was jump the occasional crater, the Mars Runner game would not be very exciting. To add a bit more drama to the gameplay, we will add a flying saucer that will make random passes across the sky, dropping bombs down at the player.

Time for action – the basic flying saucer

To add a flying saucer to Mars Runner, perform the following steps:

1. Add a new class file called `EnemySaucer.cs` to the `Mars Runner` project.

2. Add the following `using` directives at the beginning of the `EnemySaucer` class file:

   ```
   using Microsoft.Xna.Framework;
   using Microsoft.Xna.Framework.Graphics;
   ```

3. Modify the declaration of the `EnemySaucer` class to inherit from the `GameEntity` class. The new declaration should read as follows:

   ```
   class EnemySaucer : GameEntity
   ```

4. Add a constructor for the `EnemySaucer` class as follows:

   ```
   #region Constructor
   public EnemySaucer(GraphicsDevice device, Model model, Vector3
   position)
        : base(device, model, position)
   {
       scale = 0.0025f;
       yaw = MathHelper.ToRadians(180);
   }
   #endregion
   ```

5. In the `Fields` region of the `MarsRunnerPlayScreen` class, add a new field for our enemy saucer as follows:

   ```
   EnemySaucer enemy;
   ```

6. In the `LoadContent()` method of the `MarsRunnerPlayScreen` class, initialize `enemy` as follows:

   ```
   enemy = new EnemySaucer(ScreenManager.GraphicsDevice,
       content.Load<Model>(@"Models\spaceship"),
       new Vector3(0, 15, 64));
   ```

7. In the `Draw()` method of the `MarsRunnerPlayScreen` class, draw the enemy just after the rover has been drawn:

   ```
   enemy.Draw(camera);
   ```

8. Execute the game. The alien saucer should now be hovering in the sky right over the player's head as shown in the following screenshot:

What just happened?

As with adding the rover, getting the enemy saucer into the game is very straightforward using our GameEntity class. In the constructor, we rotate the model by setting the yaw property to 180 degrees. The saucer model contains a green window with an alien looking out of it, and we want this window to face the player, so we rotate the model to bring the alien into the proper orientation.

Of course, an alien ship that just sits in one spot without doing anything is not really very exciting. We need to expand the EnemySaucer class to add movement and action to the craft.

We could simply have the saucer fly across the screen in a straight line, but in order to make the alien's flight more interesting, we will compute a spline curve to give the saucer a smoother, more realistic flight path.

Time for action – flying the saucer

In order to give the saucer a more realistic flight path, perform the following steps:

1. Add a new `Fields` region to the `EnemySaucer` class, containing the following items:

```
#region Fields
private Random rand = new Random();
private int flybyChance = 2;
private float minflyByDelay = 5f;
private float flyByTimer = 0f;
private float curveProgress = 0.0f;
private float curveDelta = 0.2f;
private Vector3[] curvePoints = new Vector3[4];
public bool IsOnScreen = false;
public bool IsDestroyed = false;
#endregion
```

2. Add the `Spline Helper Methods` region and its two methods to the `EnemySaucer` class as follows:

```
#region Spline Helper Methods
public void GenerateNewCurve()
{
  curvePoints[0] = new Vector3(-60, (rand.Next(0, 3) - 1) * 25,
64);
  curvePoints[1] = new Vector3(-45, rand.Next(12, 19), 64);
  curvePoints[2] = new Vector3(45, rand.Next(12, 19), 64);
  curvePoints[3] = new Vector3(60, (rand.Next(0, 3) - 1 * 25),
64);

  if (rand.Next(0, 2) == 0)
  {
      Vector3 temp = curvePoints[0];
      curvePoints[0] = curvePoints[3];
      curvePoints[3] = temp;
      temp = curvePoints[1];
      curvePoints[1] = curvePoints[2];
      curvePoints[2] = temp;
  }

  curveDelta = (float)(rand.Next(0, 4) + 1) / 10f;

  roll = 0f;
  pitch = 0f;
  IsDestroyed = false;
```

```
        curveProgress = 0f;
        position = ComputeCurrentLocation();
    }

    public Vector3 ComputeCurrentLocation()
    {
        return Vector3.CatmullRom(
            curvePoints[0],
            curvePoints[1],
            curvePoints[2],
            curvePoints[3],
            MathHelper.Clamp(curveProgress, 0f, 1f));
    }
    #endregion
```

3. Override the `Update()` method for the `EnemySaucer` class as follows:

```
#region Update
public override void Update(GameTime gameTime)
{
    float elapsed = (float)gameTime.ElapsedGameTime.TotalSeconds;

    if (IsOnScreen)
    {
        if (curveProgress < 1.0f)
        {
            curveProgress += (curveDelta * elapsed);
            Position = ComputeCurrentLocation();
        }
        else
        {
            IsOnScreen = false;
        }
    }
    else
    {
        flyByTimer += elapsed;
        if (flyByTimer >= minflyByDelay)
        {
            if (rand.Next(0, 100) < flybyChance)
            {
                IsOnScreen = true;
                flyByTimer = 0f;
                GenerateNewCurve();
            }
```

```
            }
        }

        base.Update(gameTime);
    }
    #endregion
```

4. Override the `Draw()` method for the `EnemySaucer` class as follows:

```
#region Draw
public override void Draw(Camera camera)
{
    if (!IsOnScreen)
        return;

    base.Draw(camera);
}
#endregion
```

5. In the `Update()` method of the `MarsRunnerPlayScreen` class, update the enemy saucer right after the rover has been updated:

```
enemy.Update(gameTime);
```

6. Execute the game and drive the rover, jumping over any craters, until the saucer flies by.

What just happened?

Our code in this section accomplishes two goals. First, it determines when the saucer should perform a flyby, based on the amount of time elapsed since the last flyby was completed and a small random factor. Second, we implement the flyby itself.

In order to initiate a flyby, two things must be true. We must have had enough time elapsed since the end of the last flyby (defined as 5 seconds by the `minflyByDelay` field), and a randomly generated number between 0 and 99. The result must be less than two for a flyby to be initiated. A two percent chance of initiating a flyby may not sound like much, but remember that this check will be running 60 times per second.

This logic is handled in the second portion of the `Update()` method, when the `IsOnScreen` flag is `false`. When a flyby gets initiated, `IsOnScreen` is set to `true` and the timer is reset. A new flight curve is then generated by calling the `GenerateNewCurve()` method.

XNA includes built-in support for Catmull-Rom splines, a special-case spline type that happens to be very useful for computer graphics and animation because it provides a continuous curve between two points, with those two points guaranteed to be the beginning and ending points of the spline. Given the points of a Catmull-Rom spline and a distance along the spline, XNA can interpolate coordinates along the spline, giving us smooth, curved motion.

But if a Catmull-Rom spline uses two points that lie on the spline, why are we defining four points? The other two points are control points used by the Catmull-Rom equation. The control points define the shape of the curve, but are not actually on the curve itself, as seen in the following image:

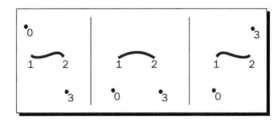

In order to generate a new curve, we just need to come up with these four points. We randomly generate their values, with certain constraints.

The first and last points (`curvePoints[0]` and `curvePoints[3]`) are the external control points. We generate these to be beyond the screen horizontally (along the X axis), and either 25 pixels above or below the origin on the Y axis. We keep the Z axis constant at 64, which is the same value we used for the rover.

The inner points that are actually on the curve are generated beyond the screen the screen along the X axis as well, with a random elevation along the Y axis. Again, the Z point is kept at 64 to keep the saucer aligned with the rover.

In the `GenerateNewCurve()` method, after the four points have been generated, we also randomly decide if we should reverse them. The way the points are generated by default, the saucer would travel from left to right across the screen. By reversing the control points, we can reverse this flight from right to left to provide a bit of variety.

Finally, `GenerateNewCurve()` resets the `roll`, `pitch`, and `IsDestroyed` fields to their defaults. We will make use of these fields later when we allow the player to shoot down the enemy saucer.

When determining the position along the curve, we keep track of a field called `curveProgress`. This number ranges from `0.0f` at the starting point to `1.0f` at the ending point. The rate that we move along the curve is defined by the `curveDelta` field, which is randomly set between `0.1f` and `0.4f` when the curve is generated. Again, this is simply to add variety to the path of the saucer across the screen.

The `ComputeCurrentLocation()` method uses the `Vector3.CatmullRom()` method to determine the current position on the curve, given the control points and the `curveProgress` field. During the `Update()` method, this value is stored into the saucer's `Position` property whenever the saucer is on the screen.

Shots and collisions

Now that we have a flying saucer to menace the player, both the alien and the player need the ability to fire shots at each other. We will implement two separate types of weapons—one for the player and one for the alien saucer.

The player's shots will travel upward at a constant rate until they either leave the screen or impact the alien saucer. The enemy's shots will act more like bombs, falling under the effect of gravity until they reach the ground.

Time for action – Shot classes

To implement the shots that the enemy and the player will fire at each other, perform the following steps:

1. Add a new class file called `PlayerShot.cs` to the `Mars Runner` project.

2. Add the following `using` directives to the `PlayerShot` class:

```
using Microsoft.Xna.Framework;
using Microsoft.Xna.Framework.Graphics;
```

3. Modify the declaration of the `PlayerShot` class to inherit from the `GameEntity` class. The new declaration should read as follows:

```
class PlayerShot : GameEntity
```

4. Add fields to the `PlayerShot` class as follows:

```
#region Fields
private Vector3 velocity = new Vector3(0, 30, 0);
public bool IsActive;
#endregion
```

5. Add a constructor to the `PlayerShot` class as follows:

```
#region Constructor
public PlayerShot(
    GraphicsDevice device,
    Model model,
    Vector3 position)
    : base(device, model, position)
```

```
    {
        scale = 0.25f;
        IsActive = true;
    }
    #endregion
```

6. Add the `ResetShot()` method to the `PlayerShot` class as follows:

```
#region Helper Methods
public void ResetShot(Vector3 position)
{
    Position = position;
    IsActive = true;
}
#endregion
```

7. Add the `Update()` method to the `PlayerShot` class as follows:

```
#region Update
public override void Update(GameTime gameTime)
{
    float elapsed = (float)gameTime.ElapsedGameTime.TotalSeconds;

    Position += velocity * elapsed;

    if (position.Y > 100)
    {
        IsActive = false;
    }

    base.Update(gameTime);
}
#endregion
```

8. Add a new class file called `EnemyShot.cs` to the `Mars Runner` project.

9. Add the following `using` directives to the `EnemyShot` class:

```
using Microsoft.Xna.Framework;
using Microsoft.Xna.Framework.Graphics;
```

10. Modify the declaration of the `EnemyShot` class to derive from the `GameEntity` class. The new declaration should read:

```
class EnemyShot : GameEntity
```

11. Add fields to the `EnemyShot` class:

```
#region Fields
private Vector3 velocity = new Vector3(0, -5, 0);
private Vector3 gravity = new Vector3(0, -30, 0);
public bool IsActive;

#endregion
```

12. Add a constructor to the `EnemyShot` class as follows:

```
#region Constructor
public EnemyShot(
    GraphicsDevice device,
    Model model,
    Vector3 position)
    : base(device, model, position)
{
    scale = 0.25f;
    IsActive = true;
}
#endregion
```

13. Add the `ResetShot()` method to the `EnemyShot` class as follows:

```
#region Helper Methods
public void ResetShot(Vector3 position)
{
    Position = position;
    velocity = new Vector3(0, -5, 0);
    IsActive = true;
}
#endregion
```

14. Add the `Update()` method to the `EnemyShot` class as follows:

```
#region Update
public override void Update(GameTime gameTime)
{
    float elapsed = (float)gameTime.ElapsedGameTime.TotalSeconds;

    Position += velocity * elapsed;
    velocity += gravity * elapsed;

    if (position.Y < -14)
    {
```

```
            IsActive = false;
        }

        base.Update(gameTime);
    }
    #endregion
```

What just happened?

The `PlayerShot` and `EnemyShot` classes share quite a lot in common. Each tracks the velocity of the shot and has a flag to determine if the shot is active or not. The velocity for player shots move upward at `30` units per second, while enemy shots begin at a downward rate of `5` units per second.

Unlike player shots, however, the velocity of enemy shots is altered by gravity over time, so an enemy shot that is falling will speed up as it falls from the sky.

Both type of shots contain code in their `Update()` methods that sets them to inactive when they have passed certain points along the Y axis, indicating that they have either left the top of the screen (player shots) or impacted the ground (enemy shots).

Finally, both types of shots offer a `ResetShot()` method, which accepts a new position for the shot and makes it active again. In the case of the enemy shot, the velocity is also reset to its default to prevent a reused shot from beginning with a higher fall rate than it should. The `ResetShot()` method will allow us to reuse shots that have expired instead of creating new ones and incurring the performance penalty of building a new object every time a shot is fired.

In order to control how shots function in the world, we will build another new class that will be responsible for managing any outstanding shots, and also for creating new ones when necessary.

Time for action – the ShotManager class

To manage how the shots will function in the world, perform the following steps:

1. Add a new class file called `ShotManager.cs` to the `Mars Runner` project.

2. Add the following `using` directives at the beginning of the `ShotManager` class file:

```
using Microsoft.Xna.Framework;
using Microsoft.Xna.Framework.Graphics;
```

3. Add fields to the `ShotManager` class as follows:

```
#region Fields
List<PlayerShot> playerShots = new List<PlayerShot>();
List<EnemyShot> enemyShots = new List<EnemyShot>();
Model shotModel;
GraphicsDevice device;
#endregion
```

4. Add a constructor to the `ShotManager` class as follows:

```
#region Constructor
public ShotManager(GraphicsDevice device, Model model)
{
    shotModel = model;
    this.device = device;
}
#endregion
```

5. Add the `Helper Methods` region to the `ShotManager` class, which contains methods to add shots to the shot lists as follows:

```
#region Helper Methods
public void AddPlayerShot(Vector3 position)
{
    bool reusedShot = false;

    foreach (PlayerShot shot in playerShots)
    {
        if (!shot.IsActive)
        {
            reusedShot = true;
            shot.ResetShot(position);
            continue;
        }
    }

    if (!reusedShot)
    {
        playerShots.Add(new PlayerShot(
            device,
            shotModel,
            position));
    }
}

public void AddEnemyShot(Vector3 position)
```

```
{
    bool reusedShot = false;

    foreach (EnemyShot shot in enemyShots)
    {
        if (!shot.IsActive)
        {
            reusedShot = true;
            shot.ResetShot(position);
            continue;
        }
    }

    if (!reusedShot)
    {
        enemyShots.Add(new EnemyShot(
            device,
            shotModel,
            position));
    }
}
#endregion
```

6. Add the Update() method to the ShotManager class as follows:

```
#region Update
public void Update(GameTime gameTime)
{
    foreach (PlayerShot shot in playerShots)
    {
        if (shot.IsActive)
        {
            shot.Update(gameTime);
        }
    }

    foreach (EnemyShot shot in enemyShots)
    {
        if (shot.IsActive)
        {
            shot.Update(gameTime);
        }
    }
}
#endregion
```

7. Add the `Draw()` method to the `ShotManager` class as follows:

```
#region Draw
public void Draw(Camera camera)
{
    foreach (PlayerShot shot in playerShots)
    {
        if (shot.IsActive)
        {
            shot.Draw(camera);
        }
    }

    foreach (EnemyShot shot in enemyShots)
    {
        if (shot.IsActive)
        {
            shot.Draw(camera);
        }
    }
}
#endregion
```

8. In the `Fields` region of the `MarsRunnerPlayScreen` class, add fields for an instance of the `ShotManager` class, and to control the player's fire rate as follows:

```
ShotManager shotManager;
float playerShotCooldown = 1.0f;
float playerShotTimer = 0.0f;
```

9. In the `LoadContent()` method of the `MarsRunnerPlayScreen` class, initialize `shotManager` as follows:

```
shotManager = new ShotManager(
    ScreenManager.GraphicsDevice,
    content.Load<Model>(@"Models\sphere"));
```

10. In the `Draw()` method of the `MarsRunnerPlayScreen` class, draw the `shotManager` after the enemy saucer has been drawn as follows:

```
shotManager.Draw(camera);
```

11. In the `Update()` method of the `MarsRunnerPlayScreen` class, update the `shotManager` and manage the player's fire rate. Place the following code just after the code to update the enemy saucer:

```
shotManager.Update(gameTime);

if (playerShotTimer < playerShotCooldown)
    playerShotTimer += elapsed;
```

12. In the `HandleInput()` method of the `MarsRunnerPlayScreen` class, add a new `if` statement to detect shots fired by the player, just before the call to `base.HandleInput()`:

```
if (
    (input.CurrentKeyboardStates[0].IsKeyDown(Keys.Space)) ||
    (input.CurrentGamePadStates[0].Buttons.B == ButtonState.
Pressed)
    )
{
    FirePlayerShot();
}
```

13. Add the `FirePlayerShot()` method to the `Helper Methods` region of the `MarsRunnerPlayScreen` class as follows:

```
private void FirePlayerShot()
{
    if (playerShotTimer >= playerShotCooldown)
    {
        shotManager.AddPlayerShot(
            rover.Position + new Vector3(1, 8, 0));
        playerShotTimer = 0f;
    }
}
```

14. Execute the game and fire a few shots from the player's cannon as shown in the following screenshot:

What just happened?

`ShotManager` keeps track of two lists of shots: shots fired by the player, and shots fired by the enemy UFO. It also stores the information needed (`GraphicsDevice` and `Model`) to create new shots as needed.

Whenever a shot is added through either `AddPlayerShot()` or `AddEnemyShot()`, the methods first look for an unused shot in the appropriate shot list. If one is found, that shot is reused instead of creating a new shot.

When we add `ShotManager` to the rest of the game, we pace player shots with a timer, which allows the player to fire one shot per second. We also offset the position at which new player shots are created by a `Vector3` value of `(1, 8, 0)`, reflecting the relative placement of the top of the cannon in relation to the rest of the rover. This makes shots appear to come from the cannon instead of the middle of the rover.

Enemy shots

Our player can now fire shots, so now it is time to even things up and allow the enemy flying saucer to fire them as well.

Time for action – enemy shots

To implement how the enemy flying saucer fires shots, perform the following:

1. Add the following fields to the `MarsRunnerPlayScreen` class:
   ```
   float enemyShotCooldown = 3.0f;
   float enemyShotTimer = 0.0f;
   int enemyShotChance = 2;
   ```

2. In the `Update()` method of the `MarsRunnerPlayScreen` class, determine if the enemy should fire a shot by adding the following code just after the `playerShotTimer` value has been incremented:
   ```
   if (enemy.IsOnScreen && !enemy.IsDestroyed)
   {
       if (enemyShotTimer < enemyShotCooldown)
       {
           enemyShotTimer += elapsed;
       }
       else
       {
           if (random.Next(0, 100) < enemyShotChance)
           {
               FireEnemyShot();
   ```

```
                    enemyShotTimer = 0.0f;
                }
            }
        }
```

3.   Add the `FireEnemyShot()` method to `Helper Methods` region of the `MarsRunnerPlayScreen` class as follows:

```
private void FireEnemyShot()
{
    shotManager.AddEnemyShot(enemy.Position);
}
```

4.   Execute the game. Enemies will now occasionally fire shots while flying past the player.

What just happened?

We use the same time-delay-with-random-element logic for allowing enemy craft to fire shots as we did to determine when an enemy makes a flyby. When a shot is fired, we leverage the `AddEnemyShot()` method of the `ShotManager` class to add it to the game.

Currently, though, our shots do not actually do anything. We will implement shot collision in two steps. First, we will allow the player shots to hit an alien craft.

Time for action – player shots versus aliens

To implement how the player shots hit an alien craft, perform the following steps:

1.   Add the `CrashSaucer()` method to the `EnemySaucer` class as follows:

```
#region HelperMethods
public void CrashSaucer()
{
    curvePoints[1] = Position;
    curvePoints[2].Y = -80;
    curvePoints[2].Z = 0;
    curveProgress = 0.0f;
    curveDelta = 0.5f;
    pitch = MathHelper.ToRadians(20);
    roll = MathHelper.ToRadians(-20);
    IsDestroyed = true;
}
#endregion
```

2. Add the `Collision Detection` region to the `ShotManager` class as follows:

```
#region Collision Detection
public bool CheckPlayerShotHits(BoundingBox target)
{
    foreach (PlayerShot shot in playerShots)
    {
        if (shot.IsActive)
        {
            if (target.Intersects(shot.Bounds))
            {
                return true;
            }
        }
    }

    return false;
}
#endregion
```

3. In the `Update()` method of the `MarsRunnerPlayScreen` class, add the following code just after `shotManager` has been updated:

```
if ((!enemy.IsDestroyed) &&
    (shotManager.CheckPlayerShotHits(enemy.Bounds)))
{
    enemy.CrashSaucer();
}
```

4. Execute the game and shoot down some aliens as shown in the following screenshot:

What just happened?

When a player shot hits an alien ship, we have the saucer tilt sideways and go into a steep dive, crashing into the ground by setting the `pitch` and `roll` fields. This alteration takes place in the `CrashSaucer()` method, where we alter the points used for our Catmull-Rom spline to make the ship's current position equal to the first point, and drop the second point downwards beyond on the screen. We also set the second point's Z coordinate to zero, causing the saucer to move downward and away from the camera.

Actually detecting the collision is a simple matter of comparing the **bounding boxes** (the total area of 3D space that an object occupies) of the enemy ship and the player's shot. If the boxes overlap at any point, we consider the player to have hit the saucer.

Note that bounding box collision is not perfect. The furthest points from the center of the model determine the size of the bounding box, and as the box is rectangular, it is possible to have two boxes that overlap without the models actually touching each other. For our purposes, the simple bounding box test is accurate enough.

Per-mesh collision testing

You could dig deeper into the bounding box testing by using the initial bounding box collision to trigger a more detailed, per-mesh collision check. Each mesh part that makes up the model could have a bounding box constructed around it, and all of the parts of the two potentially colliding models could be tested against each other. This type of testing would be quite a bit more accurate, and would allow models to be nested closer together without actually colliding, depending on the shapes of the mesh parts.

In detecting the collision of the enemy shots with the player, we will need to tighten up a bit the bounding box we are using. Players will, rightly, be unhappy if an enemy shot that they just narrowly avoided still destroys their rover because the bounding box around the rover does not represent the actual space occupied by the model.

To make things even more interesting, XNA's `BoundingBox` structures are axis-aligned (often referred to as **axis-aligned bounding box** or **AABB**). This means that the box's walls are always positioned along the world axes. Applying rotation to an AABB, as we have done with the `Bounds` property, does not actually rotate the bounding box, but rather expands the axis-aligned box to cover the new area occupied by the rotated model.

We will compensate for this larger bounding box by shrinking the bounds of the box we check for collisions when determining if an enemy shot collides with the player.

Time for action – enemy shots versus the rover

To check if the enemy shots as well as rover shots have hit their respective targets, perform the following steps:

1. Add the `CheckEnemyShotHits()` method to the `Collision Detection` region of the `ShotManager` class as follows:

```
public bool CheckEnemyShotHits(BoundingBox target)
{
    foreach (EnemyShot shot in enemyShots)
    {
        if (shot.IsActive)
        {
            if (target.Intersects(shot.Bounds))
            {
                return true;
            }
        }
    }

    return false;
}
```

2. Add a new property to the `Rover` class for collision bounds checking:

```
public BoundingBox CollisionBounds
{
    get
    {
        BoundingBox baseBounds = Bounds;
        baseBounds.Min += new Vector3(1, 1, 1);
        baseBounds.Max += new Vector3(-1, -1, -1);
        return baseBounds;
    }
}
```

3. In the `Update()` method of the `MarsRunnerGameClass`, just after checking for hits on the alien craft, check for hits on the player as follows:

```
if (shotManager.CheckEnemyShotHits(rover.CollisionBounds))
    EndGame();
```

4. Execute the game and allow an enemy-fired shot to hit the rover.

What just happened?

By adding to the `Min` and subtracting from the `Max` component of the `Bounds` property, we can shrink the bounding box around the rover, allowing the player a cushion against enemy shots that come close but should not actually hit the player.

Scoring

Our scoring system for Mars Runner will be very simple. In each update cycle, the amount of elapsed time will be added to the player's score. Each hit on an enemy ship will add 100 points to the player's score as well.

Time for action – scoring

To implement the scoring system for Mars Runner, perform the following steps:

1. Add two fields to the `MarsRunnerPlayScreen` class as follows:

    ```
    float score = 0;
    SpriteFont font;
    ```

2. In the `LoadContent()` method of the `MarsRunnerPlayScreen` class, initialize the font field as follows:

    ```
    font = content.Load<SpriteFont>("gamefont");
    ```

3. In the `Update()` method of the `MarsRunnerPlayScreen` class, inside the `if` statement that checks `playerPosition`, increment the player's score, and add an `else` condition that ends the game if the player has reached the end of the track. The new `if` statement should read as follows:

    ```
    if (playerPosition < 2880)
    {
        playerPosition += 15 * elapsed;
        skybox.Rotation += 0.1f * elapsed;
        score += elapsed;
    }
    else
    {
        EndGame();
    }
    ```

4. Still in the `Update()` method, inside the `if` statement checking for player hits on enemies, increase the player's score just after the call to `enemy.CrashSaucer()` as follows:

    ```
    score += 100;
    ```

5. In the `Draw()` method of the `MarsRunnerPlayScreen` class, draw the score to the screen as follows:

```
ScreenManager.SpriteBatch.Begin();
ScreenManager.SpriteBatch.DrawString(
    font,
    "Score: " + ((int)score).ToString(),
    new Vector2(10, 400),
    Color.White);
ScreenManager.SpriteBatch.End();
```

6. Execute the game and play it, as shown in the following screenshot:

What just happened?

Adding our scoring system just involves keeping track of the player's score and using one of the fonts that comes included in the GSM sample to display the score.

We have almost completed the Mars Runner game, but currently when the game ends we just wind up back at the main menu. As our final modification to the game, we will add a new screen to the game that overlays the play screen and displays the text **Game over!** for a few seconds before returning to the menu.

Time for action – the GameOver screen

1. Add a new class file called `GameOverScreen.cs` to the **Screens** folder of the `Mars Runner` project.

2. Add the following `using` directives at the beginning of the `GameOverScreen` class file:

```
using Microsoft.Xna.Framework;
using Microsoft.Xna.Framework.Content;
using Microsoft.Xna.Framework.Graphics;
```

3. Modify the `namespace` declaration for the class file by removing `.Screens` from the end of the namespace. The namespace line should now read as follows:

```
namespace Mars_Runner
```

4. Modify the declaration of the `GameOverScreen` class to inherit from the `GameScreen` class. The new declaration line should read as follows:

```
class GameOverScreen : GameScreen
```

5. Add fields to the `GameOverScreen` class as follows:

```
#region Fields
private float displayTimer = 8f;
private float displayCounter = 0f;
Texture2D blank;
SpriteFont font;
ContentManager content;
#endregion
```

6. Override the `LoadContent()` method in the `GameOverScreen` class as follows:

```
#region Initialization
public override void LoadContent()
{
    IsPopup = true;
    if (content == null)
        content = new ContentManager(
        ScreenManager.Game.Services,
        "Content");

    blank = content.Load<Texture2D>("blank");
    font = content.Load<SpriteFont>("menufont");

    base.LoadContent();
}
#endregion
```

7. Override the `Update()` method in the `GameOverScreen` class as follows:

```
#region Update
public override void Update(
    GameTime gameTime,
    bool otherScreenHasFocus,
    bool coveredByOtherScreen)
{

    float elapsed = (float)gameTime.ElapsedGameTime.TotalSeconds;
    displayCounter += elapsed;

    if (displayCounter >= displayTimer)
        ExitScreen();

    base.Update(gameTime, otherScreenHasFocus,
coveredByOtherScreen);
}
#endregion
```

8. Override the `Draw()` method in the `GameOverScreen` class as follows:

```
#region Draw
public override void Draw(GameTime gameTime)
{

    Vector2 screenSize = new Vector2(
        ScreenManager.GraphicsDevice.Viewport.Width,
        ScreenManager.GraphicsDevice.Viewport.Height);

    ScreenManager.SpriteBatch.Begin();

    ScreenManager.SpriteBatch.Draw(
        blank,
        new Rectangle(
            0,
            0,
            (int)screenSize.X,
            (int)screenSize.Y),
        Color.Black * 0.4f);

    string gameOver = "G a m e   O v e r!";
    Vector2 stringSize = font.MeasureString(gameOver);

    ScreenManager.SpriteBatch.DrawString(
        font,
        gameOver,
```

```
        (screenSize / 2) - (stringSize / 2),
        Color.White);

    ScreenManager.SpriteBatch.End();

    base.Draw(gameTime);
}
#endregion
```

9. In the `EndGame()` method of the `MarsRunnerPlayScreen` class, create a new instance of the `GameOverScreen` after setting `gameEnded` to `true` as follows:

```
ScreenManager.AddScreen(new GameOverScreen(), null);
```

10. Execute the game and play until it ends in one of the three possible ways.

What just happened?

We have added a completely new type of screen to the GSM system. This screen is identified in the `LoadContent()` method as a pop-up screen, meaning that it will not prevent the screens behind it from being drawn.

Instead, `MarsRunnerPlayScreen` continues to render the final scene of the game, while `GameOverScreen` overlays the whole screen with a partially transparent black texture. This is accomplished by drawing the `blank` texture, which is a blank white square included as part of the GSM resources, with a partially transparent black tint color.

The screen starts a timer when it loads, and when the timer has expired, the screen exits, allowing `MarsRunnerPlayScreen` to resume. As `gameEnded` has been set to `true`, the play screen will exit and return to the menu immediately.

Sound effects

Mars Runner is playable at this point, but like all of our games, so far it is completely silent. The audio queue provided by sound effects synced to the action in a game contributes greatly to the immersive feeling a player experiences. We can build an easy-to-use class to play sound effects that could be added to any of our games.

Generating sound effects

There are numerous sound effect libraries on the Internet that offer downloadable effects, but rarely are the license terms for these libraries very clear on the permitted usages of the sounds, especially as many of them are compilations of sounds found elsewhere and not original creations. As with graphics resources, `http://www.opengameart.org` is a great source for music and sound effects with clearly specified licenses. Alternatively, you can generate or record your own sound effects. The sound effects included with the audio package for this chapter were all generated using the **sfxr** sound generator program, available at `http://www.drpetter.se/project_sfxr.html`.

We will create a static sound effect management class that will allow us to play sounds from anywhere in our game with a single method call.

Time for action – building the SFXManager class

In order to build the `SFXManager` class, perform these steps:

1. Download the `7089_10_AUDIOPACK.zip` file from the book's website and extract the contents to a temporary location.
2. Copy the `Sounds` folder from the audio pack to the clipboard.
3. In Visual Studio, select the content project in **Solution Explorer**, right-click and select **Paste**.
4. Create a new class file called `SFXManager.cs` in the `Mars Runner` project.
5. Add the `using` directive to the beginning of the `SFXManager` class file as follows:

   ```
   using Microsoft.Xna.Framework.Audio;
   ```

6. Modify the declaration of the `SFXManager` class to mark it as static. The declaration should now read as follows:

   ```
   static class SFXManager
   ```

7. Add a `Dictionary` object to the `SFXManager` class to store sound effects:

   ```
   #region Fields
   private static Dictionary<string, SoundEffect> soundEffects =
       new Dictionary<string, SoundEffect>();
   #endregion
   ```

8. Add the `AddEffect()` method to the `SFXManager` class:

```
#region Initialization
public static void AddEffect(string name, SoundEffect effect)
{
    soundEffects[name] = effect;
}
#endregion
```

9. Add methods to play sounds to the `SFXManager` class:

```
#region Playing
public static void Play(string name)
{
    if (soundEffects.ContainsKey(name))
        soundEffects[name].Play();
}
#endregion
```

What just happened?

The `SFXManager` class, while not complicated, will allow us to play sound effects in Mars Runner (and the other games in this book if you choose to go back and add it to them) very easily. The class stores a dictionary of named sound effect, and when the `Play()` method is called, it plays back the named effect if it exists.

More advanced sound options

It should be noted that this is a very basic implementation of sound in XNA. Playing sounds directly through the `SoundEffect` class plays them in a fire-and-forget style. Once a sound effect is playing, we really cannot do anything with it, such as adjust its volume, pan the sound, and move it around in 3D space. XNA supports all of these capabilities through the `SoundEffectInstance` class, which can be created from a loaded `SoundEffect` and then the sound can be looped, started, stopped, panned, and positioned in 3D space.

Triggering sounds

In order to use our `SFXManager` class to play sounds, we need to load sounds into the class, and sprinkle calls to the `SFXManager.Play()` method throughout our code.

Time for action – playing sound effects

To add a sound effects manager to Mars Runner, perform the following steps:

1. Add a new `using` direction at the beginning of the `MarsRunnerPlayScreen` class to allow us to access the XNA Audio classes as follows:

   ```
   using Microsoft.Xna.Framework.Audio;
   ```

2. In the `LoadContent()` method of the `MarsRunnerPlayScreen` class, load the sound effects and add them to the sound effect manager's dictionary as follows:

   ```
   SFXManager.AddEffect(
       "Explosion", content.Load<SoundEffect>(@"Sounds\Explosion1"));
   SFXManager.AddEffect(
       "Jump", content.Load<SoundEffect>(@"Sounds\Jump"));
   SFXManager.AddEffect(
       "PlayerShot", content.Load<SoundEffect>(@"Sounds\Shot1"));
   SFXManager.AddEffect(
       "EnemyShot", content.Load<SoundEffect>(@"Sounds\Shot2"));
   ```

3. Inside the `FirePlayerShot()` method in the `MarsRunnerPlayScreen` class, call the `SFXManager.Play()` method just after resetting the `playerShotTimer` to `0.0f` as follows:

   ```
   SFXManager.Play("PlayerShot");
   ```

4. Inside the `FireEnemyShot()` method in the `MarsRunnerPlayScreen` class, call the `SFXManager.Play()` method after adding the shot as follows:

   ```
   SFXManager.Play("EnemyShot");
   ```

5. In the `Jump()` method of the `Rover` class, play the `Jump` effect after setting the rover's velocity as follows:

   ```
   SFXManager.Play("Jump");
   ```

6. In the `CrashSaucer()` method of the `EnemySaucer` class, play the `Explosion` effect, so the the last line of the method would read as follows:

   ```
   SFXManager.Play("Explosion");
   ```

7. Execute the game. Jump around and fire shots at the enemy saucers.

What just happened?

As you can see, utilizing the `SFXManager` class is simply a matter of loading the sounds into the manager and then scattering `Play()` calls in appropriate locations throughout our code. While not an in-depth sound system, it serves our purposes here and can act as a basis for you to expand on as you delve deeper into XNA development.

Have a go hero!

There are nearly endless possibilities to expand the Mars Runner game. Here are just a few to consider trying out:

- Right now, when the player reaches the end of the track, the game ends. Instead, display an interim screen showing the player's arrival at the Martian base and start a new level with a new track. You could increase the frequency of craters or alter the fire or flyby rates of the alien ships to make the game increasingly harder.

- Transplant the particle-based explosion system from Tank Battles to Mars Runner and apply particles at points of impact of player shots on enemies, enemy shots on players, enemy shots on the ground, and the enemy saucer's crash landing point. The particle system could also be expanded to include smoke particles, with the particles drifting upwards before dissipating.

- When an alien shot impacts the ground, have it create a new crater. The track array would need to have its segment value altered. If you have implemented the particle explosion system, the transition could be covered by the explosion and/or smoke particles.

- The GSM sample contains `PauseMenuScreen`. Allow the user to pause their game by popping up this menu screen and waiting for them to continue.

Summary

The Mars Runner project is now completed – at least as far as we will take it in this book. Where it goes from here is up to you! Try implementing some of the suggestions above, or come up with your own new ideas and work them into the game.

Over the course of Mars Runner, we have covered a number of important topics, which include utilizing and expanding the GSM system, adding a skybox to a 3D game, drawing instanced terrain meshes, abstracting support for 3D models, and bounding box based 3D collision detection.

Over the course of this book, we have discussed and implemented many of the fundamental techniques necessary to create 3D video games with XNA. While it would be impossible to cover every possible topic, I hope that you now have the foundation needed to explore the possibilities XNA brings to game development.

Index

GetHeight() method 133
GetTrackSegment() method 264
GraphicsDeviceManager class 16

H

HandleInput() method 259
HasWheelReachedTarget() method 262
Heads-up display (HUD) 10
height map
  about 100, 236
  creating 100
  terrain, generating for playfield 100
hits
  detecting, in Tank Battles project 193-195
HitTest() method 153, 160
HLSL (High Level Shader Language)
  about 48, 91, 111, 175
  for particles 180
  pixel shader 116, 117
  variables, defining for 112, 113
  vertex shader 115, 116
  vertex shader structures 113, 114
HLSL (High Level Shader Language), for lighting
    202-205

I

indices
  building 106
Initialize() method
  about 17, 49, 119
  adding, to ParticleManager class 176
  adding, to TankBattlesGame class 109
  customizing 17
  verus LoadContent() method 17
InitializeParticles() method 173
  adding, to Particle class 172
InputState class 218
InputState instance 259
installing
  Windows Phone SDK 8-10
Integrated Development Environment (IDE) 9
interface components
  about 143
  UIButtons 148-153
  UITextblocks 146, 147
  UIWidget class 144-146

interface events
  responding to 161-164
Intersects() method 29
IsOnScreen flag 271

L

left-handed coordinate system 32
lighting 198, 199
LoadContent() event 111
LoadContent() method
  about 17, 73, 132, 155, 186, 191
  adding, to TankBattlesGame class 109
  verus Initialize() method 17
Load() method 18
look at point
  implementing 39, 40

M

Main() method 16
Mars Runner game
  advanced sound options 292
  background, creating for 227
  background image, customizing for 219, 220
  BackgroundScreen class, customizing for 219,
    220
  craters, detecting on track 264-266
  design 215
  enemy shots, versus rover shots 285
  flight, providing to saucer 269-272
  flying saucer, adding to 267, 268
  GameEntity class, adding to 248-253
  GameOver screen 288-290
  gameplay screen, creating for 222, 223
  Martian surface, building 236
  menu, updating for 221, 222
  planet, animating 260
  player shots versus aliens 282, 284
  rover, animating 261-263
  rover, building for player 253-255
  scoring system, implementing for 286, 287
  ScreenManager screens, customizing 219
  SFXManager class, creating 291, 292
  shots, functioning 276-281
  shots, implementing 273-276
  skybox, creating for 228-235
  sound effects, generating 290-292

V

variables
defining, for HLSL 112, 113
vertex shader 115, 116
VertexShaderFunction() method 115, 181, 202, 208
VertexShaderInput structure 114
VertexShaderOutput function 114
VertexShaderOutput structure 116
vertex shader structures 113, 114
vertices
building, for terrain 105, 106
viewDistance field 96
ViewDistance property 96, 122
View matrix 41, 42, 116
View property
adding, to ArcBallCamera class 97, 98
visual components
drawing, for Speller game 21, 23
visual improvements, Tank Battles project
about 198
lighting 198, 199
multitexturing 207-212
Visual Studio 2010 Express 9

W

walls
cnstructing, generated maze layout used 60-63

drawing, in Cube Chaser project 64
winding order 45
Windows Phone 8
Windows Phone SDK
installing 8-10
Wings 3D 125
World matrix 116

X

Xbox 360 7, 8
Xbox Live 8
XNA
about 8
angles 36
XNA development
system requisites 8
XNA Framework 7
XNA game 10
XNA project
creating 11, 12
XNA project templates 7

Y

YawPitchRoll
verus CreateRotation 99

Thank you for buying
XNA 4 3D Game Development by Example Beginner's Guide

About Packt Publishing

Packt, pronounced 'packed', published its first book "*Mastering phpMyAdmin for Effective MySQL Management*" in April 2004 and subsequently continued to specialize in publishing highly focused books on specific technologies and solutions.

Our books and publications share the experiences of your fellow IT professionals in adapting and customizing today's systems, applications, and frameworks. Our solution-based books give you the knowledge and power to customize the software and technologies you're using to get the job done. Packt books are more specific and less general than the IT books you have seen in the past. Our unique business model allows us to bring you more focused information, giving you more of what you need to know, and less of what you don't.

Packt is a modern, yet unique publishing company, which focuses on producing quality, cutting-edge books for communities of developers, administrators, and newbies alike. For more information, please visit our website: www.PacktPub.com.

About Packt Enterprise

In 2010, Packt launched two new brands, Packt Enterprise and Packt Open Source, in order to continue its focus on specialization. This book is part of the Packt Enterprise brand, home to books published on enterprise software – software created by major vendors, including (but not limited to) IBM, Microsoft and Oracle, often for use in other corporations. Its titles will offer information relevant to a range of users of this software, including administrators, developers, architects, and end users.

Writing for Packt

We welcome all inquiries from people who are interested in authoring. Book proposals should be sent to author@packtpub.com. If your book idea is still at an early stage and you would like to discuss it first before writing a formal book proposal, contact us; one of our commissioning editors will get in touch with you.

We're not just looking for published authors; if you have strong technical skills but no writing experience, our experienced editors can help you develop a writing career, or simply get some additional reward for your expertise.

XNA 4.0 Game Development by Example: Beginner's Guide

ISBN: 978-1-84969-066-9   Paperback: 428 pages

Create exciting games with Microsoft XNA 4.0

1. Dive headfirst into game creation with XNA

2. Four different styles of games comprising a puzzler, a space shooter, a multi-axis shoot 'em up, and a jump-and-run platformer

3. Games that gradually increase in complexity to cover a wide variety of game development techniques

4. Focuses entirely on developing games with the free version of XNA

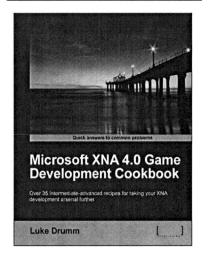

Microsoft XNA 4.0 Game Development Cookbook

ISBN: 978-1-84969-198-7   Paperback: 356 pages

Over 35 intermediate-advanced recipes for taking your XNA development arsenal further

1. Accelerate your XNA learning with a myriad of tips and tricks to solve your everyday problems

2. Get to grips with adding special effects, virtual atmospheres and computer controlled characters with this book and e-book

3. A fast-paced cookbook packed with screenshots to illustrate each advanced step by step task

4. Apply the techniques learned for wiring games for PC, Xbox 360 and Windows Phone 7

Please check **www.PacktPub.com** for information on our titles

3D Graphics with XNA Game Studio 4.0

ISBN: 978-1-84969-004-1   Paperback: 292 pages

Create attractive 3D graphics and visuals in your XNA games

1. Improve the appearance of your games by implementing the same techniques used by professionals in the game industry

2. Learn the fundamentals of 3D graphics, including common 3D math and the graphics pipeline

3. Create an extensible system to draw 3D models and other effects, and learn the skills to create your own effects and animate them

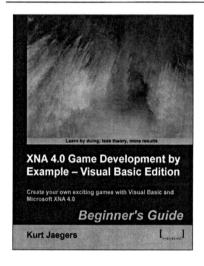

XNA 4.0 Game Development by Example: Beginner's Guide – Visual Basic Edition

ISBN: 978-1-84969-240-3   Paperback: 424 pages

Create your own exciting games with Visual Basic and Microsoft XNA 4.0

1. Visual Basic edition of Kurt Jaegers' XNA 4.0 Game Development by Example. The first book to target Visual Basic developers who want to develop games with the XNA framework

2. Dive headfirst into game creation with Visual Basic and the XNA Framework

3. Four different styles of games comprising a puzzler, space shooter, multi-axis shoot 'em up, and a jump-and-run platformer

4. Games that gradually increase in complexity to cover a wide variety of game development techniques

Please check **www.PacktPub.com** for information on our titles

Lightning Source UK Ltd.
Milton Keynes UK
UKOW03f0702010515

250692UK00001B/78/P